One of a Kind

One of a Kind

Learning the Secrets of World Leaders

Walter H. Diamond

Edited by

Dorothy B. Diamond

SYRACUSE UNIVERSITY PRESS

First Edition 2005
05 06 07 08 09 10   6 5 4 3 2 1

One of a Kind is published with the generous support
of the Martin J. Whitman School of Management
and the Office of Institutional Advancement at Syracuse University.

Unless otherwise stated, all photographs in this book
are courtesy of the author.

The paper used in this publication meets the minimum requirements
of American National Standard for Information Sciences—Permanence
of Paper for Printed Library Materials, ANSI Z39.48–1984.∞™

Library of Congress Cataloging-in-Publication Data
Diamond, Walter H.
One of a kind : learning the secrets of world leaders / Walter H. Diamond ; edited by Dorothy B.
Diamond.— 1st ed.
p. cm.
Includes index.
ISBN 0–8156–0837–3 (hardcover : alk. paper)
1. Diamond, Walter H. 2. Economists—United States—Biography. 3. United States. Dept. of the
Treasury—Officials and employees—Biography. 4. United Nations—Officials and employees—
Biography. I. Diamond, Dorothy B., 1919– II. Title.
HB119.D53 2005
330'.092—dc22   2005025976

Manufactured in the United States of America

To Dorothy, Kate, Sam, and Asher

WALTER H. DIAMOND, a widely known international tax authority and economist, is coauthor with his wife, Dorothy, of eighty-one foreign tax and trade books prepared for five legal publishers. As a UN and U.S. AID trade and investment adviser, as well as consultant to four trade associations, he has interviewed and helped more than one hundred world leaders, consisting of kings, presidents, prime ministers, finance ministers, princes, and other government officials, as to their hopes of improving living standards for their constituents. During a sixty-year period involving visits to more than 120 nations, the author served as a national bank examiner, liquidating foreign banks in the early World War II days; foreign analyst at the Federal Reserve Bank of New York; director of economics for the McGraw-Hill International Corporation; and editor of the *McGraw-Hill American Letter.* Subsequently, he became director of international taxation for Deloitte and Touche, manager of international taxes for PMG Peat Marwick, and principal of O'Connor, Davies, Mumms and Dobbins.

In handling his overseas assignments by contributing to the advances made by foreign counties in taxation, investment, banking, and trusts, Mr. Diamond received numerous citations and honorary citizenship. When serving as an officer in the U.S. Navy during World War II, he was involved in six invasions in the Pacific and European theaters, including the Normandy landings.

A native of Syracuse, Mr. Diamond graduated from Syracuse University and the American Institute of Banking and attended six years at the Syracuse University and New York University Graduate Schools. At present, he acts as chairman of the Advisory Board of the American International Depository and Trust, a Denver institution for nonresidents designed to repatriate some $6 trillion of offshore funds in order to help the U.S. Treasury reduce part of its annual current accounts deficits. Mr. Diamond is also senior vice president of the Offshore Institute, is on the editorial boards of *International Reports* and *Trusts and Trustees,* is contributing editor of *Offshore Investment Magazine,* and has written a monthly credit column for London's *Financial Times* and *Informa Magazine* for more than twenty years. He and Mrs. Diamond are professors at the Diamond International Tax Program of the St. Thomas University School of Law, from which they both received honorary doctor of law degrees. He was honored by Syracuse University as a recipient of the prestigious Arents Medal and was granted the School of Management's Achievement Award, as was Mrs. Diamond.

DOROTHY B. DIAMOND is an editor and author for Overseas Press and Consultants. As a recognized expert in developing markets for business, international corporate reorganization, free trade zones, and tax treaties, she was the first woman to address the Stockholm Advertising Club, the Caribbean Central Bank, the International Tax Planning Association, and the New York Rotary Club. Her trade column in *Tide Magazine* and *Printers Ink*, where she served as editor, won her the New York Merchandise Association Award. As an early post-World War II advocate of women's rights, Mrs. Diamond was the only woman named among the ten most influential executives in the advertising field to change consumer attitudes in Vance Packard's landmark book, *The Hidden Persuaders*. Mrs. Diamond is also coauthor (with Walter Diamond) of *International Tax Treaties of the World, Tax Havens of the World, International Trust Laws and Analysis, Tax Free Trade Zones of the World,* and the *Global Guide to Investment Incentives and Capital Formation.* She is a graduate of Wellesley College where she earned a Phi Beta Kappa key and of the Columbia Graduate School of Journalism.

Contents

Illustrations

Acknowledgments

I WOULD LIKE TO EXPRESS my deepest gratitude to my dear wife, Dorothy Blum Diamond, who contributed her journalistic skills practiced as editor of *Tide Magazine* and *Printers Ink* to reedit this manuscript. I would also like to extend my appreciation to Walter Szykitka, president of the Association for World Free Trade Zones, for assistance in providing his electronic expertise, and to the congenial staff of the Neiman Marcus White Plains men's clothing department for sharing its club room, where I wrote a good part of this memoir.

PROLOGUE

Before the War

WALTER H. DIAMOND

A TELEPHONE CALL in 1998 from Lansing, Michigan, startled me when I heard a strange voice say: "You don't know me but I'm the dean of the School of Human Resources at Michigan State University and a member of the Archives Committee in Washington. Mr. Diamond, are you writing or preparing an autobiography or biography of your life?"

I quickly replied: "Not really, but I have been thinking about it over the years, waiting for the time to work on it."

"Mr. Diamond, you should do it. We come across your name frequently from the speeches, articles, and interviews you've done for many years. If you don't, you're cheating the world out of valuable information that the government should know. The Archives Committee would like you to set your memoirs down in writing for our historical records."

Then a few weeks later I received a call from a small town in Manitoba, Canada. "I'm the son of your Canadian correspondent," the caller told me. "I've just graduated from Mount Allison University in New Brunswick, majoring in memoirs. Mount Allison's the only university in North America with a majors course in memoirs. My professors have encouraged me to make use of my education, and my mother has told me about your exploits. Could I give you some assistance in writing your memoirs?"

His follow-up calls encouraged me to proceed, but by then various bottlenecks had developed. It was not until two years later, in 2000, that I finally convinced myself that I had to cut back on the time I was spending preparing supplements for the eighty-one tax and trade books I authored with my wife, Dorothy. And that is when these memoirs began to take shape in my mind.

1. Walter Diamond pointing to bookshelves in the Diamond library housing the eighty-one books he coauthored with Dorothy Diamond beginning in 1950.

LET ME SAY FIRST that despite my training and experience as an international economist, in my heart I was always a journalist. I was born practically on the campus of Syracuse University at the Crouse-Irving Hospital and entered this world as the only male child in a family of writers. My mother's grandfather had been a Talmudic scholar whose scriptural interpretations were revered in Poland before the pogroms of the mid-nineteenth century forced him to flee to Lithuania. Faced with the discrimination and social upheaval of those times, in 1881 he chose to bring his family to the New World. On arriving at Ellis Island, he presented his birth certificate, which stated that he was originally from Kabach Province in Poland, so the customs agent listed the family name as Kabacher.

My mother was born on the ship that brought the family to America. Later she became secretary to three mayors of Syracuse. A principal task for her at city hall was writing speeches. One of those mayors, Alan Fobes, has a street in Syracuse named after him. Another mayor was Edward Schoeneck, who later became a New York state senator. She accompanied him to Albany as his secretary but left her position ten days later for New York City to become a "Gibson Girl," a glamor girl created by Charles Dana Gibson, popularized around 1900.

On the same boat that brought the family to America was a cousin, who continued on to Canada and established a successful newspaper publishing business. My two sisters were accomplished writers; one of them became an editor of *Tide*, a leading New York advertising magazine. Through her I would meet my future wife, Dorothy Blum, who became a senior editor there. Three nieces on my mother's side of the family are excellent writers.

A Scout's Code

Having been blessed with a miraculous photographic memory, I can remember perfectly almost everything I have ever seen and done since I was four years old. This astonishing gift emerged after I disregarded my mother's warning to avoid the sidewalk behind our home because a milkman's broken bottle created a hazard to pedestrians. It was already my nature to help others—a characteristic that came to full bloom several years later when I became an Eagle Scout—so I picked up a piece of broken glass to remove it from the walk and sliced the index finger of my right hand in half.

To this day I can "see" my mother pleading on the front porch with the doctor not to remove the entire finger but to take me to a hospital so that the surgeons could try to sew it back together. The resewn finger is now bent inward, and two shards of glass are still embedded in it, visible at the joints. In high school that bent finger provided me with the ability to throw an in-curve ball that few batters could hit. Some brain specialists later told me that the trauma of this event perhaps triggered an unusual photographic memory.

An "Intelligent Memory"

A question frequently posed to me concerns my combination of blending journalism and international economics into a single life. In addition to the three cardinal essentials of journalism learned at Syracuse University (source, color, and organization) that I have tried to follow meticulously, I am frequently asked, "What are the most important features that have contributed to the success of your books, interviews, and general background knowledge of international business?" For me, that question is easy to answer: memory, having an affinity to help immigrants, perseverance, and specialization.

According to a leading expert on brain responses, Dr. Barry Gordon, a professor of neurology and cognitive science at the Johns Hopkins Medical Institutions, I am one of a handful of people whose brain functions from "intelligent memory." Unlike "ordinary memory," that is, memory "heavily dependent on a relatively small section of the brain called the hippocampus, intelligent memory stems from a property of many nerve cells that are spread through the brain." In Dr. Gordon's opinion, "intelligent memory thinks on its own, connecting thoughts and ideas automatically. However, one can guide it to work better by learning to percolate new ideas."

Another indelible memory of my youth: When I was six, I wandered ten blocks from home—a reflection of my inborn wanderlust—so that I could wave good-bye to the doughboys from all over the country who had packed the New York Central trains, which were rolling along Syracuse's Washington Street track. The soldiers were destined for New York, where they would board ships to Europe in order to fight on the European front during World War I.

A third example of my phenomenal memory comes from my days in the U.S. Navy during World War II. Captain Edson Cates, my skipper on the *Kentuckian*, showed me a schematic diagram of the 5,686 ships and other vessels headed for the D-day beaches. To this day I can recall almost exactly where each of those vessels—warships, carriers, destroyers, minesweepers, and various small craft—was positioned in the largest armada ever assembled.

This rare gift for remembering was always a huge help when it came to recording interviews and events. That said, as a journalist I was well aware that careful notes of interviews, meetings, conferences, and travels were a necessity. I never forgot the sound advice I received from the president of the McGraw-Hill Book Company, Basil Dandison, whose office was next to mine when I served as director of economics of McGraw-Hill International Corporation and as editor of the McGraw-Hill *American Letter*. He knew about my work helping foreign countries and obtaining important information directly from world leaders, and he often reminded me: "Your notes may someday be an asset to posterity, especially if you put them in book form."

Affinity to Assist Foreigners

My father's parents came to America from Alsace-Lorraine via Poland. They had left Germany for Poland in the middle of the nineteenth century owing to religious persecution. After entering the United States with German passports and

2. Walter Diamond when director of economics for McGraw-Hill International Corporation in the 1950s–1960s.

their brood of seven children, they had three more in Syracuse, including my father, born on Christmas Day in 1871.

My own links to immigrants and other foreigners grew out of my father's strong commitment to helping newcomers, a virtue he had inherited from his parents. Between my tenth and thirteenth years, during summer vacation, except for the six weeks each year when I attended Boy Scout camp, I rose every morning at five and went with my father to his haberdashery to learn the retail trade. He had made it his avocation to help strangers to the New World familiarize themselves with their new surroundings and neighbors. Most of the immigrants he helped came from Italy and Poland. They poured into central New York by the thousands in the late 1880s and early 1890s. Back in their home countries, they had heard that rich farmland was available in this part of the state, and they noticed that many of its cities and towns had been named after Italian or Polish cities or historic figures: Rome, Camillus, Marcellus, Utica, Ithaca, Pompey, Warsaw, and so on. Of course, the largest contingent came from Syracuse (Siracusa) in Sicily.

My father spoke five languages fluently: Italian, German, Polish, Hebrew, and Latvic (which was spoken by most immigrants from the Baltic countries). Many poor immigrants arrived in the New World with a paper in hand with the words *Diamond, Syracuse* written on it. They would arrive at Ellis Island, get processed, and with their few possessions find their way to Penn Station, then to Grand Central Station, where they would board a New York Central train for Syracuse.

My father would send our chauffeur—be it August, Joey, or Max—to meet these forlorn immigrants at the Washington Street station. Having rounded them up, Father would help them in any way he could. He would see that they were outfitted with new clothing. The first items the immigrants asked for were "hippa boots and fleeca underwear," which is what they were used to wearing in the old country.

Soon after settling on their new farms, they would begin attending the Syracuse market, an Onondaga County landmark, every Saturday and often midweek as well. They would arrive by the hundreds in their horse-drawn wagons from all over central New York to sell their fresh produce from stalls. And each market day after the closing bell they would visit H. Diamond and Son to stock up on clothes for their families.

As a mark of appreciation, the new settlers elected father "mayor of the Italian district." Every Saturday throughout the year, when I called on them for installment payments on their credit purchases, they would welcome me with "Here comes the mayor's son." My regular contact with these hundreds of immigrants—many of them barely scraping by—was the seed of the strong desire I developed as an adult to help people in other countries. My familiarity with their customs and my awareness of the poverty suffered by so many of the world's people put me at ease when I was discussing with world leaders the approaches to improving life for their citizens.

FOR SOME REASON the label "one of a kind" has stuck with me over the years, both in my work and outside it. It was Bill Knight, my scoutmaster at Troop 21 at Nottingham High School in Syracuse, who first described me that way. This inspiring teacher, who was admired by all the parents, warned Mother that I was unique. Unlike the other candidates for Eagle Scout, "Walter is not satisfied with earning his twenty-one merit badges for the highest rank." As the third-youngest Eagle Scout in the United States, I was determined to display on my uniform every last one of the seventy-eight merit badges available in the 1920s. By the time I became assistant scoutmaster, I was wearing seventy-two merit badges on the cloth band across my chest.

A second episode that labeled me "one of a kind" arose when I gave a freak

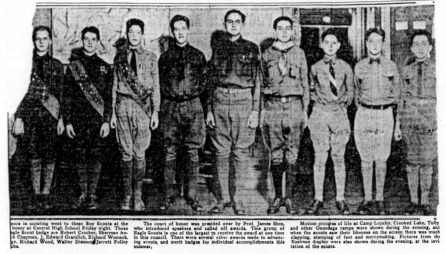

ιηεγ ἐ᾽Made Good, and Boy Scouts Win Craft's Honors

nors in scouting went to these Boy Scouts at the honor at Central High School Friday night. Those ngle Scout badge are Robert Crocker, Sherman An-lk Chapman, J. Edward Gramlich, Richard Womack, ιget. Richard Wood, Walter Diamond, Jarrett Folley obs.

The court of honor was presided over by Prof. James Shea, who introduced speakers and called off awards. This group of Eagle Scouts is one of the largest to receive the award at one time in this council. There were several other awards made to advancing scouts, and merit badges for individual accomplishments this summer.

Motion pictures of life at Camp Loyalty, Crooked Lake, Tully and other Onondaga camps were shown during the evening, and when the scouts saw their likeness on the screen there was much clapping, stamping of feet and merrymaking. Pictures from the Eastman display were also shown during the evening, at the invitation of the scouts.

3. Walter Diamond, third from right, receives the Eagle Scout Award on the stage of Central High School in Syracuse at age thirteen, 1926.

but correct answer to a trick algebra question on my New York State regents exams. Our professor, the strict Dr. Smegelsky, called Mother to tell her that I had handed in a perfect paper but he was withholding grading it 100 percent. He explained that my unique analysis of a complex algebra question was one he had never seen before and that he would have to send it to the Regents Board in Albany for review before he could hand out the perfect mark. My analysis was later approved, even though it was the first time this method of calculation had ever been submitted to the board. The ruling: my computation "only could be devised by an unusual analytical mind."

Perseverance a Key Asset

My capacity to persevere has contributed immensely to my work. I learned it from my family, but it was shaped by my long association with the Boy Scouts as a patrol leader, Eagle Scout, assistant scoutmaster, and eventually scoutmaster. I was a slender boy and also shorter than many of my friends, so I had to find my own ways to do difficult tasks—tasks that came more easily to the bigger students, many of whom were bullies.

There was one time when my closest friend and neighbor, who was a foot taller than me, became so mean and exasperating that I punched him and gave him a bloody lip. A few minutes later, his mother called mine to complain that I had "taken advantage of him." By then, Father had taught me to "always stand on my own two feet." To prepare me for any physical encounters in life, he had built a makeshift boxing ring in our backyard and instructed Max, our chauffeur and handyman, to give me boxing lessons. At one time, Max had been middleweight champion in New York State. He turned me into a fairly capable boxer. From him I learned how to duck, crouch, jab, feint, time my punches, and so on—the skills a good boxer needs to know. The terms and techniques I learned from Max were a big help years later, when I covered boxing for the Syracuse University *Daily Orange*.

Confident that I could hold my own against older, bigger, and stronger boys, when I was thirteen I applied to attend Camp Syracuse, an exclusive place for Eagle Scouts only. It was in dense woods on Browns Track Pond, three miles from Raquette Lake, a popular Adirondack resort. This camp accepted only the toughest Eagle Scouts, the roughest backwoodsmen among them. Bill Lawrence was the director of the Syracuse Boy Scouts as well as the camp director. When he learned that I had been an Eagle Scout only a few months, he told me I would have to wait a year or two. Finally, I was given special clearance to attend—all the merit badges I had earned above the required twenty-one indicated I had the stamina to survive.

When I arrived the first Sunday in August, after walking a mile and a half through the bush from the dirt road where my parents had dropped me off, all eyes were on me. Lawrence right away told me: "Go out into the woods, cut down a tree with a solid trunk no larger than six inches, find a spot in the brush, pitch your tent with the trunk as your centerpiece, build yourself a bed by using its branches and knots you've learned from scouting, and then find some balsam branches for your mattress and bedding." That was my introduction to Camp Syracuse.

There were two cliques at the camp. There were the "Southside Bums," older teenagers from the blue-collar district of Syracuse, and there were the "Northside Sissies" from the white-collar district around the university. Needless to say, I was considered one of the latter clique. I survived that month through sheer determination. In the end I was almost stymied by one activity—a three-mile swim to an island and back.

In retrospect I can say that nothing in my life would ever test my fortitude more than that swim. I was not a good swimmer, but I was going to have to finish that ordeal to earn the camp letter. I kept afloat for the entire two hours only by telling myself I could not fail. This inner thrust that I had developed by then, and that I showed that day, would become a vital asset in my career, when I sought to meet the world's leaders. I had learned the value and power of gracious persistence in achieving worthwhile results. As Calvin Coolidge once said: "Nothing in the world can take the place of persistence."

ALTHOUGH I HAD ACQUIRED some minor journalism experience on the Nottingham High School *Bulletin*, my real training did not begin until I entered Syracuse University and joined the staff of the *Daily Orange*, then one of the most highly rated college newspapers in the country. By my senior year I had worked my way up to sports editor, at which point I considered myself well versed in all the challenges—both journalistic and mechanical—I had to know how to overcome in order to be a good journalist. Little did I dream that one day computerized publishing would render useless much of what I learned about technology.

One of the most shocking lessons I discovered from my *Daily Orange* days is that you have to know who your real friends are when a news story is heading for a page 1 byline. The competition to beat your rivals to the presses can hand you an ugly reminder that "all is fair in love and war." In my junior year the senior sports editor assigned me to cover the finals in midwinter of the Intercollegiate Boxing Championship at State College, Pennsylvania. Syracuse won six titles at that event, and to make the early edition of the next day's paper, I drove all night through the Pocono Mountains in whiteout conditions with the sophomore staff sportswriter—the late Drew Middleton, who would later win a Pulitzer Prize as a *New York Times* military strategist—sprawled out on the fender of my Model-T, pushing the snow from the windshield with a rag each time the wiper went back and forth so that we could see the road.

At three in the morning we arrived back at the *Daily Orange* newsroom, where I dashed off my page 1 story revealing that Syracuse had captured six titles. When I took it down to the hot-type presses, Phil, the amiable operator, told me the story was already in print, sent up by wireless code and signed by Drew Middleton. Of course, as soon as Mike Davis, the sports editor, was notified of the awkward situation, Drew's story was yanked and mine ran in its place, complete with byline and banner page 1 head: "At Ringside."

Drew was already a seasoned journalist when he arrived at Syracuse, having worked for the Bloomfield, New Jersey, newspaper. He had also played semipro baseball, and as a catcher had had all his front teeth knocked out. Many times in the early morning, during the long, boring hours waiting for proofs to check, Drew would break the morguelike atmosphere by dropping his false teeth. When he graduated from college in 1935, jobs for journalists were hard to find; I had found that out myself the year before, while I was looking for work after graduation. Then Drew submitted a freelance article to the *New York Times* on "Old Man Jim Tenyck," the legendary rowing coach at Syracuse University. The *Times* ran it as a feature in its Sunday edition. Yet the paper still would not hire him, so he went to Europe and by a stroke of luck happened to be in Dunkirk, France, just as the British forces were being sealifted from Europe. Middleton was the only journalist at Dunkirk. The *Times* hired him the minute his riveting piece arrived on the editor's desk.

Journalism at Syracuse

In all fairness to Syracuse University, I cannot attribute my journalism skills solely to my work on the *Daily Orange*. The university had two brilliant journalism professors, who taught courses in current events and the history of journalism. In the early 1930s the university did not offer a major in journalism—this was long before it established the prestigious Newhouse School of Communications—so the best a student could do in the writing field was to minor in journalism within the liberal arts curriculum. In my senior year I was able to switch my major from chemistry to economics and my minor from zoology to writing.

Sammy Cain—known as the "mad Russian" because he had escaped the Bolsheviks in the early rounds of the Russian Revolution—was a part-time professor who was not officially on the faculty. He taught current events at Syracuse, which required him to make an arduous trip over icy, foggy, or potholed roads twice a week from Albany, where he was New York State commissioner of civil service. Sammy was deeply admired by his handful of students. He would appear each Tuesday and Thursday, no matter which makeshift room had been assigned for his class on the particular day, with a stern look but a twinkle in his eye. Every day he would greet his students with the same statement: "Middleton, Diamond. . . ," or whomever he chose, "what did I tell you, at the turn of the century, there will be only one type of government in the world—the socialists will become more democratic and the capitalists more socialistic."

Of course, the collapse of communism in Eastern Europe in 1990 would show that Sammy had been largely correct. Drew and I were hardly his favorite students; he frowned on anyone who got involved in extracurricular activities. Yet in the end, we were the only two who received an A in current events, for which students were required to submit two columns each week interpreting the political and economic news of the day.

Sammy was rough-edged and often a bully. In sharp contrast to him was our other part-time professor, Dr. Paul Paine, who was also the director of the City of Syracuse Public Library. Dr. Paine was a gentle, cultured, and compassionate man who taught us how the great publishers made their mark on the American newspaper industry. In his twice-weekly history of journalism classes, Drew and I were again the black sheep. This was not for what we did not do, but rather for what we did outside his class. When we were not attending classes or at the *Daily Orange* newsroom, Drew was usually preparing freelance articles for his New Jersey newspaper contacts. Meanwhile, I was working hard as a sportswriter for the college paper and freelancing "frosh" sports items for "Skiddy," the widely read *Syracuse Herald* sports columnist. I was also putting in considerable time as a member of the fencing and skiing teams and as a cheerleader. But when Dr. Paine's students submitted their final theses for his class, only two received an A, and only those two theses were placed on the shelves of the Syracuse Public Library at his recommendation: Drew's and my own.

The other subjects I excelled in during my senior year were two electives: history of fine arts, which was graded on the basis of a notebook I kept over the course of the year, and vocational psychology, which required each student to assemble a bookplate identifying his or her abilities and hopes. At the top of my bookplate list was a photo of three books that I had made it my life's goal to write.

Of the two journalism professors, it was Sammy Cain who had the strongest influence on me. It was he who instilled in me those three cardinal foundations of journalism, source, color, and organization. Those essentials have guided me for all my eighty-one tax and trade books, more than one hundred investment booklets, and more than five hundred speeches covering the international scene in the seventy years since I graduated from Syracuse University in 1934. I have never forgotten Sammy's words: "Every word must count." That has been my motto as an international economist and as a journalist.

From Gigolo to Pounding Stakes

Between my junior and senior years at Syracuse, the dean of women, on learning that I was a cheerleader, recommended me for a summer job as social director at

4. Walter's bookplate made in his vocational psychology class showing at the top a test tube representing his chemistry major and three books that he had set as a goal to write, 1933.

the Long Branch Hotel in New Jersey. So I joined a colleague from Brooklyn, a fraternity brother I had selected to be my partner in the venture, and we hitch-hiked there from New York. To our astonishment, we were greeted on the hotel steps by the owner's daughter, who blurted out: "This is not a social director's job — it is purely a gigolo's job."

Truer words were never spoken. The job was going to pay ten dollars a week plus full room and board (and free laundry). I was, I am sure, the envy of most American students at the time; as it turned out, the daily routine was probably the most arduous I ever faced. Every morning at four o'clock I was awakened by a hotel attendant telling me to accompany the women guests to nearby Red Bank to play golf with them. My instructions were to "be back in time to hit tennis balls" with these sophisticated women, whose husbands were mostly Wall Street financiers. During the boom years before the 1929 stock market crash, they would have spent their summers with their wives here; since the crash, they were staying close to the ticker-tape machines, hoping to recoup their losses.

Then every evening at eight, as the hotel's social director, I was expected to be on the dance floor with the "wallflowers." The bandleaders I had the privilege of introducing while I was there included Ray Noble, composer of the perennial hit "The Very Thought of You," and Isham Jones, who led another famous jazz orchestra during the depression years.

Even for a young athlete in good condition, this schedule was strenuous. After ten days racing to keep up, I resigned, just as a telegram arrived telling me that a summer job I had applied for with the Onondaga County Highway Department had come through. I dropped everything to hitchhike back to Syracuse and spent the rest of the summer happily pounding stakes for a surveying crew. I was lucky again — during the depression many students were having to leave college because they could not afford to continue.

WHEN I ENTERED SYRACUSE UNIVERSITY in 1930 I had every intention of getting a medical degree. My mother and her older sister had planned this for me since I was a child. They wanted another doctor in the family. My aunt, now living in New Orleans, having married a leading jeweler there, already had a doctor for a son — he had studied under the famous neurosurgeon Dr. Harvey Cushing of Boston's Peter Bent Brigham Hospital. My much older cousin Sydney Copeland was already making a name for himself as the head of neurosurgery at Tulane University Medical School and Hospital. Moreover, my mother, through her contacts in the mayor's office, knew Dr. Cushing, having taken her two older brothers to see him for surgery on devastating tumors. Dr. Cushing was the commencement speaker at my graduation in 1934, and when he spotted my mother sitting in the front row of the audience, he came down the ramp in his wheelchair to console her, as my father had passed away after his second heart attack the night before I graduated.

Having started out as a premed student at Syracuse, at the end of my junior year I went before the Admissions Review Board of the Medical School with faint hope of being accepted. I was nowhere near the top of the class, with a reasonable B average, and was practically thrown out after I answered the first question put to me by Dean Weiskotten, chairman of the board: "Why do you want to be a doctor, and what kind of a doctor do you wish to be?" I had been told to expect this question, and I was supposed to answer that it all depended on what I was good at and what I thought I would like and be equipped to handle after four more years of school. When I replied that I wanted to write about medicine — which was about the worst answer an applicant could give — I was politely dismissed by Dean Weiskotten (later in life I did write business articles for *Medical Economics* magazine).

Soon after, Mother was so depressed over my rejection letter that she called

Senator George Fearon, my godfather, to intercede. The senator was a close friend of my mother; she had been the mayor's secretary when he graduated from law school and had given him his first assignments as an upcoming lawyer. Whenever there was a legal problem in the mayor's office, she would call on him to consult or be the messenger.

Senator Fearon had never forgotten Kate Kabaker's kindness in helping him get his start as an attorney. As long as Mother was alive, he always was ready to help our family survive its reversals. He had attended Mother and Father's wedding in 1907, which had been arranged by the mayor at the elegant University Club, one of the first weddings ever held there. Before Fearon became head of the New York State Senate, as managing partner of Costello, Cooney, and Fearon—one of the two leading law firms in Onondaga County—he had magnanimously taken the landmark case (forgoing any fee) *Diamond v. New York Central Railroad.* The railroad was represented by the other prominent law firm in the area, Hancock, Doer, Kingsley, and Shove.

The 1929 Crash and Its Toll

In the aftermath of the 1929 stock market crash, my father suffered two heart attacks. He had been a director of the Salt Springs National Bank (which collapsed after Black Tuesday) and a close colleague of another director, who was also on the board of the New York Central Railroad. On the basis of that connection, Father had placed his life savings in New York Central stock, only to watch its value plummet after placing a sell order on October 28, 1929, at $262. It reached 261\frac{1}{4}$ before falling to $7. Eventually, it cost our family a major commercial building on the main business street of Syracuse, Salina, and a twenty-two-room house on Berkeley Drive close to the university campus, where I spent the first quarter of my life. Both were taken over by the First Trust and Deposit Company, whose president, "Ab" Merrill, lived across the street from us.

The case drew headlines because the New York Central had reneged on a contract signed by the attorneys for both parties relating to the building of six tracks on the Salina Street overpass. At the time, the railroad was being diverted from its original route through the main part of the city to the northern extremity of Salina Street. To build the overpass, the railroad would have to acquire the land under the six-story commercial building of H. Diamond and Son, which housed the haberdashery business my grandfather had started when he arrived from Poland in 1865.

Then the New York Central suddenly decided to change the width of the overpass to four tracks and laid them abutting the Diamond building. My family went to court over it, with Fearon as our lawyer. Despite the grandstand play of calling my six-year-old sister as a "star" witness (which inspired banner headlines in the daily papers), we lost the case. My father's financial woes had been ignited by the stock market crash and had been fanned by the deepening depression, which had forced him to mortgage the building to the hilt on the strength of the original New York Central offer. And now he had lost the lawsuit. All of it contributed to the heart failure that took his life when he was only sixty-three. He passed away the night before I graduated from college.

When I graduated from college in the early 1930s, in the middle of the worst depression in history, it had little meaning in the workplace. Jobs were so scarce that survival was all one could hope for. With prodding from my mother and my New Orleans aunt—both of whom were relentless when it came to making a doctor out of me—I considered applying to Tulane University Medical School, the same one where my cousin was head of neurosurgery. I had been advised that my pre-med grades, although far from top, were good enough, especially with my cousin to back my application.

Heavy financial responsibilities were hanging over me. I was the only man in the house, and my younger sister was ready for college. So I turned to journalism for my lifework. Having been the third-youngest Eagle Scout in the nation, with seventy-two merit badges out of a possible seventy-eight, and having been an assistant scoutmaster, I applied for a job with the Public Relations Division of Boy Scouts of America.

My cousin N. Wesley Markson was the comptroller of the City of Syracuse and a popular master of ceremonies at most official functions and social events in Onondaga County. He heard I was going to New York City for an interview for the Boy Scouts job, so he cabled me from aboard the *Morro Castle*. He and his wife, Mabel (the first woman automobile driver in Syracuse, defying nationwide sentiment that women should not drive), were returning from a holiday cruise. He instructed me to take his sixteen-cylinder Cadillac from its garage and meet them at the Hudson River pier in New York; from there, I would drive them back to Syracuse. As it later developed, this trip was the last complete voyage of the *Morro Castle*. That ill-fated luxury liner would sink on its next voyage after a devastating fire, taking hundreds of passengers and crew to the bottom of the shark-infested Caribbean.

Carrier Comes to Syracuse

My cousin's request did not surprise me, for two reasons. I had accompanied him when as a city comptroller he had visited Carrier Corporation in Newark to entice that company to move to Syracuse. The city offered to hand the company the Franklin automobile plant in the South Geddes Street area, which had become derelict since the city sequestered the property for back debts after Franklin filed for bankruptcy and closed down. The cost to Carrier would be one dollar, to show for the record that it was a binding sale. The implications of this "sale" were far-reaching: Carrier's future expansion would bring great financial rewards to both the company and the city; more important, it would put hundreds and eventually thousands of unemployed Syracusans to work.

Second, I was very close to both my mother's family and my father's. It always puzzled me why they had chosen me as their favorite child among the many other offspring nieces and nephews from my father's nine brothers and sisters and my mother's five. Looking back, I do remember making the family rounds every Sunday morning with my father, who would call on as many of his family as possible. After my father passed away in 1934, I continued the custom by myself right up until I left Syracuse two days after Pearl Harbor. I simply believed it was the right thing to do, what my father would have wanted. It was a rare week that I was not invited to dinner by my aunt Theresa or by my lovable aunt Margaret. As nurse and housekeeper to my ailing grandparents, this devout Irish Catholic with her County Clare brogue ran the original huge Diamond homestead on Jefferson Street that had once housed my grandparents and their ten children.

At the pier where the *Morro Castle* was berthed, I was surprised when Wesley and Mabel introduced me to William T. McCaffrey, the obese president of the Lincoln National Bank of Syracuse. Wesley explained that McCaffrey had been with them on the ship and would be joining us for the drive back to Syracuse. We had left New York behind and were in Westchester County when Wesley, a director of the Lincoln Bank, asked me what I was doing in New York. When I replied that my interview with the Boy Scouts for a job writing copy and press releases had gone well, he immediately told me: "Walter, you shouldn't leave Syracuse. With your father gone, your mother will need you. Bill here will give you a job at the bank." He turned to McCaffrey: "Isn't that right, Bill?" Our passenger did not seem to object: "Come in to see me next week," he blurted out. And that was the beginning of my banking career, which would occupy me for the next twenty years, except for nearly four years in the U.S. Navy during World War II.

But before starting at the bank, I made one more stab at becoming a sports-writer. As sports editor of the *Daily Orange* in my senior year, at a Syracuse-Columbia game at Baker Field, I had enjoyed the opportunity to work as a football spotter for Eddie Dooley of WOR Radio Network. Dooley was one of the three most popular radio sports announcers in the country, along with Ted Husing of CBS and Graham McNabee of NBC. Broadcasting had a strong appeal to me. Years later, as a director of the Syracuse Junior Chamber of Commerce, I would appear on station WSYR, on its regular Sunday night panel, covering business issues of the day. My mother arranged an interview with the publisher of the *Syracuse Post-Standard*, Jerome Barnum, whom she knew from her days at the mayor's office. Her motto was, "Always go to the top. Take nothing less if you want the right answer." The publisher told her that "unless Walter could be another Grantland Rice," who was the greatest sports columnist of that era, "he should forget being a sportswriter." So I took the bank job.

5. Syracuse Junior Chamber of Commerce directors, including Charles Schoeneck Jr., who later became a New York state senator and senate leader. *Syracuse Journal,* 1940.

An Avocation Begins

It was not exactly a happy marriage for me at the bank. As a bank messenger, from the start I encountered obstacles to my progress. In the past, the bank had extended its messengers six months' training; I was kept at that lowly post for more than a year. To me, the eleven dollars a week still looked good. More than half of the two thousand graduates of Syracuse University—the largest graduating class since its foundation in 1871—were still seeking work. At long last, I was promoted to be a block bank clerk. That involved balancing daily credits and debits. Fortunately, this gave me a freak opportunity to use my writing skills.

The bank's chief officer, the aforementioned McCaffrey, had been president of the Lincoln Alliance Bank in Rochester, New York (now a Chase bank). After the failure of the Salt Springs National Bank in Syracuse, the Monroe County Republican chairman, Clarence King, had spread his wings to Onondaga County. King believed that the city of Syracuse could use another commercial bank. With the help of A. Dean Dudley, chief executive of Niagara Hudson Electric Power, and Huntington Beard Crouse, president of Crouse-Hinds and a Syracuse University trustee and philanthropist, he started a bank and recruited McCaffrey to run it.

Through his contacts in Rochester, McCaffrey persuaded National Cash Register, Eastman Kodak, and Bausch and Lomb—all Rochester-based manufacturers—to design a combination camera and calculator that would eliminate the despised routine of hand-listing every daily bank check, deposit, debit, draft, and other transactions. The result was the Recordak machine, which was a great invention at the time. As a trained journalist with "a nose for news," and as the upstate correspondent for the *American Banker*—the only banking daily in the world—I prepared an article on the Lincoln Bank's new experiment.

What I did not know, and did not learn until later, was that McCaffrey's right-hand man, Charles Maltby, was ghostwriting an article about the Recordak (for McCaffrey's byline) for *Banking Magazine* of Philadelphia, scheduled for publication in January 1938. I had already asked Clinton Axford—editor of the *American Banker*—to run my article without a byline. It was not the first time that Maltby had been involved in preparing a manuscript for McCaffrey.

In 1937, McCaffrey was attending the Rutgers University Graduate School of Banking, a one-year course for the top bankers in the country, one of whom was David Rockefeller. To graduate, a student had to prepare a thesis in book form on a significant topic of the day. Although McCaffrey was a domestic banker, he had the courage and foresight to select a topic rarely before addressed in the United States: "A Comparison of the British and American Banking Systems." Considerable research was necessary, and when Maltby—who was assisting McCaffrey in its preparation—was stymied, he came to me for help, since he was aware of my background in international economics. The thesis was a resounding success and was placed on the shelves of the Rutgers School of Banking Library, alongside the theses of David Rockefeller and a few others.

Displacing Bank Tellers

Meanwhile, on December 30, 1937, my own article on the Recordak appeared as the lead story on page 1 of the *American Banker* under the headline "Lincoln of Syracuse Uses Gimmicks and Gadgets to Displace Six Tellers." That same morning, calls began coming in from all over the country and from as far away as Alaska, Hawaii, Australia, and South Africa. Over the next two weeks a steady flow of bankers from everywhere visited the bank to inspect this new invention.

No one at the bank had the faintest idea who had written the story. I kept hearing scuttlebutt that "it had to be an inside job." Of course, I did not mention a word of what I knew. At the same time, the officers were happy to see a relatively new bank draw worldwide attention, since correspondent banks quickly began responding with a much higher level of respect, which in the end meant more business for the Lincoln Bank of Syracuse.

Two weeks later, after several sleepless nights, while I was standing at the platform desk of the senior vice president, Cyrus Hawkins, where a copy of *American Banker* with the headline was displayed, I exclaimed: "Oh, they didn't run that article I sent them, did they?" Hawkins looked shocked. He pointed his finger at me and cried out: "You wrote this? A lowly bank clerk? Come with me." I trudged behind him to the president's secluded office at the front of the bank. After receiving a severe reprimand from McCaffrey, I retreated back to the block section, understanding that my future at the bank was to be short-lived. This was the only time in my many years at the bank that McCaffrey would ever speak to me; generally, he was accessible only to the bank's directors and a few officers. He died in 1939 from obesity and a liver ailment.

Soon after this embarrassing episode, Charlie Maltby, a close ally by then, let me know that the Lincoln Bank was not for me and that I would be wise to keep my eyes peeled for other work. During my six years at Lincoln Bank, I had been attending courses offered by the American Institute of Banking (AIB) at the

Syracuse University Graduate School of Extension. Courses were conducted at the downtown School of Law Building, diagonally across from the University Club and less than ten minutes' walk from the bank. The university had a unique arrangement with the institute: the AIB member banks paid the small sum of five dollars for each course an employee took; the employee could receive credits from the graduate school provided he or she paid the remainder of the thirty-five dollars that each course cost.

The director of the AIB curriculum, a brilliant and compassionate man who taught all the classes, was Dr. William Morton. He was also a finance professor at Syracuse University. Dr. Morton later became president of the Onondaga County Savings Bank. As the first comptroller of J. C. Penney and Company, he leaned heavily on myriad ingenious techniques of retailing—techniques he had learned from J. C. himself. Three evenings a week, from six to ten o'clock, I attended his classes in banking, finance, accounting, advanced economics, and international business. Usually I had to leave my day's work at the Lincoln Bank unfinished so as to hear his opening lecture, in which he always discussed the headlines of the day. Often I would have to return to the bank after classes to finish posting my assigned accounts as one of four bookkeepers. Many a time after midnight, I trudged through the snow in thirty-five-below weather the two miles up "the Hill" through the desolate university campus before reaching home for a night's rest.

As I plodded on sagging legs across the "Old Oval" of the campus, I would remember my childhood, when I had the vitality to play at the bottom of the fifty-foot-high coal pile outside the School of Forestry, which supplied the heat for the entire university. And I would remember how my younger sister and I once skied down from the top of Mount Olympus onto the campus while the students— many of them southerners who had never seen snow or heard of skiing before— lined up on both sides of the passage made for us to applaud our efforts.

In the late 1930s, while I was still working at the bank, Bill Tilden and Ernie Kozloh, several times Wimbledon singles and doubles champions in the 1920s and 1930s, made a promotional tour of upstate New York. They were scheduled to play at the elite Sedgwick Club in Syracuse. This incomparable pair had almost never lost a set. A coworker and friend, Joseph Nicholson, who later became president of the Merchants Bank in Syracuse, had teamed with me to win the AIB city championship, so we were selected to be the unfortunate opponents of the world champions of the 1920s. Needless to say, we did not win a single game, but at least we got to show our fortitude by appearing with them on the same court.

The Lincoln Bank had only one other staff member and two officers with an AIB degree, yet my achievement made little impression on the bank president and the other senior executives. Still determined to become a successful banker, I set out to become a state bank examiner. Each morning as I left my home on Berkeley Drive for the long trek to sign in at the bank by eight fifteen, I had with me the New York State Banking Code; my goal was to memorize the law. I learned a section each day in preparation for the three-part exam, which was famously difficult, so much so that few bank employees ever attempted it. Sure enough, I finally took the exam, and received mediocre grades, ranging from 35 to 42 percent (65 was considered a pass, and very few did). The Lincoln Bank's assistant cashier, with his twenty years of banking experience, did not do much better than I.

A Lucky Courier

Having given up on becoming a New York State bank examiner, I applied for an appointment as a national bank examiner. During the depression years, there were few dependable messenger services, and the most practical way for banks to register treasury securities was for the officers to physically carry these paper equities to the Federal Reserve Banks or to the Treasury Department in Washington, D.C. Charlie Maltby usually was the carrier for the Lincoln Bank, since he often visited Washington on the bank's business and for lobbying purposes. When I told him I was planning a trip to Washington, he quickly agreed to let me serve as a messenger. It would save him the chore of carrying one month's transactions to Washington—a bulky bundle of treasury bonds and certificates.

As a member of the bank's pistol team, I already had a pistol permit, issued by the county registrar. So off I went with my .38 H&R (Harrington and Richardson) strapped to the gearshift of my car for easy access if necessary. After I delivered the bonds to the correct window of the Treasury Department, I dropped in unannounced at the Office of the Comptroller of Currency. The comptroller, Franklin Delano, was a cousin of President Franklin Delano Roosevelt. After we shook hands, he introduced me to the assistant comptroller, Clarence Goff, who placed my job application in his files. This innocuous encounter turned out to be a key event in my life.

On December 7, 1941, Pearl Harbor Day, I had been helping install a ski tow as a member of the Cazenovia Ski Club. In the early 1940s, radios in auto-mobiles were quite new and rare, so we knew nothing about the sneak attack on Pearl Harbor until we returned home that evening. There I found waiting for me a telegram. The comptroller of currency had just appointed me an assistant national bank examiner. A few hours after his "Declaration of War Address" to the nation, President Roosevelt had issued orders that the holdings of Japanese, German, and Italian banks and businesses be sequestered as enemy property. It would be my task to help liquidate those entities.

Two days later I resigned from the Lincoln Bank, where I had worked my way up to head of cash items (now called adjuster) and director of research. However, I was still earning the eleven dollars a week at which I began as a messenger despite my completing the AIB courses, earning me six years of credits toward my Ph.D., and serving as a director of the Syracuse Junior Chamber of Commerce as well as the Lincoln Bank consul to the AIB. The rest of this book is a chronicle of what I have seen and done since that telegram arrived on the evening of Pearl Harbor Day.

Breaking the Glass Wall

DOROTHY B. DIAMOND

*B*EFORE MARRYING WALTER and becoming his coauthor, I enjoyed an independent career as a journalist dating back to when I was twelve. My parents had switched me from public to private school, where I was not only the youngest in the class but also the brightest, leading to my being bullied by older girls. My gloom was relieved by the friendship of Maxine Marx, Chico's daughter, who had been sent east to be educated in our New York City suburb. Chico often visited the academy, where he played the piano and flirtatiously pinched the French teacher's backside.

On Saturdays my mother escorted me to the children's concerts in Manhattan's Carnegie Hall. I confess that, while I liked Mozart and Beethoven, for me the high point of the performance always came when the audience folded their programs into airplanes and sent them sailing through the enormous auditorium. Midway in the series, the conductor, Ernest Schelling (successor to Walter Damrosch), told us about the concerts' annual notebook contest, and I submitted an entry. One of the greatest surprises of my life was receiving a telegram from Dr. Schelling himself congratulating me on winning the gold medal and inviting me to accept it on the Carnegie Hall stage. A photo of the event appeared in 1931 in the *New York Times'* Sunday edition.

For my high school education, I returned to public school and a more diversified student body. A chagrined academy administrator warned me: "You will not get into the college of your choice." Although our high school courses were less advanced than the academy's, we had wonderful teachers who made their subjects interesting and who were friendly, inviting us to visit them at home after school. My father urged me to take practical courses, specifically typing and shorthand. That's how I came to be the only college-bound student to venture

TALENTED YOUNG-
STERS OF LONG ISLAND WIN MUSICAL AWARDS: BERTRAM AND
DAVID PRESKY
of Brooklyn, Dorothy Blum of Woodmere and Constance Merce of Brooklyn
Receiving Medals From Director Ernest Schelling at the Children's Concert of the
Philharmonic-Symphony Orchestra in Carnegie Hall, New York.
(Brown.)

6. In 1931, twelve-year-old Dorothy Blum (Diamond) receives the coveted
award on the stage of Carnegie Hall in New York for preparing the best
notebook on the famed children's concerts in the 1920s and 1930s.

into the Commercial Department. Learning typing was fun because we did it in
unison. A teacher would read sentences in a stentorian voice, and we would re-
spond with uniform clacking of the keys.

Shorthand presented a problem for me. After two days of memorizing Gregg
symbols (and believe me, it was not easy), I was asked to drop out so that the
teacher could concentrate on fewer students. "You will never need to use this,"
she said. I would remember her comment when I was covering Washington press
conferences and envied other young women reporters calmly writing symbols in
their loose-leaf notebooks, recording exact quotes, while I frantically scribbled
hieroglyphics I would have to translate later.

Getting into an Ivy League college was highly competitive even then, although we were at the end of the Great Depression and many families were still
struggling financially and could not afford the fees. At Wellesley, my first choice,
the annual fee was one thousand dollars, half for courses and the other half for
dormitory living. Remembering the pessimistic prediction of the academy administrator, I went to an on-campus interview feeling somewhat nervous. How-

ever, a cordial woman admissions officer put my mother and me at ease and encouraged me to apply. My other applications went to Smith and Cornell. On the fateful day when the decisions arrived in the mail, I received three fat envelopes, meaning acceptance, and immediately chose Wellesley.

At my graduation ceremony I delivered the valedictory speech and won a twenty-five-dollar science prize donated by William J. Fox, a movie magnate who owned an estate in our town.

In 1936, Wellesley was a strict college. It imposed a curfew, required us to sign out at night, and set a quota for how many times we could go out on evening dates. The one advantage of the system was that, if you didn't like a blind date, you could remind him you needed to get back to the dormitory by a certain hour. Close supervision prevailed until Hilary Rodham Clinton (class of 1969) staged a revolution.

Madame Chiang Kai-shek's Professor

I majored in English literature and minored in economics. One of my most colorful professors was the redoubtable Annie Tuell, who taught a course on the rise (always pronounced "rice"} of the novel. If dissatisfied with a student's paper, she sometimes expressed her contempt with a scathing F-minus-minus grade. But she had a pleasant social side, entertaining us with teas in her dormitory apartment. Refreshments, consisting of Chinese tea and an anchovy-style paste spread on crackers, were provided by one of Miss Tuell's protégées, Mei-ling Soong, class of 1917, better known as Madame Chiang Kai-shek.

In our senior year, a normally staid economics professor became atypically emotional, complaining that our class was receiving an excellent education we would never use because we would all be getting married. She condemned our Wellesley schooling as a "waste of time" and hoped that in the future we would spend fifteen minutes a day on intellectual activities. Usually astute, she had no inkling that World War II was going to enable women to break the glass wall then separating us from exciting, responsible positions in a variety of occupations. Contrary to what had been predicted, women retained their positions after the war, and we entered an era of acceptance that women could do almost everything except fill top CEO positions. At that exalted level, the glass ceiling is just now being broken.

After my excellent and in-depth English-lit courses, what I enjoyed most at Wellesley was working on the *Wellesley College News*. I served as feature editor and helped cover exciting campus news: an imposter from Harvard disguised as a woman undergraduate winning the annual hoop race; and Sergei Rachmaninoff arriving on campus in a blizzard to play his sonatas.

In my senior year, choosing a career became an important issue. I had an excellent scholastic record, which led to admission to Phi Beta Kappa, but I was uncertain about how to blend academic accomplishments with the practical skills required for a job. Becoming a teacher or a secretary (even at the executive level) or a social worker did not appeal to me. Three years of law school was out of the question. Journalism tantalized, but I knew how hard it was to get an entry-level job.

My father, a prominent patent and trademark lawyer, heard from a Hollywood friend a story about a Beverly Hills teacher who assigned her class to write an essay called "The Poor Family." One student wrote: "The family was very poor. The Father and Mother were poor. The butler was poor. The cook and the maids were poor." Etc., etc. This anecdote does not sound hilarious today, but I sent it to the *New Yorker*'s "Talk of the Town" and received a form acceptance note with a ten-dollar check. It was my first paycheck and, undaunted by the small amount, I thought, "This is a good way to earn a living."

After Wellesley, Columbia Journalism

Soon afterward, Professor Eleanor Carroll of the Columbia Graduate School of Journalism arrived on campus to recruit students. During an interview, we discussed the increasing importance of the nonpress media, and she told me about Columbia's placement service. I submitted an application to the "J" School and was admitted to a class of 125 students, of whom 11 were women, 3 of them Wellesley graduates. Annual tuition was five hundred dollars (compared with fifty times as much today), and I did not have to pay a dormitory fee because I was living at home. I walked every day from our Manhattan apartment overlooking the yacht basin in the Hudson River to Broadway, where I boarded a streetcar that took me to Morningside Heights.

Classes took place in a "city room" furnished with rows of desks topped with office typewriters. No grades were issued except for courses in history of journalism and the legal aspects of libel and slander. For our first assignment, a professor recited the bare facts of a news event, which we had fifteen minutes to write up and hand in. Our efforts were then critiqued by a professor, who might be a Pulitzer Prize winner. It was a horrendous experience. Another day the professor

WELLESLEY COLLEGE
WELLESLEY, MASSACHUSETTS

OFFICE OF THE DEANS

June 29, 1939

Miss Dorothy Blum
316 W. 79th Street
New York City, N. Y.

Dear Dorothy:

It is a real pleasure to me
to find such splendid records as yours
among those for the Class of 1940. I
hope that the senior year will bring you
similar rewards and an increasing intellectual satisfaction in your academic work.

Cordially yours,

Helen T. Jones

Helen T. Jones
Dean of the Class of 1940

HTJ:RM

7. Letter to Dorothy from the dean of the class of 1940 at Wellesley College.

recited a chorus girl's adventure. The male student who wrote the least got the highest praise, because he realized that this was just a publicity stunt.

Interview with Eleanor Roosevelt

Later, we went out into the city to cover stories, which were then printed in our class newspaper. The assignment I most enjoyed was mingling with professional reporters at an interview with the first lady, Eleanor Roosevelt. Usually, reporters are not photographed, but a picture was taken of me with Mrs. Roosevelt.

Among the precepts handed down to us by our J School professors were the following:

• Develop your own specialty.

• You should be able to write a story after doing a half hour of research (which is certainly not true in this high-tech age).

• Get to know everyone in an organization.

• From Walter Pitkin (author of the book *Life Begins at Forty*): write all the facts of your story first, then the lead will come naturally. (Sometimes . . .)

My classmates included Helene Kazanjian, former editor of the *Wellesley College News,* and Helen Markel, daughter of Lester Markel, editor of the Sunday edition of the *New York Times.* Helen invited me and my friend Frances to dinners at her home, where we had the pleasure of conversing with her parents.

Our class included a clique of foreign students, who had enrolled in order to remain in the United States during World War II. A stunning blonde German woman was questioned in class about her Nazi friends. "Charming," she replied when asked about Göring, Goebbels, and then (pause) Hitler. To our disgrace, no one contradicted her. Later, the secret service became alarmed when the same blonde became a good friend of President Kennedy.

Toward the end of the school year, classes fizzled out as several faculty members rushed to volunteer for the war effort. Only two weeks after graduation, I was seated in another newsroom in another city working as a cub reporter for a tabloid newspaper. I arrived at one in the afternoon and stayed until ten. My first story, headlined "Silk Stockings Go to War," went out on the Associated Press wire. Our newspaper and the AP shared office space, separated by a wall of filing cabinets. Soon after my article was dispatched, the face of a young man appeared over the wall of cabinets and a recent Princeton graduate asked, "What are you doing here?" We became friends, and he saw me home most nights after work, so I was not endangered by street crime.

Much as I enjoyed the excitement of a daily newspaper, nighttime hours and impending cold weather made me realize that I had better move on. With the help of Columbia University's placement office, I landed a job on a youth magazine, *Young America,* located advantageously in the heart of Manhattan's art and fashion world, at the junction of Madison Avenue and Fifty-seventh Street. The building housed the Parke Bernet auction house, a Rolls-Royce showroom, and an art gallery where Greta Garbo and Marlene Dietrich dropped in to browse.

I shared a double desk with the magazine's editor, the son of a *New Yorker* columnist. My job was to help produce the magazine and write a column for it. Everything was satisfactory except that, after a year, I was earning only $22.50 a week, which was less than the prevalent entry-level wage. I made an appointment to talk with our usually courteous publisher, a favorite golf partner of Edward, duke of Windsor (formerly King Edward VIII), and an heir to the R. H. Macy department store fortune. If a staff member could not pay for, say, root-canal work, the publisher was known to help out by sending the employee to his own dentist and taking care of the bill. Committing himself to a raise, even a small one, was another matter. "Do you live at home?" he asked. Upon receiving a "yes" answer, he retorted, "Then you don't need any more money."

After hearing about this conversation, my editor naturally concluded, "You are not going to get anywhere here. I am going to call a friend who edits an advertising trade magazine named *Tide*. He won't hire you, because you know nothing about business, but he knows everybody in town. I'll make an appointment for you." This single kindhearted phone call set the course of my life—both my career and my marriage.

Finding a Niche in Journalism

Tide could no longer hire male writers because they were involved with the war, either by choice or from the draft, so its editor was hiring women, predominantly those who were tall and long-legged. I fitted into this category and joined the staff as an associate editor.

My first day on the job, someone handed me a press release and asked me to rewrite it. I dashed out some copy, and soon the editor arrived offering lavish praise for my work. I had found my niche in journalism as a business writer.

A young woman my age stepped in from the neighboring cubicle to say hello. She told me she had an older brother, and she would introduce me to him. Her name was Faye Diamond.

Interviewing Business Leaders

Tide had been founded by Time, Inc., but was now owned by Raymond Rubicam, head of Young and Rubicam, one of the world's largest and most prestigious advertising agencies. Thanks to the magazine's excellent reputation, it was easy to get interviews with prominent businessmen. From our offices on Thirty-seventh street off Madison Avenue, one day I took a taxi south to the financial district to interview E. F. Hutton, who obligingly brought me uptown in his chauffeured Rolls-Royce. A few days later I was heading north to talk to CBS executive Frank Stanton about the impending arrival of color television. During an especially hot summer, the best place to schedule an interview was in NBC's Studio H, where Arturo Toscanini conducted his concerts at night. It was one of the few air-conditioned spots in town.

Occasionally while I was visiting Faye I met Walter, but we exchanged only perfunctory greetings. The first time he called me for a date, a woman informed him "Dardi no here" and hung up. Walter thought this was my mother and decided not to get mixed up with a family that didn't speak English. Actually, the phone had been answered by our beloved Hilda Reffler, a superb cook and housekeeper, who was a wizard in the stock market but never mastered the English language. Thus, my first date with Walter didn't take place until two years later.

Meanwhile, the business world was preparing for the postwar years. My father astonished me by saying that housewives would no longer need to go through the drudgery of squeezing orange juice, but instead would be able to buy it in concentrated frozen form inside a small cardboard cylinder, an invention of his client Clarence Birdseye.

New vacuum cleaners and other household appliances were not being manufactured because factories were being used for wartime purposes. An enterprising Long Island bank, Franklin Square National, promoted a layaway savings plan so that depositors would have the funds to buy appliances as soon as they became available.

During a weekend visiting my friend Frances, now a *New York Herald Tribune* woman's page writer living in her parents' Long Island home while her husband was overseas, I mentioned my Franklin Square business article to her. We agreed that the topic would be of interest to a national magazine and promptly drove to the bank to interview the manager. Our joint effort was accepted by *Collier's*, a general interest magazine.

Hitting the Big-Time Media Market

From there we went on to become busy freelancers, selling numerous articles during the absence of other journalists covering the war. One of our articles, "Ladies May Lobby," appeared in *Mademoiselle*. Inspired by a Broadway musical comedy hit, *Bloomer Girl*, we wrote a piece called "The Real Amelia Bloomer." She was a suffragette from upstate New York who promoted the wearing of bloomers, an abbreviated outer garment designed to release women from the confinement of long skirts. Made of navy blue or black serge, bloomers were cinched at the waist, puffed out at the sides, and then fastened daringly above the knee. I wore them at gym classes and summer camp. We thought the article was suitable for the *New York Times Sunday Magazine* and sent it to Lester Markel. He wrote back graciously, remembering "the Dorothy and Frances I used to know," and accepted the article.

Raymond Rubicam was asked to contribute a chapter on advertising to a book to be titled *While You Were Gone*, which was being written for people who had been posted overseas during the war. He asked me to help compile it. The chapter praised individual advertisers and the Advertising Council for their contributions to the war effort, but lacerated companies running offensive "brag" advertising.

At the age of fifty-three, Mr. Rubicam decided to retire from the advertising business and move to Phoenix, where he would develop the Valley National Bank as well as Scottsdale. He also wanted to write intellectual articles and suggested that I join him in Phoenix as his assistant. I preferred to work for a company rather than an individual, and so politely declined.

On to Washington

My editor was disappointed with the coverage he was receiving from a Washington correspondent and asked me to open and run a one-woman news bureau in the Capitol. I hesitated about moving to a city where housing was extremely difficult to find, where hotels rationed how long guests could stay, and where I knew only a few people. But after much soul-searching, I agreed to accept the challenge.

In April 1945, I took a morning train to Washington. That same evening I went to a crowded cocktail party. "If you take one step backward, you'll be stepping on the vice president's foot," a guest warned me. The next day I accompanied a group of businessmen to the White House for an appointment with our new president, Harry Truman, who had been in office only one week following President Roosevelt's death. Greeting another newcomer, the president put his arm around me and escorted me to a chair next to his desk. What a wonderful welcome!

I soon made an appointment to interview the renowned poet Archibald

MacLeish, head of the Office of War Information. While I was seated in the waiting room, a dapper man came out to screen me. I stiffened and asked, "And who are you?" He replied, "Just Adlai Stevenson, a Chicago lawyer." We became friendly, and after his defeat in the 1952 presidential race, I wrote him. He promptly replied with a handwritten letter.

During the ten days the Wardman Park Hotel permitted me to stay as its guest, I placed an "apartment wanted" ad in the *Washington Post*. Out of fourteen responses, I chose a summer sublet in former slave quarters located in the rear of a handsome Georgetown mansion. When the lease expired, I joined a group of journalists living in the southwest area. Then Christine Sadler, a top reporter for the *Washington Post*, rented me an apartment on Adams Mill Road near the zoo. At night I could hear the lions roaring. The zookeeper, who lived in the building, tried to raise a baby tiger in a bathtub but was unsuccessful.

The Hidden Persuaders

I needed a few bottles of liquor for entertaining in my apartment and searched in vain for any advertising addressed to women. In a dispatch from Washington, I wrote: "If I were to become acquainted with American drinking habits merely from advertising, I would assume that whisky and gin are consumed mostly by men." This was at a time when, in a survey of liquor stores, 38 percent reported that half their customers were women. It turned out that the Treasury Department had an excise tax rule that prohibited women from being mentioned or shown in advertising promoting alcoholic beverages. The rule has since been revoked. The fracas over appealing to women as purchasers of liquor was reported in Vance Packard's landmark study on motivational research, *The Hidden Persuaders*.

I had office space near the Willard Hotel, but my real hangout was a newsroom in the Social Security Building, where I mingled with representatives of the major newspapers. One reporter, who was required to file a daily story, began to submit a story one day and then deny it the next. This subterfuge was soon discovered, and he was fired.

By now I was getting to know important people. I just missed being on the first *Meet the Press* broadcast, lunched with Agnes Myer (Katharine Graham's mother), and was approached about becoming a pioneer television critic. But I really wasn't happy living and working alone, and I transferred back to Manhattan.

Faye Diamond had taken another job, but Walter called to invite me for a dinner date at the romantic Silvermine Tavern in the Connecticut woods. He was so kind to me and so skillful at making me feel comfortable that I was instantly attracted to him. As he carried me over a rustic bridge spanning a pond, the much-talked-about chemistry between two people came into play. After dinner I went with him to his apartment, where he asked me to type a report on Argentina for him. A portent of things to come.

A Unique Proposal

Walter and I have many similar interests, but skiing is not one of them. I took ski lessons, but I am not athletic and never progressed beyond slow intermediate turns. In April we drove to Manchester, Vermont, for spring skiing at Snow Valley. While we rode a lift up the mountain, it was snowing lightly, but soon a blizzard descended upon the area. I huddled under a tree on the Bulldozer Trail until Walter skied down to meet me. He proposed marriage, and I accepted enthusiastically, without delay, so that we could hurry to a sheltered place at the bottom of the mountain. As Walter now tells it, I have been "bulldozed" ever since.

Our news was received with jubilation by my parents and brother, by Dad's partner and his wife (good friends), and by Hilda. We were married in June at home in a small family ceremony, which was followed by a reception and dinner for more friends and family at the Plaza Hotel. For our honeymoon, we drove through Lake Placid to Gray Rocks Inn, a ski resort in the Laurentian Mountains north of Montreal. Our sports activities consisted of renting a canoe and my paddling Walter around Lake Ouimet.

Just before our wedding I was asked to become the first woman marketing editor of *Business Week*. I turned down this tempting offer because a challenging new job and a new marriage seemed like a risky combination. Fortunately, I was to receive many offers of part-time jobs and freelance work over the coming years.

Dexter Masters, editor of *Consumers Union*, asked me to take a part-time summer job writing articles and helping put the annual *Buying Guide* to press. I especially enjoyed subscribing to a fruit-of-the-month club and comparing the taste, ripeness, and appearance of the fruits against the club's claims for them.

Revealing the "Woman's Viewpoint"

A marketing specialist, Charlotte Montgomery, engaged me to help her with various projects, including learning how women felt about cigars (hatred was the al-

Magazine Editor Engaged

Dorothy Blum, of "Tide," Fiancee of Walter Diamond, Economist

Mr. and Mrs. Asher Blum, of this city, announce the engagement of their daughter, Miss Dorothy F. Blum, to Mr. Walter H. Diamond, former Maritime Service and Navy officer, son of Mrs. Samuel C. Diamond, of Syracuse and New York, and the late Mr. Diamond. Miss Blum, Wellesley College alumna and a Phi Beta Kappa, received the master's degree from Columbia Graduate School of Journalism and is a senior associate editor of "Tide" Magazine and a contributor to magazines.

Mr. Diamond, a graduate of Syracuse University and the American Institute of Banking, took post-graduate studies at Syracuse and is foreign economist for the Public National Bank and Trust Company of New York. He served in Europe and the Pacific during he war.

Ira L. Hill
Miss Dorothy F. Blum

8. Dorothy's engagement announcement. *New York Times,* 1947.

most universal response) and launching a campaign promoting soup for break-fast. (It flopped.) Charlotte had originated a column, "The Woman's Viewpoint," for *Tide,* and when she was invited to become a *Good Housekeeping* contributor, she recommended me as her replacement.

During several years of writing the column, I approved of small cars, frowned on dramatic television commercials unrelated to the products they were supposed to promote, expressed irritation at heavy packaging that prevented access to products, and left hungry after a press luncheon at which all the food was made from soybeans.

The column led to my becoming the first woman speaker at the Atlanta Advertising Club. Afterward, I took off to meet Walter in Mexico City. To my horror, the air trip involved three flights with stopovers in poorly furnished Quonset huts baking in the glaring sun. When the plane landed at Mexico City airport alongside a tropical garden at one in the morning, I noticed in the waiting crowd an affable red-haired man. I thought, "I wish he were meeting me." It was mental telepathy. He came right over, introduced himself as Rudy Fauchey, a McGraw-Hill representative, and drove me to the Hotel Reforma.

The next morning I met a government official I'd known in Washington, and he advised me to move to the renovated section of the hotel. The reservation clerk failed to record the change, and that is how Walter was told, "The lady is out for the night," when he arrived in the evening.

The editor in chief of the magazine *Modern Floor Coverings* asked me to write a column with the alliterative title "Candid Customer Comments." My first column, about a carpet shopper's grievances, must have hit the right note, because the next issue's cover announced in huge red letters, "Dorothy Is Back!" To obtain material for the column, while traveling abroad we visited carpet factories, including one near the Taj Mahal, where we recoiled at the sight of rows of young children injuring their eyesight by weaving rugs. Child labor was also exploited in Greek rug factories.

McCall's asked me to publicize its Woman's Congress devoted to improving the status of women. Eleanor Roosevelt was honorary chairman, and I found her pleasant, obliging, cooperative, undeniably an aristocrat. The same magazine asked me to write an article, "Be Your Own Decorator." When the check arrived, Walter asked: "What are you going to do with it?" "Hire a decorator" was my reply. And so I found a decorator who loved to browse in musty Third Avenue antique shops. She and her brother, who owned a Manhattan store specializing in decorative accessories, helped us refurbish our apartment, which was located on the former Warburg estate in Hartsdale, New York (where George Balanchine presented his first ballet in the United States). Later, they helped us decorate the colonial house we built nearby on a street headed by an eighteenth-century cottage where George Washington and General Rochambeau met to plan the Battle of White Plains.

The *New York Times* travel section ran my articles on Malta and Yugoslavia. For the *New York Post* I covered Antigua, Banff, and Norfolk. I also wrote chapters on Malta, Cyprus, Ecuador, Greece, Turkey, Iran, Israel, Australia, New Zealand, and other countries for *Pan Am's World Guide* and did a series of foreign-city profiles for TWA.

An editor for the floor coverings magazine, Larry Shelton, had become a reading-rack publisher supplying leaflets to employers for distribution in their cafeterias and recreational areas. I wrote fifty booklets for him, including three offering recipes for budget, meatless, and fish cooking. I also instructed readers about how to lose weight, give good parties, safeguard their home, refinish furniture, stop smoking, and prevent dental problems. Most valuable to me was a booklet on street safety, which helped me ward off a Madison Avenue mugger.

In December 1973, we were just leaving on a trip to Taipei when Larry telephoned to tell me he was quitting the reading-rack business to become a professional in his hobby, collecting rare birds. "What next?" I wondered about my future career.

Becoming Walter's Coauthor

I never dreamed that in a few days I would be switching to international affairs as coauthor of *Tax Havens of the World.* In dealing with this controversial topic, we have always been impartial and have reported in detail the "harmful" lists, blacklists, and sanctions imposed by the Organization for Economic Cooperation and Development and the Financial Action Task Force. Professor William Byrnes of St. Thomas University has praised *Havens* as the only "quality" work in the field.

9. Walter H. Diamond and Dorothy B. Diamond, authors of eighty-one international tax and trade books published by five law publishers as described in a feature article defining their contribution to overseas operation of U.S. and European industry. *New York Times,* 1989.

I am also coauthor of *International Trust Laws and Analysis*, *Global Guide to Investment Incentives and Capital Formation*, and *Tax Free Trade Zones of the World*. In a conference with Oceana Publications as to who would annotate eighteen hundred treaties for *International Tax Treaties of All Nations*, Edwin Newman, Oceana's vice president, chose me, to the relief of everyone else. I was appalled, but decided to make the best of it by varying my vocabulary and giving as much background history and analysis as possible. When I emerged from the ordeal, I had the reward of being a more facile writer.

Walter and I have worked together happily for more than thirty years, and people sometimes wonder how we manage it. When I recently had an appointment with a new doctor, he asked: "What do you do?" I replied: "I write books on international finance with my husband." A look of horror came over his face, as if I had said I walk barefoot over hot coals. Actually, we find that our collaboration has strengthened our marriage by adding common interests and giving us joint satisfaction from our mutual achievements. One thing is sure: we never run out of things to talk about.

PART ONE

World War II

⇒ 1 ⇐

The War at Home

*I*T WAS THREE DAYS after receiving the telegram from the comptroller of currency that I reported to the New York Federal Reserve Bank. Ninety-six bank examiners—two from each state—had assembled for orientation. We were about to be taught how to "take over" the German, Italian, and Japanese banks and businesses that had been shut down by federal agents on the night of Pearl Harbor. Our "simple" mission was to find the record books, collect all documents, block all bank accounts, look for violations, and take note of all questionable transactions.

Unraveling Espionage Devices

Officially, we were employed by the Comptroller of the Currency Office; in practice, our boss was the Alien Property Custodian, the charismatic Leo Crowley. Crowley had advised us through Federal Reserve channels that when we entered an alien bank or business, we were to explain that we were making a normal accounting investigation under the authority of the Federal Reserve Bank and the Treasury. We were absolutely not to tell them we had been sent by the Alien Property Custodian. Often we would be accompanied by FBI or Treasury agents, but we were not to identify those people as such.

Actually, my introduction to the world of espionage came the first night after arriving in New York. My initial assignment was an order to visit B. Westermann's bookstore, a popular and respected seller of all types of books. The store was in Radio City just off Fifth Avenue. I was to secure the company's accounting ledgers, using my U.S. Treasury identification for entry. Unbeknownst to me was that the FBI strongly suspected that this store served as the principal drop point for a Nazi espionage ring.

Soon after confiscating the accounting records and other documents—

Walter Diamond To Aid in Figuring Jap Banks' Assets

Walter H. Diamond, of 1301 E. Genesee st., for the past eight years connected with the Lincoln National bank,
yesterday was appointed an assistant national bank examiner by the comptroller of the currency. He left immediately for New York city, and today will begin work in the foreign funds control department of the Federal Reserve bank.

W. H. Diamond

Diamond's immediate task will be to assist in the examination of Japanese banks whose assets were ordered "frozen" at the outbreak of hostilities.

Graduated from Nottingham high school in 1930, Syracuse university in 1934 and the American Institute of Banking in 1939, Diamond began working for Lincoln bank as a messenger. He is a director of the Syracuse junior chamber of commerce and editor of that group's official publication, former editor of The Syracuse Banker, and a frequent contributor to The American Banker magazine.

10. Article concerning Walter Diamond's appointment as an assistant national bank examiner. *Syracuse Post-Standard, 1941.*

Diamond Leaves Lincoln Bank for Federal Reserve Job

Appointment of Walter H. Diamond of 1301 East Genesee Street to assistant national bank examiner was announced by the Comptroller of Currency in Washington yesterday. Mr. Diamond, who has been with the Lincoln National Bank and Trust Company of Syracuse for the last eight years, will be connected with the foreign funds control division of the Federal Reserve Bank of New York.

Due to the present war emergency, Diamond was requested to report immediately by the Comptroller's office, and will take over his new duties at the Federal Reserve Bank Friday morning.

Diamond is a graduate of Syracuse University and the American Institute of Banking. He is former editor of the "Syracuse Banker" and an upstate correspondent for the "American Banker." He also was a director of the Junior Chamber of Commerce and consul of the Syracuse Chapter of the Institute of Banking for the Lincoln Bank.

11. Article concerning Walter Diamond's appointment as an assistant national bank examiner. *Syracuse Herald, 1941.*

which I reviewed and then handed over to the Federal Reserve Bank of New York, as was the usual procedure—the FBI found proof of its suspicions. On the bookstore shelves, in well-secluded spots, they found dozens of coded messages placed on pages of ordinary books. The "spymaster" at Westermann's was apparently a Mr. Helmater, an employee there. Helmater was a leader of the German Bund and was using the store as a distribution point for Bund pamphlets and papers. Helmater, along with his underling, Schutz—a known Bund member with Mafia connections—later served prison sentences for their espionage activities.

I knew nothing at the time about how important the Westermann raid would be to the U.S. war effort. Later, I would be described as the government agent who slept with his feet against the door "scared [expletive]," as reported afterward by John Ray Carlson, the author of *Undercover*, which became a best-seller when it was published just after the war. The FBI arrived the following morning to relieve me from my post. Later, after examining the ledger entries for suspicious transfers, I became certain that the store owner had no idea that his well-respected business was being exploited by the Nazis.

My New York colleague Howard Shulman, a bank examiner from Brooklyn, had been available to report for work on Pearl Harbor night. When I finally arrived and met him, he quickly adopted me as his "younger brother." He lost no time telling me all the fascinating details of his first assignment, which he had carried out even while the world was still waking up to the details of the Pearl Harbor attack. On that very evening, only hours after FDR's address to the nation declaring "this day of infamy," Howard was ordered to go to the Nippon Club, a circle of local Japanese businessmen. As usual, "Geisha girls" were gathered in the elegant 1912 brownstone house at 161 West Ninety-third Street. Howard and the other examiners were astonished to find a dozen geisha girls perched on the floor of the main hall in their traditional Japanese position with their legs crosswise; clearly, they were apprehensive about their American callers. The examiners had been tipped off that at the club they would encounter a number of important Japanese business executives who would have had inside information about Tokyo's war plans. Later, when examining the books, we found that the club had been disseminating a great deal of Japanese propaganda about American "transgressions."

On the Friday morning after Pearl Harbor, all ninety-six bank examiners reported to the Federal Reserve Bank of New York for their first assignments. We were divided into six groups of roughly fifteen agents; each of the teams was assigned to take over a single foreign bank. The Yokohama Specie Bank, because it was the largest, was assigned to twenty-five agents. The other four banks were Mitsui, Mitsubishi, Banco di Napoli, and the Deutsche Bank. The sixth group was assigned to take over the Allied Chemical Corporation in New Jersey, an affiliate of a giant German producer of chemicals and pharmaceuticals.

Liquidating Foreign Banks

I was directed to the Yokohama Specie Bank, which occupied several floors of 120 Broadway, at that time one of Wall Street's largest and most modern buildings. It was suspected (and it turned out to be true) that a large part of Allied Chemical's production was being shipped to third countries but ending up in Germany, where it fed the Nazi war machine — in particular, its chemical warfare program.

At the Yokohama offices, I was told to take over the assistant manager's desk. I opened the top right-hand drawer expecting to find records of important financial transactions. What I found instead were some scraps of cockroach-infested food and a photo tabloid; I began turning its pages and found one sheet after another of Japanese pornography. I counted 138 positions. Of course, the other examiners crowded around, eager to absorb a taste of Japanese "art."

Because of all the books, food, garbage, and dirt we found at Yokohama, we were ordered not to report for work on Saturday: the entire bank was to be fumigated. When we returned the following Monday — now eight days after Pearl Harbor — we were not allowed to enter until noon. There was a six-inch layer of dead cockroaches outside the several doors of the bank.

The headquarters of the Yokohama Specie Bank were, obviously, in Yokohama, which was Japan's largest port at the time as well as the hub of the nation's commerce and trade. Much the greater part of Japanese imports and exports were processed through that city. Yokohama Specie's staff were well schooled in the handling of trade documents and consequently were some of the world's most sophisticated bankers. We saw numerous signs of their business expertise in the many letters of credit we found — letters that covered payments for American exports, which were confirmed by European banks and by some Latin American ones, mainly in Argentina. Most of these shipments represented sales by major American manufacturers of strategic materials, including chemicals, pharmaceuticals, machine tools, light arms, ammunition, and agricultural equipment (mainly trucks and bulldozers). Almost all bills of lading were processed through third frontiers, but the goods themselves eventually came into the hands of the Nazis or their Italian Fascist allies.

When we liquidated the Yokohama Specie Bank (and, later on, other alien banks), what surprised us most was that these institutions seemed to be running normally and efficiently under the guidance of low-echelon officers — generally assistant managers. We investigated and quickly learned that the top officials —

from the managing directors and their deputies down to the vice presidents—had all left the United States when the last transport ship sailed for Japan from the United States on July 31, 1941. That was the date Roosevelt decreed all Japanese citizens must leave the United States or face internment.

By six months after Pearl Harbor, almost all the foreign banks in the Second Federal Reserve District had been liquidated by Crowley's office. At that point all of the examiners were withdrawn from the banks, except for one or two in each. These examiners were kept on hand in case the FBI asked for supporting information for their investigations. Security guards were also posted at each bank, and the entrances were padlocked.

The eighty-odd examiners involved in liquidating the five sequestered banks agreed unanimously that these institutions had been administered by shrewd managers who had been taking orders from their headquarters staff, who in turn had been directed by their respective governments. Operations were generally carried out in a gray area; we often found that these banks had been violating U.S. commercial laws.

The key conclusion the examiners reached, after thorough investigation, was that each Japanese bank had government agents on the staff who were well aware of Japan's aggressive intentions. Managers of these banks showed no surprise and expressed no remorse over Pearl Harbor. Actually, the Japanese banks, like the American branches of the Deutsche Bank and the Banco di Napoli, had been serving as spy nests for the Axis powers.

While we were uncovering one dubious or illegal transaction after another, we were puzzled by one fact: how could everyone in the United States in a position to know or to ask have missed what these banks were doing? The politicians in Washington had not known, and neither had American businesspeople. Our conclusion: American politicians, bankers, and business executives were more naive than anyone had ever realized.

An Italian Front

On the last day of my assignment at Yokohama Specie, I was about to leave the bank when I received an emergency call from my reporting officer at the Federal Reserve Bank, Jim Carroll, a gentleman of the old school admired by all the examiners for his habitual kindness. To this day, sixty years later, I remember him as the finest boss I ever had. Apologizing for the call, he told me that Crowley's office had called him and that he needed someone to go immediately to the offices of Francisco Renzuli, executive director of the Federation of Italian World War I Veterans, on the sixth floor of the RCA Building at Radio City. It was urgent. The harrowing investigation would turn out to be of immense importance to the war.

After I knocked several times on the door, it was answered by a stunning Sicilian woman with long, braided blonde hair. She reluctantly allowed me to enter after I flashed my Treasury agent's ID. I quickly did the usual—gather the office books and search the desk drawers for tip-off documents—and while doing so found several surprises. First, deep in a drawer were stacked a dozen savings bank books and many receipts for U.S. war savings bonds. The bonds reflected large accounts at Radio City's most respected bank, the Colonial Trust Company, and at the Banco di Napoli. These would serve as springboards for the subsequent investigation of the federation.

While liquidating the Banco di Napoli, the examiners had noted daily transfers of funds to European banks, mostly Swiss ones, for the account of the Italian government at the headquarters offices of the Banco di Napoli or for that bank's branches in Sicily. Many of these remittances—so it was learned after the Allied occupation—had been directed to the personal accounts of Mussolini. Therefore, it was not a complete surprise to me to find that there was millions of dollars in bank deposits representing the federation's routine collections from families of Italian World War I veterans in the United States. These collections were supposed to be deposited in blocked accounts in Manufacturers Trust Company safe deposit vaults under a license granted by the U.S. Treasury Department, as authorized by the Alien Property Custodian. Yet I could find no deposits or Treasury bond receipt slips confirming it had been done. However, I did uncover certificates indicating that these monies had been deposited at the Federal Reserve Bank of New York in unblocked accounts, as well as finding records and more passbooks representing savings accounts at Colonial Trust.

After admitting me to the federation offices, the Sicilian office secretary called Dr. Renzuli at his home in Tuckahoe, New York. By the time I returned from blocking the accounts at Colonial Trust, he was there to meet me. Needless to say, he was indignant that his books and records were being investigated. He declared that he would be contacting his attorneys. As usual, I brushed aside these threats of legal retaliation, as we had been instructed to do. Soon after, though, I learned that this case had many more ramifications than either the Treasury or FBI had anticipated.

A Narrow Escape

Early the next morning, Jim Carroll called me to report to headquarters immediately. "A problem developed during the night." Always considerate to his subordinates, he added: "Don't be alarmed. The problem has already been solved." Of course, I knew that when I was blocking the federation's accounts at the Colonial Trust the evening before, I did not have an official warrant to do so. The federation's lawyer had contacted the attorney general's office in Washington, D.C., to file a strongly worded complaint. Soon after, official authorization was released by the Treasury to block the accounts.

When I arrived at Jim's office, I was greeted by a burly man with an anguished look on his lined face. Blocking my way toward Jim's desk, he thrust his finger at me, shouting: "You had no right to block our accounts!" He then reached into his coat pocket and pulled out a .38 H&R pistol, which he aimed at me. Two security officers standing at the door rushed him and knocked it from his hand. To my utter dismay, Jim told me who the triggerman was: the controversial and infamous former judge Joseph Mancusco, who had been a powerful figure in Jimmy Walker's day and who had attracted headlines as an alleged accomplice of Murder Inc. and as an associate of the Al Capone gang.

When the FBI reviewed my report and case history (all bank examiners were required to submit them promptly), it came out that Justice Department personnel as well as J. Edgar Hoover himself had long suspected the Mafia was deeply involved in the many German Bund cells scattered around the country. The Mafia's purpose in doing so was to help the Fascists interfere with the U.S. war effort. My examination of the federation's books revealed the presence of Sicilian employees both at the federation and at the Banco di Napoli, as well as a heavy outflow of transfers to Sicily, Naples, and Rome. As soon as Hoover heard about it, he asked for more details from his agents.

An Ambassadorial Exchange

All of these events sparked an investigation of the whereabouts of Antonine Corregliana, general manager of the Banco di Napoli in New York, who had signed almost all of the dollar transfers to Italian banks. Corregliana were a major player both on Wall Street an in New York's Little Italy. The Immigration and State Departments eventually located him on Ellis Island, where he was waiting to board the first available Europe-bound freighter; undoubtedly, he was heading for Italy. Orders to detain him were immediately issued by immigration officials. I accompanied two FBI agents to Ellis Island to serve him with an arrest warrant. I went along because that warrant was based on my report on the federation.

Meanwhile, the State Department had been trying to end this turmoil by negotiating the release of the U.S. ambassador to Italy, who was being held at his residence in Rome as a hostage. The Swiss were the intermediaries in this negotiation. By the time we arrived at Ellis Island, the State Department had arranged an exchange of "prisoners": the ambassador for Corregliana.

My next assignment would help roll up one of the most cunning and harmful espionage networks in the country. Late in the day after I returned from Ellis Island, Leo Crowley called me. This call was the first time I had spoken to him since I joined the examiners' team. He told me to be waiting at the northwest corner of Forty-fifth Street and Lexington Avenue at 5:55 P.M. There I would meet two U.S. Treasury special agents; each would be carrying a briefcase in his left hand. On the southwest corner, I would see two photography experts from the Treasury Department; each would be holding his hat in his right hand and would join us. Then, from the northeast would appear two FBI agents, each wearing a white handkerchief in his left breast pocket. These handkerchiefs would be folded neatly to display four points representing East, West, North, and South. By protruding one of the folds, an agent might confirm the direction of a specific rendezvous or activity. (Hoover required all his agents to fold their handkerchiefs this way in order to facilitate identification; I have followed the same habit to this day.)

A German Cell Exposed

At precisely 6:00 P.M., as instructed, our seven-man contingent entered the Graybar Building at 405 Lexington Avenue and knocked on the door of the eighth-floor offices of Lexington Model Photography. We were greeted by Hans Kohlman, a robust German, who admitted us effusively as if he was expecting us.

Kohlman led me to what he said were the files. While I was requesting the company's books, I heard chattering in the back of the room. On investigation, I found behind a drawn curtain several models preparing to leave the office, having finished their day's poses for pornographic media. I was certain these leggy Rockette lookalikes knew nothing about this operation, so I gave them permission to leave the premises.

After leafing through the files, I was startled to find enlarged photographs of many American historic and strategic sites. They included the White House, the Washington Monument, Mount Vernon, the Brooklyn Bridge, the Empire State Building, the Statue of Liberty, and San Francisco's Golden Gate Bridge. Also included were many important sites for the war effort, such as Forts Bragg, Benning, Dix, and Sumter and the ports of New York and Boston, as well as the Stony Point Naval Arsenal, where dozens of World War I vintage Liberty ships were moored in storage.

On the reverse of each photograph was a code number and a name. These names were later determined by the FBI and U.S. Board of Economic Warfare as belonging to German Bund agents in Lisbon, to whom the photos were being sent. The enlarged photographs of America's key landmarks were being sold in Lisbon (the World War II center of espionage activities) to Nazi and Fascist agents. It was later learned that these photographs were highly coveted by the Germans; clearly, they were photos of intended military targets.

It is worth noting that the well-staffed Board of Economic Warfare in Lisbon (the center of America's own European espionage operations) was purchasing— often by rather devious means—photographs of German and Italian strategic targets: the ports of Hamburg, Bremen, Bremerhaven, Cuxhaven, and Eindhoven and their important shipbuilding facilities; various government buildings in Berlin, including the Reichstag; several sections of the Rhine, including the Remagen Bridge; parts of the Maginot Line and other fortifications; numerous steel and artillery production sites; and even Hitler's Eagle's Nest retreat at Berchstesgaden.

Fooled by the Axis

The Board of Economic Warfare in Lisbon did not know that German and Italian agents—some of the best ones the Axis had—were playing both sides; that is, they were buying American photos even while providing their go-betweens with "valuable goods," which the U.S. Board of Economic Warfare then acquired.

Of course, my mission during the Lexington Avenue raid was simply to gather accounting books and other documents. Judging from Leo Crowley's tone of voice when he assigned me this task, the agents accompanying me were fishing in deeper waters than I was; they must have had a mystery to solve. Someone must have tipped off the FBI; Hoover was already famous for running down any speculative rumor. In early 1941, American spies were anything but seasoned professionals. The CIA would not be founded until after the war, and the Office of Special Services, its wartime predecessor, was barely beginning its work.

When it was obvious there were no accounting records, balance sheets, or other business papers in the files that contained the photographs of models and strategic targets, I told Kohlman to direct me to where they really were. He pointed to a medium-size safe deposit vault in the corner of the room. I fiddled with the wrong numbers he gave me and then demanded the right ones. He fed me wrong ones again, and they failed once more. Then he came over to the dial, kicked me in the shins, and pushed me aside. At that point the two FBI agents standing at the door rushed over with their pistols drawn and forced him to open the steel door.

Tucked in a back corner of the vault were the objects of my search: a half-dozen accounting books recording transactions with Bund members in Portugal. I stuffed them into my briefcase to prepare a report on them that evening and turn them over the next morning to Jim Carroll. Kohlman turned his flushed face toward me and howled: "Those are my private books and I demand them!" The last time I saw this Nazi spy he was being frog-marched from the studio by two Treasury agents.

THE BANK EXAMINERS all knew that the liquidations would soon be over, the alien banks and businesses padlocked for the war's duration when I embarked upon my final assignment. Rogow and Fuse, Japan's largest zipper outlet in the United States and a substantial dollar earner for the Japanese, was located on Fifth Avenue between East Twenty-eighth and Twenty-ninth Streets—the heart of the retail area at that time. In the roomy seventh-floor offices of the firm, I flashed my Treasury ID and warrant papers at a nervous young Japanese, who identified himself as Hideo Yamaguchi, the recently appointed president of the company.

On this assignment, I was the lone examiner and fully expected a rapid liquidation. I never imagined the repercussions that would arise from it or that it would draw the attention of Henry Morgenthau Jr., secretary of the Treasury. Hideo had been appointed president of Rogow and Fuse shortly after July 31, 1941, which was the day the U.S. foreign-asset property law became effective. The real Japanese top-echelon staff had left the United States, leaving Hideo nominally in charge. It was a year later. Hideo lacked any business experience at the time his superiors left, and he knew nothing about the company's operations, but he was born in Japan and thus had been selected to serve as the company's front man.

Hideo was the perfect front man for the operation. Since he had a Japanese birth certificate, the firm qualified as a foreign establishment. He was especially loyal to his peers, always responding to requests with "I do." His courteous manners permeated the business. Fascinated by the tales that reached him, Morgenthau requested a case history of this "unusual character." When I asked Hideo to put his life down on paper, he flashed his wide, familiar smile and raised his thick eyebrows. By then he realized he was a vital cog in the business, not just a dupe. He prepared a fifty-page history of his life, in longhand, some passages of which brought tears to the eyes of even sophisticated Treasury officials. On rereading it sixty years later, I still cannot imagine how this unfortunate orphan survived his life's hardships. As a six year old he had roamed the Japanese countryside, riding the rails, jumping from boxcar to boxcar to avoid capture, and scrounging for food with his "stomach extended out three feet" from a chronic case of beriberi—an illness common among his "homeless and filthy" companions. Hideo became an "unsung hero" in the eyes of the Treasury Department.

Flagrant Violations

The actual brains behind Rogow and Fuse were two lawyers and two accountants. All four resided on Riverside Drive in Manhattan. Before leaving the United States in July 1941, the two key Japanese officers of the company had legally assigned its operations to these four Americans. The company books were written partly in Japanese and partly in English—just enough for me to uncover the shenanigans that had occurred. All told, the company had committed thirty-three illegal procedures.

The first that I uncovered was also the most flagrant and was instrumental in sending the four Americans to prison for two or three years each, besides generating fines. The import documents revealed that the company had avoided high customs duties on zippers by declaring on the invoices, forwarders' papers, and letters of credit that the goods purchased were items carrying lower tariffs than zippers. This procedure netted Rogow and Fuse an annual income of $750,000. It should be noted that the leading producer of zippers in the United States was Talon, at least until the war, when it ran out of inventory for private consumption

owing to priority military contracts for the war effort. Talon met around 90 percent of the U.S. market for zippers largely because of tariff protections extended
to it by an isolationist Congress.

Further examination of the financial records showed that import licenses approved by the Department of Commerce and the Alien Property Custodian for
purchases of goods to be exhibited for display, not sold for consumption, were repeatedly violated. Put simply, goods were being brought in for display but then
being sold. Not only that, but the company was hiding its assets through illegal
accounting dodges similar to the ones we read about in the business pages today.

On reviewing Rogow and Fuse's banking transactions, I quickly discovered
that the four professionals running the firm had avoided completing transaction
applications with the Federal Reserve Bank of New York, the agent for the Alien
Property Custodian, whose official order of July 31, 1941, froze all assets of alien
entities. The "caretakers" of America's largest supply of zippers had opened up
personal accounts in several New York banks. When the company's funds were
being deposited, they regularly transferred sums to foreign banks in Argentina,
Brazil, and Venezuela, all of which ended up with the actual owners of the business, who by then were back in Japan. Unwittingly, Hideo had assigned powers of
attorney to his four bosses; as a consequence, these transactions seemed valid to
the banks. In some cases, dummy accounts had been opened under false names.
Where the Federal Reserve Bank had approved licenses for essential operating
materials and equipment, often it was found that these permits were being used
for goods to refill depleted inventories or for private purposes.

I discovered a litany of other illegal practices that would bring a gleam to the
eye of any district attorney with political ambitions. They included various forms
of misconduct, including defalcation and breach of trust, fraudulent activities,
attempts to conspire with one or more persons to carry on fraudulent activities,
failure to maintain proper accounting records, and violations of disclosure rules.
The four Americans had falsified their books, faked or padded sales to phantom
buyers, circumvented their tax obligations, bloated their credit evaluations marking debts, distorted accounts, and siphoned off funds. All these charges were
listed in the brief presented to the courts. Eventually, the evidence sent the four
men to prison.

Alien property liquidations rarely made a "profit" for the Treasury Department. Rogow and Fuse was an exception. There was scarcely a zipper to be
found in the warehouses or on the shelves of any U.S. manufacturer of this
widely sought item. Most American department stores were clamoring for this

valuable product. Word quickly spread in the New York's garment district that a Japanese firm had large stocks up for liquidation.

From the phone calls I received and the path that zipper manufacturers were beating to my door, I quickly realized just how strong the demand for zippers was. Following the usual practice at Treasury, I ran ads in various media announcing that zipper auctions were to be held. As I expected, the race between Talon and New York Merchandise to capture the largest share of Rogow and Fuse's stock drove up the bids. In the end, I was able to turn over $750,000 to the Treasury. This fortunate outcome prompted my superior at the Federal Reserve Bank Jim Carroll to describe me in his reports to Treasury as "one of a kind."

I was to have another encounter with the duped messenger from Rogow and Fuse. After Rogow and Fuse was liquidated, Hideo was sent to an internment camp for Japanese near Provo, Utah, where he spent the next three and a half years. In 1946, shortly after he was released from the camp, I heard a loud knock on my hotel apartment door. There, to my astonishment, attired in the traditional dark Japanese suit handed to him by the camp officials, was the broad smile I recalled from nearly four years before.

An Offer Turned Down

"Do you remember me?" he asked. "I am Hideo Yamaguchi. I have come to be your valet for the rest of my life since you saved me from prison." Needless to say, I did not accept his magnanimous offer. But I did show him my appreciation by offering to help him find employment. My reward came in the form of a letter of commendation signed by the secretary of the Treasury, expressing his gratitude to me for an extraordinary service rendered to the United States of America on carrying out a most successful liquidation.

Hideo Yamaguchi seemed so cheerful, and so happy to have survived the camps, that I asked him about his treatment as an internee. As the world now realizes, it was President Roosevelt more than anyone else who had made the decision to intern thousands of Japanese who had become American citizens. The president realized that some Japanese-born Americans were of questionable loyalty. And he firmly believed that the loyal ones were at heavy risk of their lives because of anti-Japanese protests and that it was necessary to protect them by creating the camps.

What I learned from Hideo indicated that FDR had every right to worry. He told me that in the camp he had been treated "fairly and with respect" — something he had never encountered since his orphan days. Even his three meals a day meant more to him than to an ordinary citizen. During his struggles to survive in the United States as a handyman in the vicious garment wars of New York, a full stomach was never ensured. More significantly, Yamaguchi told me about some of the questionable activities he had observed among his Japanese American colleagues while an internee.

Hideo had been trained to listen carefully and say little. He remembered hearing grumblings from other internees about the U.S. war effort. Infused with loyalty to their emperor, these "prisoners" at Provo often spoke freely about their families and relatives in Japan, and about the two-way communications that had escaped censorship before and during the war.

Many of these Japanese Americans publicly declared their support for the United States, yet they had known more about the Japanese plans to attack the United States than officials in Washington, which had no intelligence network in Japan before the war. Yamaguchi had no doubt that many important American plans and actions had been channeled to the Japanese authorities by way of internees' contacts in Japan. In other words, Roosevelt had been right.

I knew from the start that Rogow and Fuse was going to be my last assignment as a liquidator, so it was most timely when the Federal Reserve Bank of New York offered me the position of foreign analyst. My predecessor, Andrew Overby (later to become the Treasury Department's assistant secretary for international affairs), had been called to Washington to join the Armed Forces' Office of Information with the rank of captain. His assistant, Walter Rozell, subsequently became the governor of the Central Bank of Ethiopia. I was thrilled at the opportunity to involve myself more closely in the international scene.

Of the ninety-six bank examiners handling the liquidations early in the war, I was the only one with a background in both journalism and economics. That is how I caught the eye of the Reserve Bank's senior vice president, L. Werner Knoke. A brilliant, sophisticated Swedish banker, Knoke's evaluations of international operations commanded the attention of American bankers and also that of the Treasury secretary, Henry Morgenthau Jr. I was later told that the president of the New York bank, Alan Sproule, had been expressing concern about the millions of dollars in foreign securities that we liquidators had been uncovering in the asset portfolios of the dissolved banks, especially the Mitsubishi and Mitsui Banks and the Banco di Napoli.

Except for two American bankers, Andrew Gomery (senior vice president of the Manufacturers Trust Company's international department) and Wilbert

Ward (head of National City Bank's foreign operations), American bankers were relatively unsophisticated in international matters. Gomery was chairman of the Standstill Agreement, through which the international financial community hoped to settle the World War I bond obligations of Germany and its European partners. However, it was not until 1963 that Gomery's commission was successful in settling the World War I Germany debt, with 33 percent payment to the creditors. Ward's profound knowledge of international business later earned him the executive directorship of the U.S. International Chamber of Commerce.

But at that time, no one in Washington—and that includes the Internal Revenue Service and the Treasury Department—and not a single person in the American banking industry knew what to do with the foreign securities we were finding in the portfolios of the liquidated alien banks. Sproule learned of my background and called me to his office one day. "Diamond," he told me, "I want you to find out and keep a record of all the foreign taxes to which these sequestered securities are subject." Little did I foresee that this task was my first step toward the career that has absorbed me for most of my life.

One of the first actions I initiated was to draw up two charts showing twelve categories of taxation for all the Western European and Latin American countries. Basically, this chart expressed all that needed to be known in order to accomplish a complete liquidation of the assets of the sequestered banks. It became the Treasury Department's guide when it came to ascertaining the dividend and interest withholding taxes applicable to the foreign securities acquired by the Treasury through bank liquidations. These charts would become the basis for Matthew Bender Law Publishing's first international book, *Foreign Tax and Trade Briefs*, which is known as "the bible in the field" and is still kept current today through bimonthly supplements.

While foreign analyst at the Federal Reserve Bank before joining the military service, I was exposed almost every day to confidential discussions between Knoke and Morgenthau or his able assistant Harry Dexter White, an aggressive but compassionate statesman with a brilliant mind. It was White who actually formulated this country's capital and foreign exchange policies during the war. Many of his telephone calls to Knoke were routed to Rozell or me. Rozell usually took down White's instructions, with me listening in, since it would be my task to handle the research for White's schemes. White often called me directly to ask how my research was progressing or to offer ideas that he and Morgenthau had generated during their own discussions.

Most of my assignments from White involved the repercussions of capital transfers to the Central Banks of the other Allied countries. Foreign exchange support of the U.S. dollar and Allied currencies was high on the agenda. One must recall that during the war, the Federal Reserve Board was relegated to a secondary power agency. U.S. international financial policy was being shaped mainly by the Treasury and the New York Federal Reserve Bank. From my frequent conversations with White, I quickly surmised that various members of Congress and the Senate and House Finance Committees were growing concerned about how the world's exchange rates would be stabilized after the war.

Drafting a Sample Currency Model

President Roosevelt had instructed Morgenthau to find ways to avoid a currency debacle of the sort that had followed World War I, when the German mark became worthless. In turn, White instructed those of us at the Fed to design exchange recommendations for the postwar era. Some of us detected an aura of martyrdom in White's instructions to us, however eager he was to carry out his assignment. Rozell and I resorted to scanning Adam Smith, Thomas Malthus, and the money theories of John Maynard Keynes as if we were back in Economics 101.

Knoke and Horace Sanford, the vice president of the Federal Reserve Bank's Foreign Department, had urged Overby, Rozell, and me to attend Marcus Nadler's evening courses on foreign exchange and capital movements at the New York University Graduate School. That course was held annually at the Corn Exchange in lower Manhattan. Nadler, a prominent finance professor at Rutgers University and an economics consultant to Manufacturers Trust, was considered the leading authority in the field at that time. It became a ritual for the Fed's foreign analysts to attend these courses annually; some of us repeated them as many as three times.

Rumors were flying that Morgenthau and his staff were enmeshed in some sort of a currency scheme that would be ready for the Allies to consider after the war ended. One person who was determined to test the Treasury Department's strategies was Sylvia Porter, an exceptionally energetic and loquacious employee of Irving Trust's Foreign Department. Later, she would become financial editor of the *New York World Telegram* and a senior policy maker for the New York State superintendent of banks. Almost every week this highly capable woman—a rarity in the higher echelons of New York banks in the 1940s—would call or visit Knoke, Sanford, Rozell, or me to ask questions that would sometimes have broken confidentiality if we had answered them. On one of her visits to Sanford, the vice president and second-in-command of the Fed's Foreign Department, she threatened to go to Washington to see Morgenthau himself if the bank could not provide the answers to her inquiries. Sure enough, she went to Washington the next day, had a personal interview with Morgenthau, and returned to the Federal Reserve two days later to provide us with previously undisclosed information.

❧ 2 ❧

The War in Europe

_M_ORE THAN A YEAR after Pearl Harbor Day, the draft board caught up with me. I joined the U.S. Naval Reserve as a third-class petty officer. It did not take the U.S. Navy long to notice that it had a unique enlistee on its hands. I had signed up after the draft board refused to wait any longer for my officer's ranking to come through from Washington. Previously, I had escaped being drafted, my duties as a bank examiner having been considered essential to the war effort.

The morning after I enlisted, I woke to a ferocious pounding on the door of my Ruxton Hotel apartment. Two burly shore patrolmen demanded, "Come with us." I had no inkling as to why. They escorted me to Naval Headquarters at 90 Broad Street, where I was taken to the lieutenant who had accepted my volunteer application. He barked that I had violated the Naval Code and threatened to throw me in the brig for giving false information on my application. Specifically, I had given him the wrong birth date. Then he explained that the birth certificate on file in the Onondaga County Registrar of Births office stated that I had been born on January 31, 1913, not on February 1, which is what I had written on my application.

As it turned out, the Crouse-Irving Hospital in Syracuse had recorded the time of my birth as 12:00 P.M. on January 31, even though the doctor and my mother had always considered the time to have been 12:00 A.M. on February 1, 1913. That was the birthday I had celebrated for the first thirty years of my life. In the words of the naval officer who swore me into service: "This is the first time in millions of inductee applications over the years that a sailor had two birthdays." Once again, I was marked as one of a kind.

Acting as Chaplain

One day, while I was serving at Sheepshead Bay, Brooklyn, as a petty officer in the disbursing department, I was told to report to Naval District Headquarters at 90 Church Street. There, a Captain Thompson, chief chaplain of the Third Naval District, told me I was being withdrawn from my present duties to become librarian of the base, which had twelve thousand "boots" in training. Navy regulations required one chaplain for every thousand personnel of a specific faith. At the time, there were several Christian and Catholic chaplains at the base (headed by the warmhearted Chaplain Harpole). However, the eight hundred Jewish "boots" and administrative personnel did not warrant an official chaplain. Because I had recently held an important post in the Treasury Department—for which I received two commendations from Henry Morgenthau Jr. himself—I was to "act as a chaplain arranging and running appropriate religious services."

Captain Thompson introduced me to Commander Joshua Goldberg, a well-known and beloved clergyman from the New York area. I was to serve as his

12. Walter opening the door for Elijah to enter at the U.S. Naval Maritime Base Passover seder that Walter was asked to run when he was assistant chaplain by the commandant of the base (a former captain of a German U-boat in World War II who became a U.S. citizen and acted as master of ceremonies at the affair), 1944.

man Friday, meaning to use my own discretion but not to "overstep my authority." Specifically, it would be my job to approve emergency "chits" (passes) permitting leave from the base "as I saw fit." This job, of course, involved practicing eternal patience while I listened to the most remorseful stories about ailing grandmothers, battered wives, and unfortunate trysts with girlfriends left behind.

After many months Stateside as a disbursing officer, librarian, and assistant chaplain at the U.S. Maritime Base at Sheepshead Bay, I sailed to Europe on the *Kentuckian*.

Aboard the *Kentuckian*

It was shortly before D day when I was assigned to the *Kentuckian* and shipped out to England. We were delayed while loading sixty Seabees and their gear at the Naval Seabee base at Davisville, Rhode Island, so we had to race to catch our convoy, which was assembling in New York. With 169 ships, it would be the largest ever to assemble at that port. After disembarking from the *Kentuckian* to file the usual shipping documents at the Naval Registry on City Island, I was rushed by speedboat to my ship, which had taken its allotted space in the convoy and was already a few miles off the mainland. A dangling rope ladder was waiting for me, and with the *Kentuckian* steaming along at eighteen knots an hour, I grabbed it and painfully climbed aboard, briefcase tied to my arm.

At this point it was too dark for me to see just how huge the convoy was — there were battleships, cruisers, dredges, aircraft carriers, and minesweepers, all placed so as to protect one another from German submarines. Three times during the voyage the minesweepers were used near the *Kentuckian*, close enough for me to be thrown out of my bunk each time.

WHILE WAITING FOR A BERTH to open at Milford Haven, the *Kentuckian* was anchored off Plymouth. By then, the Luftwaffe had almost leveled that port. When we anchored out in the harbor (the berths closer in were mostly assigned to troop ships and heavily armed vessels), our crew was told there would be little to do onshore. All the theaters and nightclubs had been flattened by the Luftwaffe, and only a single church was still standing. I was ordered to stop each sailor as he went ashore and make him sign a log entry stating that he would stay away from Thompson Street. Of course, the sailors guessed why and went straight there. Thompson was famous across the seven seas for its many brothels.

Later, when they were examined by doctors aboard the *Aquitania*, eleven of the twenty-four members of the *Kentuckian*'s armed guard were found to have a venereal disease.

A prominent local resident, Lady Astor, well knew how depressing a town Plymouth now was, so she opened the country mansion, Cliveden, where she lived (although given to the British government in 1942), high above the town, to the thousands of military personnel in the district. With the *Kentuckian*'s radio operator, every day I climbed the endless steps from the citadel to her home. She was a gracious hostess whose regal bearing was awe inspiring. This elegant, statuesque lady was always standing at the door to greet the hundreds of daily guests, and her first words were always: "Please make yourself at home. Help yourself to some refreshments." Several large rooms in her home were always crowded with GIs, munching on the sandwiches, sweets, and tea that had been laid out for us.

To this day, I could never understand why, despite her close association with the Prince of Wales (who was Edward VIII until he abdicated to marry Wallis Simpson), Lady Nancy Astor, the first woman to sit in Parliament, was sometimes the target of cruel slurs, based on the false rumor that she had Fascist sympathies because of her friendship with the Prince of Wales, who had been accused of being sympathetic toward the Nazis. Whatever her politics, to many of the thousands of enlisted men who enjoyed her hospitality, she will always be remembered with both fondness and awe.

WHILE WAITING FOR NAVAL ORDERS, I was playing in a ship's tennis tournament in Plymouth when a harsh voice startled me from the back court: "You, are you a padre?" I turned around and saw an ancient groundskeeper pointing his finger at me. "No," I told him, "but I'm the ship's chaplain." "Come with me," he said. We stepped into his booth, where he handed me a gigantic gold-leafed Old Testament dated 1674. "This book was found in the rubble of the attic of my mother's home," he told me, "when it was destroyed by German planes." He asked my name, then opened the volume and inscribed it: "To Ensign Walter Diamond, from the heart of the British people to the heart of the American people."

At that moment I had no idea of the book's value, but after the match, the port's ship chandler raced up to me and on the spot offered me 100 pounds for it (then $403). The book was strapped to my back when I jumped into the English Channel on D day. More about this later.

A Jules Verne Feat at the Normandy Beachhead

Winston Churchill was visiting Franklin Delano Roosevelt at Hyde Park in December 1941, shortly after Pearl Harbor. The two were meeting to plan a strategy for the war. From the veranda, they watched the oil barges coming up the Hudson River. Churchill turned to his host, flicked his fingers three times, and declared: "This is how our boys will go back to the Continent."

When Churchill saw these barges, he envisioned concrete caissons pieced together to form a breakwater that would allow heavy war equipment—trucks, bulldozers, artillery pieces, and so on—to be taken ashore after the first wave of infantry had secured the beaches. Later on, his concept was tested at various ports in England. It was learned that the heavy currents of the English Channel would quickly force water through the joints of these concrete caissons. No makeshift pier would be able to withstand the constant pounding of the sea.

After much prodding by Churchill himself, the British and U.S. naval commanders found a solution to this problem. Some ninety Liberty ships built in Towson, Maryland, near the end of World War I were now serving in the European theater as cargo ships. With Washington's quick approval, the American naval commanders posted in London ordered all available World War I Liberties to the Irish Sea port of Milford Haven. There, the engines were removed from thirty of them. These hulks would be towed over to Normandy immediately after the Allied landing, positioned alongside the artificial harbors, and sunk between the concrete caissons just deep enough to serve as breakwaters. For the most part, those barriers would hold.

Years later, cadets at the U.S. Military, Naval, and Merchant Marine Academies would hear the Mulberry harbors (so they were called) referred to as "the Jules Verne structures that made the Normandy landings possible." To this day, I look back at that miracle and wonder how the gigantic concrete blocks destined for those harbors, each the size of a city bus, had been floated across the Channel to the beachheads. (To be candid about it, six-by-eight-foot rubber balloons were used, the same kind that frogmen depend upon today to raise sunken ships.)

My commanding officers knew that before joining the navy I had been a bank examiner for the U.S. Treasury. From their perspective, that qualified me to arrange the voyage home for the sailors of the Liberty flotilla after it was deliberately sunk. I did not look forward to the task. The captain of my ship, the *Kentuckian*, was Edson Cates, a genial and soft-spoken mariner from Edgartown,

Massachusetts, who had rarely left his ship since joining it in 1918. The *Kentuckian* was one of the few Liberty ships to have escaped mothballing at Stony Point between the wars. "There are no volunteers for the task from any of the pursers of the Liberties to be sunk," he told me. By then I was an officer in the U.S. Naval Reserve as well as purser, chaplain, and hospital corpsman on the *Kentuckian*, so I had no say in the matter—the U.S. Navy Headquarters in London had given a clear order.

So be it, and my duties began immediately, in Milford Haven, while my shipmates and their counterparts on the other doomed vessels waited on their ships for another week, enduring the stench of iron ore smelting and the crunching of steel beams. Living in Cardiff, a few miles from the Milford Haven shipyard, was the chief ship chandler, who walked three miles every morning from his home where I stayed to make sure there would be a quart of scarce milk outside my door each day when I woke up. (The navy doctors had prescribed it to subdue my ailing stomach.) My main task was to arrange for the crews' personal effects and the ships' sextants (vital to navigation) to be shipped to Bournemouth on England's Channel coast. There, the eighteen hundred survivors of the sunken flotilla would hole up until London could arrange transportation back to the United States.

Getting the eighteen hundred crew members back Stateside was a challenge from the start. First, of course, we had to sink the Liberty ships along the Normandy coast. To that end, we left Milford Haven in the early morning hours of June 6. For the task at hand, the navy seemed to have far too few tugboats, which had been sequestered from firms along the Irish Sea coast. Once at sea, the *Kentuckian* had to find its place in the convoy, which was like scrambling for the correct piece in a jigsaw puzzle. Captain Cates had shown me a schematic diagram of the 5,686 vessels—from LSTs to carriers—that made up the greatest naval armada in the history of mankind.

We arrived a few hundred feet off the beach, where the *Kentuckian* discharged its complement of sixty Seabees and their equipment. Now we discovered that the piping structure that was intended to carry oil and water onto the Mulberry section adjacent to Omaha Beach was too long to be removed from the ship, and we were forced by this circumstance to withdraw a few kilometers to deeper water. After the proper dredges with three necessary derricks arrived to carry the pipes to the Seabees on the beach, we continued on to our destination. The *Kentuckian*'s crew watched with admiration while the tugboat crews maneuvered our ship over its graveyard spot at the corner of two caissons.

Faced with a Ship on Fire

Once the ship was positioned, we clambered down the rope ladders—a maneuver I had already practiced once. It did not faze me until I reached the last rung, where I saw that I would have to jump into the churning water. We were all standing in three feet of water off the Normandy Coast when we were horrified to see the *Kentuckian* catch fire. Ours was the only Liberty that did not go down as planned. Faulty wiring had ignited a fire on B Deck before the explosives we had planted could sink it.

After clambering back up the rope ladder to extinguish the blaze, which turned out to be minor, we watched from close-up while GIs scrambled across our ship and down a plank to the sandy beach. Their faces were intense. Frozen in my memory is the sight of a burly sergeant dashing through the ship, grabbing a roast turkey off the dining room table like a football under his arm. Jesse, our chef, had made sure the larder was clean before we consigned our home to the sea. He had prepared us a feast for our last night aboard. Now his bright smile told us how happy he was that his turkey was making a contribution to the landing forces.

My biggest concern at that moment was the 1674 Old Testament that was strapped to my back, wrapped in several layers of burlap. I did not want it to suffer any water damage while I was floundering in the sea.

Leading Survivors Back to the United States

Bringing the eighteen hundred sailors back from the sunken Liberties was a daunting task—one setback after another. First, there were not enough LSTs to get us back to England. Many of them lay on their sides or were below the water's surface, casualties of the pounding waves. The usual gangplanks were missing, which meant that most of us had to be pulled over the gunwales by our belts. When we touched ground again back in England, we were surprised to find ourselves in the remote village of Portland, a few miles from our destination. Needless to say, the navy's plan to meet us with jeeps had gone awry, so we had to hitch rides to Bournemouth, where we should have landed. The navy had sequestered the luxurious Ambassador Hotel for us. Most of the sailors—many of them former longshoremen from small American ports—were startled to see how well affluent people lived.

Forced to wait in Bournemouth for more than a week before London found a transport ship large enough to carry all eighteen hundred of us back to the United States, we spent a quiet week, except for the constant complaints about the delay. Of course, the problem was that the British trains were busy carrying Allied troops toward the beachheads and wounded GIs back from them. Understandably, merchant seamen were not the highest priority.

At the time, I was better nourished than most. During our Bournemouth days, most of the ship's officers were hanging out at the British Women's Service Organization (the WSO, equivalent to America's USO). Word leaked out that there was a tennis player of some note among the Americans. In fact, rumor had it "he once played in a doubles match against Tilden and Kozloh."

On that basis, the West Hants Tennis Club in Christchurch, a suburb of Bournemouth best known as Percy Bysshe Shelley's burial place, invited me to spend a few days at the club as its guest. I was chosen as a practice partner for Thelma Long, the women's Wimbledon champion, who was then the professional at the club. Every day at four o'clock sharp, at the ringing of a gong, British etiquette required me to drop my racket whether the point was finished or not and rush to the veranda, where I sampled tea sandwiches and cake along with the traditional tea.

This bliss continued until Thelma Long's day off from practice—a day I have recalled thousands of times, because it was the day the club arranged for the mother of one of the WSO hostesses to show me Shelley's grave at Christchurch Cemetery. There we stood at the foot of the great poet's resting place overlooking the English Channel. My grand hostess pointed toward the Isle of Wight, a few miles away, and told me: "That is where we used to spend our Sundays picnicking with the family before the war." Tears streaked her face as she added: "I wonder if we'll ever be able to return." I promised her she would. I *knew*. I had seen the ferocious resolve in the eyes of the American GIs as they stormed the Normandy beaches, and they were not going to let her down. Although the Isle of Wight was never physically captured by the Nazis, it was occupied by the Germans with little resistance.

The south coast of England had suffered some of the nation's heaviest casualties in the early part of the war. The Luftwaffe pilots made a sport of strafing the weekend beachcombers with machine-gun fire. The Germans' merciless "calls" had resulted in constant blackouts; shortages of food and medical equipment; bans on theatrical, musical, and other gatherings; and strict laws against recreational activities. The husband of my hostess was a mild-mannered manager of Otis Elevator and an ardent classical music lover. He told me that his sole wartime recreation was to stay up every Saturday night until three in the morning to listen on his shortwave radio to the Boston Symphony Orchestra, which was then led by Serge Koussevitzky, "the greatest conductor in the world."

V-2 Rockets Get the Marble Arch

During our layover in Bournemouth, I was lucky enough to visit London briefly. This day in early June 1944 turned out to be a memorable one for the British — it was the night the Germans "got the Marble Arch." The Germans had developed their V-2 rocket by then. Hitler was pinning his hopes on it, predicting that the new weapon would break British morale and retard the Allies' advance on the continent. An Australian infantry captain and I were making our way through Hyde Park to Paddington Station after attending a Royal Albert Hall concert when we felt the earth shake as bombs rained down on the docklands and commercial areas.

After boarding the train for Bournemouth, I quickly found that the first twenty-odd miles through Reading were a lesson in British fortitude — the V-2 rockets were landing on both sides of the train. At Salisbury at four in the morning, a large group of stevedores and construction workers boarded the train. Most of them were well past draft age. As we rode to Plymouth together, they told me: "We hear the Jerries were over London again last night." They did not realize that the "Jerries" were actually V-2s.

Back in Bournemouth, the Liberty crews were growing incensed at the delay. Except for the naval gunners, almost all of them were hardened merchant seamen, many of them former dockworkers or stevedores. I knew they lacked military-style discipline, but I had to at least try to calm their protests and bring some order. Finally, after days surviving on Spam, crumpets, and tea, the listless crews of the sunken Liberties were told that a train had been assigned to take them to Scotland, where their ship home was waiting.

When our train stopped in Bath, we were met by dozens of British Volunteer Corps women with mugs of tea and crumpets instead of coffee and doughnuts as promised. Somehow, this only fanned the anger of the sailors. Back on the train, mutiny almost broke out, with the thirty captains of the sunken Liberties looking for some way to quell the brawls that were breaking out in several of the cars. Needless to say, the crews were focusing their anger on the *Kentuckian*'s purser" since I was in charge of arranging their return. The captains, worried about my safety, locked me in a separate compartment, and a navy patrol was assigned to guard me.

Finally, after two days marked by dozens of sidetrackings and detours, our caravan of famished sailors arrived at the port of Greenock on the outskirts of Glasgow. When we stepped down from the train at five in the morning, we were greeted by another group from the British Women's Auxiliary Corps. This time they handed out coffee and doughnuts. The turnaround defied belief: eighteen hundred hardened merchant seamen, many with tears streaking their bewildered faces, hugged and kissed these matronly British women in their fifties and sixties.

We quickly boarded the tenders, which carried us out to the *Aquitania*. As I watched Glasgow's billowing smokestacks in the early morning sunrise and looked around at my happy comrades, the outlook brightened. But it did not last long.

A Sorrowful Crossing

Also aboard the *Aquitania* were several thousand wounded veterans just back from France, most of them infantry casualties. They filled the ship's once sparkling ballroom and elegant restaurants, which had been converted into hospital wards. Dozens of military nurses and American Red Cross workers were rushing around desperately trying to keep their patients alive. We were directed to see a seasoned old salt from the original *Aquitania* crew, who barked out instructions as to our "bedding quarters." On reaching these once luxurious staterooms, which had been divided into eight-by-ten cubicles, each to house twelve sailors in triple bunks, the mood of the eighteen hundred Liberty crewmen again darkened.

The sailors realized soon enough that they had been better off waiting at the Ambassador Hotel. For me, I could only imagine the once magical luxury of this ship. With no sea or air escorts to guard the *Aquitania* on its return voyage, strict blackout regulations were in effect; none of us could go up to the deck or wander through the ship unless called to meals. The voyage took us nearly six days instead of the usual five. We were forced to follow a zigzag course to avoid German submarines; their home ports had by then been destroyed by Allied bombers. I stared at the ceiling from my bunk with little to occupy my mind except the chief mate's occasional observation — "There we go again" — each time the ship veered off course to avoid being sighted by a German submarine. So I had plenty of time to lie on my third-tier bunk and reflect on my misfortune in being stuck with this assignment.

❧ 3 ❧

Bretton Woods

A Wartime Interlude

*H*AVING BEEN INVOLVED in crafting foreign-exchange recommendations for the Treasury Department before joining the military service, I
was eager to find out what contribution the U.S. would make to the postwar
world. When I returned to the U.S. after D day, I had not yet been reassigned to
the Pacific theater or to my new ship, the *Utahan*. So I was able to coax a two-day
pass from my commanding officers and attend the Bretton Woods Conference,
where the postwar world monetary regime was about to be born.

Armed with a bundle of ID cards, including entry permits for the U.S. Treasury and the Federal Reserve Bank, along with all my various navy IDs and press
credentials from the *Syracuse Herald* and *American Banker*, I bundled together
four years' worth of gasoline coupons and added a few from friends. My 1940
Dodge had been parked for most of the war in a free lot under the West Side
Highway viaduct at 125th Street in a space designated by Mayor Fiorello La
Guardia, one of his many deeds to make life easier during the war for his thousands of admirers. While I fretted about whether I would be admitted to the conference as a reporter rather than an invited delegate, the sinuous, potholed roads
of the White Mountains battered my car. The road could have been improved
through funds still available from Roosevelt's Public Works Administration, but
because of the war, there was no manpower to do the work.

When I arrived at the Mount Washington Hotel in the isolated town of Bretton Woods, I found out quickly that my naval officer's uniform was all I needed to
bypass the very loose security. I stood at the back of the jammed hotel ballroom
and observed that the panel on the dais was apparently being led by Harry Dexter
White, although Henry Morgenthau Jr. himself was the official leader of the
large American delegation.

Finding a Currency Solution

White was Morgenthau's indispensable deputy, and he showed unremitting de-
votion to the task of creating a better postwar world by providing it with financial
stability. In no way was White a communist. But largely because he insisted that
the Soviet Union be permitted to help reconstruct Europe, he was persecuted by
the House Un-American Activities Committee during the infamous witch-hunts
of the McCarthy era. In the 1950s, McCarthy's vicious targeting of White drove
the brilliant economist to suicide. He jumped to his death from a hotel window
in Newark.

John Maynard Keynes was at Bretton Woods, which raised the tone of the
conference. In retrospect, though, Morgenthau and White through their careful
planning did more than Keynes to shape the postwar recovery. Of course, both
the delegates and the press sought out Keynes's views at every opportunity, and he
was the constant focus during huddles in the hotel corridors.

I was shocked by the disagreements among the Allies over the two main issues being discussed. Both ignited heated debate during the one day I was able to
attend the conference. The U.S. delegation was insisting that the gold standard
be kept and that a fixed exchange rate be established with a 5 percent spread over
and under par. By the time the Bretton Woods meetings were over, there was a
general agreement that a 2.75 percent leeway below and above par would be recommended to the conference of Allied finance ministers and treasurers, scheduled for San Francisco for later that year. Also, the Allies agreed unanimously to
maintain the gold standard intact, and to set the rate at thirty-five dollars an
ounce, as called for by the Gold Reserve Act of 1934.

In San Francisco a few months later, at the St. Francis Hotel on Union
Square, the world's heads of state and foreign ministers met to adopt the United
Nations (UN) Charter. At the same meeting, the International Monetary Fund
(IMF) and the International Bank for Reconstruction (now the World Bank)
were approved. At those meetings the currency spread was adjusted to 2.25 points
above and below par. This fixed percentage would stay in place, notwithstanding
the controversy surrounding it, until 1971, when President Richard Nixon and
his Treasury secretary, George Shultz, abandoned the gold standard.

By coincidence, I was in San Francisco at the same time as the UN Charter
meeting, awaiting orders to sail on the *Utahan* bound for the Pacific theater.
Much to my disappointment, the *Utahan*'s captain would not spare me from my
purser's duties so that I could go and observe. In his opinion, completing the

many documents required before we could sail was far more important than "one of those stodgy political meetings."

When I resumed my post as foreign analyst at the Federal Reserve Bank after the war, my colleagues told me that the San Francisco meetings establishing the IMF and International Bank for Reconstruction had essentially rubber-stamped a program that had already been designed with little acrimony among the delegates. In comparison, Bretton Woods had involved much more brainstorming, with ideas, many of them brilliant, being tossed out spontaneously for heated debate.

Great Minds Convene

Bretton Woods truly was a historical milestone, mainly because of the great minds that convened there. I would never forget the thrill of listening to Keynes, the master economic sage of the twentieth century, tell his rapt audience of government officials from forty-four nations that "as goes capital expenditures, so goes the economy." Later, in expounding on his exchange theories, he declared with eerie accuracy that "no matter what kind of rates you have, whether fixed or managed, you are going to hurt someone. If you have fixed rates, the banks will suffer, and if you have floating currencies, then business will suffer."

Capital Spending, the Key to Prosperity

As a bank, government, and UN economist for nearly sixty years since Bretton Woods, I have followed closely Keynes's prophecy that when private capital spending heads downward, an economic slide is sure to follow. By relying on Keynes's philosophy, I personally benefited from his theory. In fact, in 2000, when capital expenditures showed the first signs of dropping to an 8 percent rate from the prior ten-year average hovering in the 14 percent range, it was not difficult to foresee what was ahead. As corporate profits plummeted and employee dismissals skyrocketed, business spending for expansion and modernization dipped to 4 percent in 2001 before leveling off at practically 0 percent in 2002. To quote the *Wall Street Journal* on the recession: "The real cause looks to have been the abrupt halting of capital spending by business after technology and telecommunications companies in the late 1990s over-borrowed and over-built." As was confirmed from the corporate scandals that pervaded the world in the early years of the 2000s, CEOs and others in the top echelons of multinational corporations have held back on allocating outlays to capital expansion or modernization when they see their profits falling six months before the public is aware of any dip in revenues.

Keynes's second perception that left a lasting impression on me was explicitly borne out three decades later in 1973, two years after Nixon abandoned the gold standard. After consistent prodding from the U.S. Treasury, the IMF discarded fixed exchange rates. Immediately after this controversial action, U.S. exporters, importers, and commodity traders who had been accustomed to calculating invoices at a single stable rate suddenly found themselves at sea when it came to handling pricing structures.

Hedging Risks

All they could do was hedge their currencies by buying and selling futures. For the first several months in this new era of free exchange rates, unsophisticated traders suffered substantial losses; these people had yet to be convinced that hedging could be their salvation, whatever its risks and costs. Meanwhile, shortly after the return to floating rates, the commercial banks began to reap large profits through their foreign departments. Almost all the banks with foreign exchange divisions happily watched their overseas earnings skyrocket from 20 percent to 60 percent of total financial profits, with currency trading alone accounting for 70 percent of foreign income. This sudden boom in exchange activity swelled the banks' coffers so suddenly that they had to expand their foreign-currency trading staffs almost exponentially. For example, Citibank increased its foreign exchange department from a staff of five to some seventy in the first year after fixed rates were abolished.

→ 4 ←

The War in the Pacific

$\mathcal{B}$ACK IN NEW YORK after Normandy, I was determined to preserve the Old Testament Bible (printed in 1674) that had been given to me in Plymouth. So I arranged a day off from the *Utahan*, my new ship, and took my bible to the Sheepshead Bay Maritime Training Station in Brooklyn, where I had served before being assigned to the *Kentuckian*. The base by then had a permanent Jewish chaplain. I wrote in the Bible: "To the chaplain from Ensign Walter Diamond for safekeeping for the duration of the war."

The chaplain was from Utica, New York. Months before, I had called on him to conduct the Passover seder, which the base commander had ordered me to arrange. Actually, I was not the best choice; even the traditional opening of the door for "Elijah to enter" was more familiar to hundreds of Jewish sailors than it was to me. Also, the commander was a Captain von Schneidern, who had captained a German U-boat during World War I. The day of the service, to the surprise of the sailors on the base, he stood next to me on the dais and listened attentively to the readings and prayers.

The Vanished Bible

Unfortunately, I never saw my precious Bible again. After I went to retrieve it after the war, it had vanished. When I asked the chaplain where it was and reminded him that I had inscribed it with both his name and mine, he retorted: "What Bible? You never gave me a Bible. I don't know what you're talking about." He told the same to FBI agents when they questioned him later at the request of staff members of the Jewish Theological Seminary in New York, which I had anticipated would be the book's permanent home. Since it was the chaplain's word against mine, the FBI dropped the search, declaring it "insoluable."

The *Utahan* raised anchor the next day, en route to Davisville, Rhode Is-

13. Lieutenant Walter Diamond with his mother and sisters after returning from Normandy landings and before sailing for the Pacific theater, 1944. Sisters Faye (Syracuse University, 1940) and Marion (Syracuse University, 1930) are in the center of the picture from left to right. Marion was the first convocation chair of the newly established Hendricks Chapel in 1930, and Faye, like her brother, was on the staff of the *Daily Orange* and a cheerleader.

land. There, we were to pick up sixty Seabees and their equipment for the Pacific theater. On our way to Davisville, we took an indirect route set by the navy in order to avoid the German U-boats we knew were lurking within sight of the coast. Earlier in the war, they had torpedoed hundreds of Allied ships. Washington did its best not to publicize this fact. Even so, to this day many New Englanders remember hearing the roar of planes from Mitchell Field and the echoing boom of depth charges as the army hunted the submarines that were seeking us. In the first six months of the war, off the U.S. East Coast, 397 American ships (more than 2 million tons total) had been sunk by German U-boats, and more than 5,000 American lives had been lost, almost twice as many as the unfortunate victims who did not survive in the September 11, 2001, World Trade Center disaster. During those same months, only seven U-boats were destroyed by the U.S. Coast Guard. Clearly, U.S. naval defenses were weak. By the end of the war, 733 American merchant ships had been sunk and 8,785 American sailors had lost their lives trying to keep the supply lines open for our troops. According to the American Battle Monuments Commission, "Merchant Marines suffered the highest casualty rates of any service branch."

After the war, it became known that Hitler had plans to attack New York with long-range bombers, hoping to "see New York skyscrapers blazing like torches." He ordered airplanes to be designed that had sufficient range, but fortunately he lost the war before any could be built.

We spent five days at Davisville loading the Seabees and their equipment. On the third day, I was outside the base a few miles north of Davisville in Providence, arranging for the delivery of provisions when I received an urgent call from the ship's master to return at once.

I arrived back at the ship fifteen minutes before the worst hurricane in Rhode Island history. The *Utahan*'s sailors were frantically tying down the ship with every spare piece of rope or chain available. Then the storm struck, and for almost an hour the ship pitched and yawed in the violent waves while raindrops the size of golf balls pounded us. Then the sea fell calm, which terrified even the most hardened sailors among us—the eye of the hurricane was passing directly over us. We looked up and saw a brilliant full moon in the deep-blue heavens. And then the wind, waves, and rain started all over again. To this day, nearly sixty years later, plenty of Providencians remember the killer hurricane of September 1944, which the U.S. Meteorological Survey listed as the seventh deadliest ever to strike the United States.

As the *Utahan*'s purser and supply officer, it was my job to register the ship's departure from American waters at City Island, situated in Long Island Sound. This time, however, the *Utahan* slowed down to a snail's pace so that I could use a set of steps instead of a dangling rope ladder. That had not been the case on the *Kentuckian* six months earlier.

Robbing Gatun Lake of a Victim

But by the time we reached Colón at the northern entrance to the Panama Canal, my luck had run out. During the war, ships passing through the canal were required to keep a strict schedule that allowed only a few minutes leeway. We were warned that if we were late, we would "disrupt the entire war effort of the U.S. in the Pacific area." Once again, with the ship in motion, down the precarious rope ladder I went in order to register our documents with U.S. authorities. And climbing back was even worse. A navy jeep drove me thirty miles at racing speed to catch the *Utahan* as it emerged from the Gatun Locks onto Gatun Lake. There, a speedboat rushed me to the ship. Once again, I grabbed for a dangling rope ladder, burdened by the weight of my navy satchel, which kept slipping down my left arm, while the crew leaned over the side, placing bets as to whether I would live or die. By sheer luck I grabbed the lowest rung while the ladder swung back and forth. With the crew cheering me on, I finally made it to their outstretched hands, which hauled me over the side. Gatun Locks had been cheated of another victim.

Needless to say, it was huge relief to me when we reached Balboa at the canal's southern end. There we docked to load even more provisions. Many of the crew took advantage of the stopover to visit Panama City's infamous red-light district.

The harbor pilot guided us out into the Pacific and waved good-bye and good luck, and Captain Bryant ordered full speed ahead. Captain Cates, my skipper on the *Kentuckian,* had been a quiet and easygoing gentleman from an old seafaring family on Martha's Vineyard; he had spent most of his time at sea on the bridge, charting course and keeping a sharp eye on the helmsman. Unlike Captain Cates, Captain Bryant was a ruthless sailor and a gregarious man, who could be found almost every evening in the officers' mess seeking a bridge game. He was happy to be alive: his previous ship had been torpedoed by a U-boat in the Barents Sea off Murmansk. He and most of his crew had been plucked from the frigid waters by the Russians. Yet he harbored little gratitude for this rescue. Almost every evening, while he fingered his cards, he would tell us: "Those commies are all alike, they're up to no good. When they boasted of their great country and offered us the opportunity to see it, they'd blindfold us before jamming us into open trucks and race us around the countryside at sixty miles an hour." Despite his outgoing personality, Bryant was adept at keeping his crew in the dark. We still did not know that the *Utahan* was destined for the Pacific island of Tarawa, the site of one of the bloodiest beach landings of the war.

"Tokyo Rose," a Bizarre Thorn

For five days we battled Pacific gales and twenty-foot waves. In her inimitable way, "Tokyo Rose" taunted us about the "great feats" of the Japanese, who were "repelling the attacks of those misled American doughboys." Finally, Bryant received orders from U.S. Naval Headquarters in Hawaii to alter course for a little-known island that Tokyo Rose pronounced "Taryaya," where United States Marines, she said, were being slaughtered.

We dropped anchor off Tarawa two days after the initial American landing, to find that the marines were well in control on all fronts. For the next few days, while anchored less than a mile offshore, we heard sporadic cannon fire. As we unloaded provisions, neighboring hospital ships were busy taking aboard marine and infantry casualties. The Seabees the *Utahan* had picked up at Davisville lived up to their reputation—within two days, every piece of equipment we had transported, down to the last nut and bolt, had been landed and was in its proper place. The complete base was up and running within forty-eight hours.

While they were accomplishing this feat, some of the *Utahan*'s crew gathered pieces of Tarawa's sparkling coral from the beaches. Combining these with colorful stones and shells, they produced attractive necklaces, bracelets, earrings, and rings, which they sold to the rest of us. All the while, navy planes were making repeated sorties over the island, snuffing out the last isolated pockets of resistance. Some Japanese units held out for days.

We raised anchor and set a course directly for San Francisco in order to load another cargo. It would be a harrowing voyage for me. I was also the ship's hospital corpsman, even though I had not yet taken the Merchant Marine Hospital Corps course at Sheepshead Bay in Brooklyn. A few days out, a young mess man complained to me of excruciating pain in his right side. Captain Bryant ordered me to treat him according to the *Hospital Corps Handbook of the United States Navy*, a copy of which was in the sick bay.

I diagnosed this case as acute appendicitis. After I consulted by wireless with the nearest naval hospital (on Guam, two hundred miles to the west), I was almost certain that peritonitis had set in. The *Utahan* was forbidden to make any unscheduled stops at any port or to drop anchor at any location except for approved emergencies involving war activities. Fortunately, the Guam hospital base was able to furnish a helicopter, which flew out to us and picked up the mess man by lowering a basket to a spot above the ship's bow. After several attempts, we shoved the stretcher with the patient onto the floor of the basket. This procedure should have been executed more skillfully. When it wasn't, Captain Bryant flew into a rage because jarring the basket was bound to worsen the patient's condition.

Captain Bryant's temper sometimes stung, and the crew usually took it out on me, since they perceived that I was his right-hand man. Other times, though, he seemed overcome with sadness, especially when he talked about the loss of his ship on the Murmansk run and the many crewmates he lost that day.

When the *Utahan* tied up at San Francisco, to our surprise there was the mess man waiting to rejoin us. A successful appendectomy in Guam and a military air transport had him back in San Francisco before us, looking cheerful and well tanned. I asked Captain Bryant what he would have done had a rescue heli-copter not been available. He pulled his gun from its holster, pointed it at me, and said with a straight face: "You would have done the job, with my supervision."

The *Utahan* had been sequestered from the American Hawaiian Steamship Company. Our next naval orders as transmitted through American Hawaiian's West Coast headquarters at 90 Market Street came quickly. We had four days to load our next cargo and take on a Seabee complement and its equipment. Again, we were not yet told which island we were taking it to. "Most important," we would be carrying equipment and ammunition to Pearl Harbor, from where it would quickly be transferred by military transport to Makin Island, because Japanese stragglers in caves were still putting up sporadic resistance.

A Sad Reminder

A few days later, we arrived at Pearl Harbor to discharge our cargo. That moment was unforgettably sad. The port was so congested that cargo vessels could not penetrate the entrance channel, and wreckage covered much of the harbor. We dropped anchor a mile from shore, and from there we took motor launches. The only "piers" available were the hulks of the *Arizona* and *West Virginia*. Those two ships and the capsized *Oklahoma* were just three of the many casualties of the Japanese attack that launched the Pacific war. As we walked across the decks to jump ashore, we could only imagine the "body parts, corpses and letters from home strewn across the decks," as described in the media after December 7.

The next voyage back to the States was uneventful but still an eye-opener for me. With our cargo holds empty and the ocean relatively calm, we made good speed for San Francisco. Soon we spotted the Golden Gate Bridge in the late-autumn sun, its suspension cables glistening like strings of Indian jewels. The last time I saw a photograph of the Golden Gate, I had been liquidating a photo stu-dio on Lexington Avenue. Now I knew why the Nazis saw it as a prime target for destruction.

Again we loaded cargo in San Francisco. This time our destination was Port-land, Oregon, where we were to pick up another Seabee crew bound for yet an-other recently captured island. I took advantage of a weekend pass to go skiing at Mount Hood.

Because of the government's wartime restrictions on manpower, the road from Government Camp near the base of the mountain could not be plowed. Government Camp was a major base for nondraftee volunteers seeking work in the Public Works Administration. Twenty-foot snowdrifts had piled up over a four- to five-foot base on the roadway, which made the climb and subsequent descent through the virgin pine forest the strangest skiing experience I ever encountered. The next week, I went skiing there again and once more was overpowered by the backbreaking ascent on skis and formidable descent.

Both times, the *Utahan's* navigator came with me. I was teaching him to ski as a quid pro quo for instructions in navigation. The second time, he urged me to join him on a side trip to Rhododendron, a hamlet a few miles from the mountain, nestled in the woods on the placid Zigzag River.

There, he negotiated the purchase of a cozy cottage on the river's bend. The cost: one thousand dollars. He paid part of it on the spot. To cover the balance, he asked me to endorse a loan from a Portland bank for five hundred dollars. He knew I had once been a national bank examiner, and he had surmised there would be no difficulty obtaining a loan as long as I guaranteed it. When the Portland Trust Company explained it would take two weeks to process the documents and check on his credit, the disappointed ship's navigator, certain we would be shipping out in a few days, suggested that I share the property with him.

So I provided the remaining funds he needed to close the deal with the Rhododendron real estate broker. That is how I came to own 50 percent of a cottage on a bend of the Zigzag River. Four months later, back in the States again, the navigator picked up his paycheck and paid his debt to me. Just after the war I got a note from him saying that he had sold the property for six times what it cost him.

Unknown Pacific Invasions

The *Utahan* set sail from Portland fully laden, and we took a zigzag course with no escort, on our way to Honolulu. We had been advised that Japanese submarines were lurking off the West Coast. In fact, rumors that torpedoes had been found along the Washington and Oregon coasts later turned out to be true. Our second arrival at Pearl Harbor provided the same obstacles as the first: to set foot on land, we had to anchor offshore, take a launch to dry land, and clamber over the destroyed *Arizona*. I asked the port captain about it, and he told me that because of the war, "he just didn't have the manpower to clean up the wreckage."

After ten days in the port taking on more material for the deck—mostly ammunition, small vehicles, and airplane parts—we set sail on New Year's Eve 1944 for what would have been a challenging voyage for the most hardened sailor. To begin with, the chief mate and his crew, not being sure if they would survive to celebrate the next New Year, had become inebriated before sailing. The *Utahan's* pilot, who was required to follow a zigzag course to avoid wreckage in the congested harbor, got little help from either the helmsman on the bridge or the crew in the engine room.

Central Pacific Naval Headquarters had the distressing habit of keeping their ships' routes a secret because of the presence of Japanese submarines, so it was several days before we realized that our first destination was the vital military base at Enewetak, a coral atoll in the Ratik Chain of the the Marshall Islands. Although only fifty miles in circumference, the atoll consists of some forty islets surrounding a large lagoon.

Enewetak, which had been mandated to Japan by the League of Nations in 1920 after World War I, was captured by the Americans in early 1944. The Japanese defenders had been few in number and had offered little resistance, according to the marines who greeted us when we arrived two days after the invasion. In the words of our hosts, the Japanese had seemed more concerned about losing their beautiful beach—one of the loveliest in the Pacific—than relinquishing the island. Besides, the Japanese were in no position to wage a strong defense.

The Americans had chosen Enewetak as a vital armory for war materials to feed the forthcoming Pacific offensive. It would also serve as a transfer station, R & R stop, and staging area for American soldiers preparing for or returning from action. Few local people were available to help off-load the *Utahan's* cargo there, so the troops already on the island did the job, clearing the jammed deck in record time. There was an urgent need for the vehicles and ammunition we had brought.

Enewetak is better remembered today as this country's testing ground for atomic bombs in 1948, 1951, and 1953. In 1954 the first hydrogen bomb was tested there. Before conducting those tests, the American authorities moved all the local people to less attractive islands—to be candid, it evicted them from their homes. The thousands of people affected have resented the U.S. government ever since. The Enewetakens were allowed to return to their island some fifteen years later, but even today they maintain that the beauty of their island has been shattered, that its fishing industry has been ruined, and its once fertile crop-growing land has been poisoned. All of this misfortune has blighted their lives, making once cheerful people an unhappy lot today.

Eniwetok had been mostly subdued by the time the *Utahan* arrived there. Our next stop was Kwajalein, the largest atoll in the Marshalls, covering six and a half square miles. When we arrived there to off-load the bulk of our cargo, the battle for the island was still raging. The Japanese had been using this large, flat disk of land as a naval and air base. Tokyo had ordered its defenders to hold it to the last man, and every available means was being used to defend it. But the Japanese were greatly outnumbered by fresh American troops, who were strengthened by the vehicles and supplies the *Utahan* had brought, and the Nipponese troops finally surrendered.

The booming of Japanese artillery did not stop some of the *Utahan's* crew from sneaking ashore to grab pieces of Kwajalein's renowned coral, its principal revenue earner. Again, they would spend much of their time at sea turning their haul into costume jewelry and selling it to their crewmates, and to people in the United States once they were ashore.

On Kwajalein, Captain Bryant bumped into an old sea buddy who was now a navy pilot. This pilot invited him on an observation flight over Makin Island, a patch of land of little strategic value that had just been taken from the Japanese. It had been reported that a sole Japanese survivor was hiding on Makin in a secluded cave. Whenever an American plane appeared, he invariably left his hideout to fire off a few rounds. Bryant needed little coaxing to join his friend. The two climbed into the two-seater, and while the mechanic was checking the propeller, they turned to me and waved for me to join them. Trembling with fear, since this would be my very first time in a plane, I squeezed into the cockpit for a fifteen-minute flight over land and sea. To my great relief, the cave dweller did not come out that day. Some twenty years later his existence was confirmed when the American military stationed on Wake Island revealed to the press that a World War II Japanese soldier had finally emerged from his "cannibal life" on Makin to surrender to the American forces.

Today, the U.S. Navy uses Kwajalein as an antimissile installation. A military base known as USAKA (U.S. Army Kwajalein Atoll) is also located there.

Makin had been captured by U.S. forces forty-eight hours before our arrival. After a brief stop there to unload much needed supplies, we left for Nauru. Originally named "Pleasant Island" by a naval captain who discovered it in 1798 and was impressed with the cordial welcome given to his crew, Nauru has been known as Phosphate Island since early in the twentieth century, when Europeans discovered valuable phosphate beds under the desolate interior plateau. Nauru was the *Utahan's* final scheduled stop on this voyage. Here we had to depend on the local people to discharge the remaining cargo; the American troops had landed only a few days earlier and were too busy mopping up the last Japanese resistance. According to marine officers we later met, the "going was as tough as any yet encountered in the Marshalls."

Unconventional Stevedores

Nauru is a thin ring of fertile ground shaded by palm trees, twelve miles around, enclosing an arid phosphate plateau. There were no docking facilities and no deepwater approaches—which was often the case in the Pacific. So we dropped anchor outside the reef, and the crew got busy unloading the *Utahan*'s cargo, guided by the few local men, who knew how to maneuver boats through the surrounding inlets. In the Pacific area we usually had to depend on the locals to transfer cargo from the holds to flat-bottomed rafts, which the natives built out of local hardwood timber. Generally, the local stevedores were the strongest native men, but Nauru was unique: to our astonishment, husky middle-aged women naked from the waist up boarded our ship each morning to do a full day's manual labor with their callused hands. Each morning some two or three dozen of them tied up their canoes to the ship and climbed our gangway, greeting us with broad smiles, eager and happy to do the job. The Nauru men, for their part, were busy guiding the marines through the dense inland woods and clearing out wreckage.

Every sunset, after the women left the ship, the mood of the *Utahan*'s crew darkened. Consequently, the ship's officers sought an escape from the ship's routine. They looked for some sort of local entertainment at the makeshift officers' club, which had been installed in the only building on shore left standing after the invasion. Every evening the ship's motor launch would deposit us on the black volcanic rock that was used for mooring. To reach the club we then had to traverse a piece of ground the length of a football field covered with two to three inches of recently deposited bird droppings. The guano bird, which is native to Nauru, is responsible for the island's wealth, which at one time was the reason the people of the island had the highest per capita annual income in the Far East: twenty-three thousand dollars. After the droppings hardened, they turned into a high-quality phosphate that was in great demand around the world for manufacture of aluminum or for fertilizer or munitions.

Ten days after we off-loaded the last of our cargo at Nauru, the *Utahan* lifted anchor with a high-spirited crew. We all felt proud of our contribution to the war effort. We had delivered our urgently needed cargo "without mishap," as Captain Bryant put it in his usual dinner wrap-up of the day's activities. We sailed for San

Francisco in a happy mood, never dreaming how close we would come to not making it back.

Four days out of Nauru, northeast of the Hawaiian Islands, at four in the morning, a tremendous explosion rocked the *Utahan* with enough force to throw many crew members (including me) from their beds. The ship's engines had been knocked out by a Japanese torpedo. The chief engineer and his crew quickly found a gaping hole in the stern a few inches above the waterline below the aft deck. It did not seem too severe to them. For four hours we lay idle while the hole was welded shut, a job made simpler by a calm sea. The ship's engines were started again.

Just as we were restarting the engines, at eight in the morning, our radio operator picked up an SOS. A U.S. ship carrying two thousand troops, most of them infantry and marine replacements for the universally dreaded invasion of Japan, was sinking after being struck by a torpedo from a Japanese sub. It was calling frantically for all vessels within two hundred miles to rush to its assistance and pluck any survivors from the sea. Captain Bryant was now certain that the *Utahan* was the victim of a torpedo from the same submarine.

Tokyo Rose later told us that Captain Bryant had guessed correctly: a Japanese sub had fired its next-to-last torpedo at us, then its last one at the troop ship. From the press, we also learned later that when the submarine rose from the sea after firing its final torpedo, its crew had machine-gunned the two thousand Americans floating among the wreckage, killing around half of them. To this day, the U.S. military has never been able to explain why it failed to provide a naval escort for the troop carrier.

Surviving on Salt Water

As Captain Bryant put it, we were lucky to have suffered only an aft-side scrape — that damage, however, had been enough to knock out our evaporator, which was our source of potable water. By this time the captain and "Mac," the chief mate, had closely inspected the hole from a rope ladder thrown from the deck and were certain the damage to the *Utahan* was only slight and that our voyage would not be imperiled. However, the jolt to the engines meant we could only make twelve knots at top power. Captain Bryant radioed Pacific Naval Headquarters requesting that we be allowed to tie up for repairs in Honolulu or another Pacific island. He was turned down; we would have to limp back to the States.

Our real problem, we soon found out, was the shortage of drinking water. As purser and hospital corpsman, it was my job to see that sick-bay patients took priority when it came to getting fresh water. Now the evaporator was broken, and boiling seawater was a poor alternative. The salt that remains in boiled seawater shrinks one's esophagus—a problem that to this day has kept me from consuming some kinds of foods, especially spiced and creamed ones.

We were lucky with the torpedo damage but not with the weather. Behind us a typhoon spawned near the Philippines was at our stern, while in front of the bow loomed a hurricane from the Gulf of Mexico. There was no point in trying to change course, so for five days—roughly a thousand miles—the *Utahan* pitched and tossed at heaven's mercy. After three days of towering waves, Captain Bryant ordered the lifeboats released from their stations, to be ready for boarding at any moment. The skipper was thoughtful enough to bring out a few maps to explain to the crew "where the Japan Current would probably take us." He pointed to the Cape of Good Hope at the southern tip of Africa. But fortunately, it never came to that.

Saved by the Russians

Captain Cates and I had become close friends while serving on the *Kentuckian*. In the five months since, he had been convalescing from pneumonia at his family home on Martha's Vineyard. Now he had a new ship, the *Logan Victory*, and was waiting in San Francisco to take it on its maiden voyage. He was happy and well rested from his first vacation since 1917, and he had requested that he not be required to fill his complement until I returned to the United States. I did not yet know that he had arranged my transfer to the *Logan Victory* as purser and supply officer.

While all of that activity was going on, the *Utahan* was still forty-eight hours out of San Francisco. Captain Bryant received orders from Naval Command to sail north to the Astoria bar at the mouth of the Columbia River in Oregon. This sudden change in course did not please him—he knew very well how dangerous that course was during heavy weather. To seasoned sailors that part of the coast was known as a "ship's graveyard" because of the dozens of wrecks protruding from the rocky coast there. In fact, the legendary Columbia River Bar is called the "Graveyard of the Pacific." Captain Bryant was certain we would never make the narrow entrance at the Astoria bar owing to the ferocious waves. But we managed to reach the mouth of the Columbia, where we spotted the U.S. Coast Guard cutter that was awaiting us.

After throwing out lines and guiding us into the treacherous mouth of the Columbia River, the cutter halted long enough for us to take aboard our guests: fifty well-dressed Russian officials. They would be our guests for the twenty hours it would take to reach Vancouver, Washington. The *Utahan*'s crew were not told—but found out anyway—that Washington had signed our ship over to the Soviet Union under the Lend-Lease Agreement. FDR had maneuvered this controversial act through Congress after Winston Churchill convinced him that it was vital to England's survival.

During the night, Captain Bryant asked his crew for volunteers to man the ship on an important mission, one that would take the *Utahan* through submarine-infested waters, around the Aleutians, and through the Bering Strait all the way to Murmansk, Russia's vital northern seaport and naval base. We all knew how grueling this voyage would be. In the end, only the chief mate, a hardened sailor who had spent most of his life at sea, agreed to go along.

But by the time we arrived at Vancouver early the next morning, the chief mate's brave offer had been forgotten. By then the Russians had thoroughly inspected the *Utahan*. Having noted its smashed evaporators, its ancient galley (1917 vintage), its deteriorated infrastructure, and its poor plumbing, among other flaws, the Russians said *naj spasebo*—"no thanks." We heard some muttering that morning about the lend-lease offer.

The Lend-Lease Agreement would provide a crucial eleven billion dollars of financial aid and assets to the British and Russians and help end the war sooner. It is also the reason I am alive to write this book, and here is why: When Captain Bryant was ordered by U.S. Naval Headquarters to divert the *Utahan* to Oregon, Captain Cates, waiting in San Francisco, was compelled to fill the vacant purser's post on the *Logan Victory* with someone else. Loaded completely from lower holds to the top deck with munitions, the *Logan Victory* headed straight for Okinawa, a Japanese island regarded as a vital stepping-stone to Tokyo. On the first day of the invasion of Okinawa, with Captain Cates on the bridge, a kamikaze struck the *Logan Victory* directly amidships, blowing it to pieces. It never had a chance to complete its maiden voyage. Captain Cates's body was found floating in the water along with the rest of the ship's crew and the navy gunners and Seabees it carried.

Navy headquarters in Washington advised Captain Cates's sister in Edgartown, Martha's Vineyard, that her brother's body would be returned for burial in the family plot by the autumn of 1947, three years after the *Logan Victory* exploded. When my new mate, Dorothy Diamond, and I visited Edgartown in October 1947, his body still had not been returned home.

WITH THE *Utahan* in a Seattle dry dock for repairs, I was instructed to report to Sheepshead Bay for the three-month medical course. I graduated from there with a full U.S. Merchant Marine/Navy Hospital Corpsman Certificate and a Senior American Red Cross License and was assigned to a two-month internship at the U.S. Coast Guard Hospital at Stapleton, Staten Island, New York. There, I made the rounds of the wards twice a day, at six in the morning and four in the afternoon, to give the ailing GIs their vitamin B injections. The routine quickly bored me, especially when I compared it to the demands of my duties during the Pacific invasion.

In the mid-1940s, penicillin had not yet been discovered as a cure for venereal diseases. The five hundred patients I injected with vitamin B twice a day were victims of the worst types of venereal diseases, from gonorrhea and syphilis to lymphoma venerium and granuloma venerium. Most of them had picked it up in North Africa or southern Italy. The *Hospital Corps Handbook of the United States Navy* indicated that verium sulphanides were to be used to treat VD, but the Staten Island Coast Guard Hospital did not have any available at the time. Supplies of these antibiotics were limited, and the overseas military clinics and infirmaries held most of the inventory for acute cases among the troops abroad.

A Medical Diploma

In August 1945, just as I received my Navy Hospital Corps diploma, a few days after President Truman decided to drop two atomic bombs on Japan, the war with Japan abruptly ended. Truman's difficult decision about the atomic bomb was a wise one, I believe, as well as a blessing for the one million GIs whose lives were undoubtedly saved. Earlier in the war, Captain Bryant had shown me a radio-transmitted communication from Admiral Chester Nimitz "to all ships in the Pacific to expect a total of two million casualties [once the invasion began] in the planned strategy to penetrate the long and narrow entrance into Tokyo harbor."

After celebrating the Japanese surrender in Times Square with a million other happy GIs and civilians, their faces all reflecting relief that nearly four years of hardships, tears, and sadness were at an end, I was assigned to a new Victory ship, which was in its Brooklyn berth awaiting its first orders. My new captain told me we would be sailing to Ceylon (now Sri Lanka) and that I had to prepare departure documents immediately and interview all the crew members to ascertain the state of their health. Five days later, having done all of it, I was caught off guard by a knock on my office door. Standing there in his new full-dress uniform was another lieutenant, who told me he had just arrived from Boston and who showed me his orders, which were to replace me as the ship's purser and supply officer.

With the war over, I was anxious to return to my duties as foreign analyst at the Federal Reserve Bank of New York. Only forty-eight hours before, I had filed a request for early discharge from the merchant marine. I had already received my official honorable navy reserve termination.

As eager as I was to return to civilian life, I still felt regret when I accepted my honorable discharge and commendations. I had been looking forward very much to a last voyage through the Suez Canal and the "exotic" (at the time) Middle East ports before reaching Colombo. On the other hand, I had worked with the U.S. Treasury earlier in the war in planning foreign exchange policies for the postwar era, and I was ready to help take on the challenge of assisting in building a new world.

✻ 5 ✻

Return to Civilian Life

I RETURNED TO THE FEDERAL RESERVE BANK of New York, where I
had been upgraded to senior foreign analyst. My former colleague Andrew
Overby had decided to remain in Washington, D.C., where he later became assistant treasury secretary. Another colleague, Walter Rozell, had been appointed
governor of the Central Bank of Ethiopia. At that time, the Truman administration felt obliged to acknowledge the help of Emperor Haile Selassie, the hero of
modern Ethiopia, for supporting the Allies against the Axis countries. Mussolini
had invaded his kingdom in the 1930s as a test run for his armed forces in
Europe's coming war, and the American people remembered that the emperor's
troops had been among the first to take up arms against fascism. Now, with the
war over, the Truman administration was looking for ways to help the nation re-
build itself. One means was to assist it in rehabilitating its finances, and that is
how Rozell ended up in Addis Ababa.

The United States Aims to Become a World Trade Player

Prior to the war, the United States had barely figured in world trade. The Treasury and Commerce Departments were now determined to change that situation
and to make this country a key player in the world's trading and financial markets. With the cooperation of the twelve Federal Reserve District banks and some
fourteen thousand private commercial banks, both departments sought ways to
make the United States a leader in international trade.

Washington top officials believed that "at least there was an opportunity to
get a foothold in future European markets" by encouraging American industry to
gather all its wartime resources to help reconstruct Europe. Congress quickly approved requests by Truman and Henry L. Stimson, the secretary of war, that it allocate billions of dollars (some of which came from lend-lease funds) to finance

14. Walter Diamond addressing the executive committee of the International Executives Association, for which he served as an international trade consultant, when they visited McGraw-Hill to discuss adopting policies that would help its members find more markets abroad for their products, 1953.

the conversion of American manufacturing from a wartime to a peacetime footing. This change would boost the construction and road-building sectors and spur the manufacture of farm implements as well as consumer goods for Europeans. In this way, the seeds of the life-saving Marshall Plan were germinated at the war's end. At the same time, the *Gray Report* of the early postwar years recommended that emergency economic assistance be extended to those parts of Europe that had been devastated by the war. Also, Nelson Rockefeller's International Advisory Board and the Latin American Commission were urging that a single development authority be established to foster higher living standards in remote regions (what we now call the Third World) by offering development aid. The goal of all of these projects was to contain aggression and foster peace by offering aid in the form of capital investment.

In the early postwar era up until the mid-1970s, the Annual International Monetary Fund and World Bank Conference was one of two places where world trade policy was established. The other was the National Foreign Trade Council Convention, held annually at the Waldorf-Astoria in New York. After that, other conferences began to compete. One was the General Agreement on Tariffs and Trade, established in Montevideo and now known as the Uruguay Round. Another was the World Economic Forum in Davos, Switzerland, where nowadays the world's top government, banking, and industrial leaders mingle to recommend policies for coping with the world's economic challenges.

The National Foreign Trade Council, which had an administrative board composed of key American leaders from government, education, and industry, maintained tremendous clout in drawing presidents and prime ministers as annual speakers or panelists. On one occasion at the Waldorf-Astoria, the luncheon speaker was the Soviet leader Nikita Khrushchev. He was loudly and rudely interrupted by a gang of young anticommunists who had commandeered the ballroom's balcony. After they had shouted him down and tossed papers at him, they were ejected from the ballroom by security officers. Fifteen minutes later they returned, this time shoving chairs over the balcony before they were collared for good.

On another occasion, at a reception prior to the final dinner, I was talking to Jim Farley, the former postmaster general and close friend and political adviser to FDR, who was munching oysters Rockefeller ("my favorite passion," he told me), when Farley was approached by a stranger. "I'm John O'Donnell of the *Daily News*," he said, and reached out to shake hands. Farley quickly turned away. O'Donnell was a widely read columnist known for his acid attacks on FDR and his administration, especially Eleanor Roosevelt. O'Donnell seldom wrote a column that did not malign her.

Stamped a Free Trade Zone Expert

Washington also made it a key project to help American industry develop its overseas markets through trade and investment. Therefore, it did not surprise me when the Treasury suggested to the Federal Reserve Bank of New York that it undertake a study of export and foreign investment incentives, both existing and potential. As a senior foreign analyst at the bank, I was eager to get busy again, so I accepted the assignment with enthusiasm. Little did I realize that after my report was published in the *Federal Reserve Bank Annual Report* several months later, I would be stamped for life as an expert on free trade zones and as a specialist in foreign investment and trade development.

Not long after my article on foreign trade and investment incentives appeared, Washington, through the European Recovery Program (ERP, subsequently called the European Economic Administration, now known as the Agency for International Development, or U.S. AID) and the UN, asked me to help with the economic development of countries around the world—in the end, 100 of them. Through these assignments, I have met, interviewed, dined with, and forged economic plans with more than 120 foreign leaders, including presidents, prime ministers, kings, princes, and finance ministers. My journey began with President Arnulfo Arias of Panama in the early 1950s and was still going strong decades later when I met some of central Europe's postcommunist leaders in Bulgaria, Lithuania, and Romania.

Marshall Plan Changes World Trade Outlook

Despite Washington's efforts, at the end of World War II there was barely any enthusiasm among American corporations and banks for expanding their activities abroad. But after the Marshall Plan began allocating financial aid so that the Western European countries could begin rebuilding their destroyed economies, American industrialists began retreating from their isolationist mind-set. One of the businessmen who saw opportunities in this new attitude was Jack Bender, president of Fallon Law Book Company, renamed Matthew Bender and Company in the 1950s.

Bender and his executive vice president, Bill Vanneman, were certain that America's industrialists would have to expand their activities overseas, so they drew upon their courage and published the charts I had devised for the Treasury Department during the war, having converted them into a heavily annotated two-volume book. Bender's decision was made only a few days after the Public National Bank, where I was serving as the economist, reversed its plan to print the charts in summary form for distribution to its customers. Mats of the charts had been made by the bank's advertising firm. Now the bank's president, Chester Gersten, suddenly realized the risk involved. "What happens," he demanded to know, "if Diamond is not around and we can't keep the tax rates current?"

My return to the Federal Reserve Bank of New York as senior foreign analyst after the war had not been as rewarding as I had anticipated, and the unsophisticated foreign departments of the American commercial banks were clamoring for economists who had been trained in international finance, so I grabbed the opportunity to participate in the postwar recovery by moving to the Public National Bank as the economist. The core of this medium-size bank—which had foreign deposits of roughly five hundred million dollars—was a dozen or so far-sighted and aggressive former officers of the ill-fated Bank of the United States. That bank's failure had been one of the reasons Roosevelt declared a bank moratorium in 1933.

Not long after I joined Public National, my "clear and concise analyses" (as evaluated by Washington trade analysts) of the economic and credit conditions of foreign countries where overseas borrowers were located stirred interest among Public's competitors. In the early postwar era, Manufacturers Trust was one of the five largest and most internationally active banks. It was also a leader in arranging overseas financial assistance to help the Allies lift themselves out of their economic quagmire. At the time, Europe's commercial and banking industries had almost entirely broken down. Manufacturers Trust now dominated international banking, largely because of the reputation of Andrew Gomery, its senior vice president.

The Standstill Agreement

Gomery's acumen in overseeing the Standstill Agreement settling the Axis's World War I debt was admired by all bankers. As chairman of that agreement, he had almost single-handedly eked out an unexpected settlement: a 33.33 percent payment on the hundreds of millions of dollars of defaulted bonds (mostly German, but a few were Italian) that had been floated in the early decades of the century. The American creditors were delighted to recover even a fraction of the outstanding debt that had lingered for more than thirty years.

Gomery's reputation became known to Dr. Alan Valentine, president of the University of Rochester, who was Truman's choice (after Paul G. Hoffman resigned in 1950) to become head of the Marshall Plan (subsequently it was called the European Recovery Plan, European Economic Administration, the International Cooperation Administration, and the Agency for International Development). John Hartstone was Valentine's assistant at the time. On Gomery's recommendation, he approached me about becoming the economist for the first European Recovery Plan mission to the Netherlands. That country had been selected as the ERP's guinea pig because it had not been devastated as badly as some other Allied nations, such as Belgium, France, and Luxembourg.

Having spent so much time overseas during the war, I declined the invitation to move to Europe. I stayed with Public National Bank, partly because it was closer to Washington, D.C., which was the center of the growing demand from foreign governments for economic and financial assistance. While Public Bank's merger with Bankers Trust Company was pending, I joined McGraw-Hill as director of economics of the McGraw-Hill International Corporation and editor of the McGraw-Hill *American Letter*. Bankers Trust already had an economist of note, and at that time in the early post-World War II period only four banks had their own economists. Aside from Public National Bank and Bankers Trust, the other two were National City Bank and Chase National Bank, where David Rockefeller was the economist until being promoted to senior vice president.

Specialization Required for Successful Writing

It was at McGraw-Hill that I discovered the power of specialization in writing and economic forecasting. Whereas my previous position at Public National Bank as foreign economist and international credit manager involved country analyses and financial ratio computations in preparing lines of credit for some two hundred banks abroad, all the final recommendations submitted to the board of directors for approval followed the same pattern. Now as editor of the McGraw-Hill *American Letter*, as well as director of economics for the McGraw-Hill International Corporation, I was given a free hand to revive an ailing publication prepared exclusively for overseas readers.

The remedy was quickly determined: we would publish twenty editions every two weeks. Each was to be specialized in name by calling it a specific country edition of the *American Letter*—for example, the Argentinean, Brazilian, Indian, Pakistani, Philippine, or Taiwanese edition of the *American Letter*. The immediate results were staggering; circulation skyrocketed, with overseas subscribers, especially foreign governments, eager to read our interpretations of the effects that U.S. and world events would have on their interests.

Not long after our switch to special editions, foreign newspapers began quoting the *American Letter* regularly in front-page stories. As demand spread for relevant information, particularly on each nation's commodities, I was forced to expand my staff. Fortunately, we were able to attract Flora Lewis, the future prizewinning distinguished journalist who later became chief European editor of the *New York Times*, to help prepare copy for the special editions.

Flora had just arrived from Mexico, where her family had lived while her husband, Sidney Gruson, of the *New York Times*, was covering Central America. Gruson was in Guatemala in the late 1950s and early 1960s during the bloody dictatorships of Presidents Armas and Fuente. The future vice president of the *New York Times*, Gruson was taken into custody by the armed military troops after he was grabbed on the steps of the capitol as a "political spy" and imprisoned. It took the Canadian and U.S. governments (Gruson held a Canadian passport) a great deal of maneuvering to eventually get him released.

In view of the success of the specialized editions of the *American Letter* that kept the publication in the black, in 1962, ten years after my taking over the newsletter, McGraw-Hill's publishing committee decided to merge it with *International Management Digest* in order to boost that monthly's sagging circulation and advertising revenues.

A McGraw-Hill Episode

While at McGraw-Hill I was involved in another situation that had wide implications. Soon after arriving there in 1952, I met Clifford Montgomery, the former quarterback of the Columbia University football team that upset Stanford in the 1933 Rose Bowl. Cliff, whose office was next to mine, became the hero of that game by calling the much heralded trick hidden ball play, known as a "naked reverse," which scored the only points in the contest against Stanford, actually a far stronger opponent than coach Lou Little's Lions. Aware that I had been a sportswriter and spotter for the Syracuse University Orangemen while working with Eddie Dooley in his Columbia radio broadcasts, Cliff greeted me early one Monday morning with an enthusiastic description of a high school game he had refereed on the previous Friday. A highly successful space salesman for McGraw-Hill's *Business Week* and *Automotive Magazine*, since his fame in the New York area enabled him to obtain advertising contracts simply by visiting prospects, he spent his Saturdays working as an official intercollegiate-association referee, frequently volunteering his services for high school games on Fridays.

When Cliff came into my office, he began, "Walter, I refereed a high school game Friday afternoon at Manhasset, and there was a heavy-set African American with legs like pistons and a body frame like a bulldozer who, if he went to college, would be an all-American, and if he played professional ball would be the greatest player of all time. His name is Jimmy Brown." As a former sports editor of

the *Syracuse Daily Orange* and freelancer for the *Syracuse Herald* covering fresh-
man sports, I quickly called Coach Ben Schwartzwalder, the Syracuse head
coach known for his daring exploits as a paratrooper in World War II, to report
this find. The Syracuse sports staff had heard of the "Manhasset Mauler," as he
was called, and Schwartzwalder sent his assistant, Reeves Baysinger, to Manhasset for a talk with Jim Brown's coach. Baysinger carried considerable weight in
eastern football since this former stellar back was known for guiding the 1926
Syracuse team to an almost perfect season had it not lost to Army in a fierce
27–21 struggle at West Point after a referee named Schwartz penalized Syracuse
305 yards. Army scored the winning touchdown in the final minutes when the
referee called a questionable penalty.

Baysinger reported that Brown already had twenty offers of scholarships from
such powerhouses in those days as Stanford, Oklahoma, Michigan, and even
North Texas, a school that had never booked a game with an opponent having an
African American on its team. There was no chance at all that Brown would select Syracuse until it was learned that a leading judge in Manhasset was a former
captain of the Syracuse lacrosse team in the late 1920s.

With Judge Kenneth Malloy now on the Syracuse side, Brown finally chose
to go there after the district mayor had declared a "Jim Brown Day" and honored him with a "Jim Brown Parade" to the city hall, where at a ceremony the
mayor handed him the keys to the city and Brown was awarded eleven block letters, including basketball, baseball, track, lacrosse, and football. Jim Brown set
all kinds of records at Syracuse, one of which was his last game against arch rival
Colgate when he scored six touchdowns and kicked six points after the scores for
a total of forty-two points, a record still never equaled by any other Syracuse
player.

U.S. Creates Export Insurance System

Following the merger of the *American Letter* with the *International Management
Digest*, I resigned from McGraw-Hill to become the director of the Foreign
Credit Insurance Association (FCIA), at the request of the Export-Import Bank
in Washington, D.C. The Eximbank shared 50 percent of the FCIA ownership
with some twenty-two major insurance companies. This association was the first
official U.S. organization to insure exports, issue guarantees, and finance transactions of American companies selling abroad. Aware that I had previously pre-

15. Walter Diamond, as director of research for the Foreign Credit Insurance Association, with Lynn U. Stambaugh, senior vice president of the Export-Import Bank of Washington, D.C., and John A. Barry, chairman of the New Orleans American Institute of Marine Underwriters, after addressing New Orleans-area industry executives on how covering export risks with insurance would boost their business and the U.S. economy, 1962. *New Orleans States-Item.*

pared a study of export credit insurance of the world that include an in-depth analysis of the British Export Credits Insurance Department for the Federal Reserve Bank when I was foreign analyst there, the Eximbank tapped me for its venture. England's system, the oldest guarantee program of this nature in the world, was established in 1917.

PART TWO

Post–World War II Assignments

❧ 6 ❧

Helping Developing
Countries Fight Poverty

Panama

*A*MONG THE FIRST foreign governments to contact me for assistance in seeking ways to improve their industrial development programs and therefore be able to absorb the growing numbers of unemployed workers was Panama, which felt that the United States owed it something. Panama had opened its territory to U.S. military bases during the war and had worked hard to keep the Panama Canal operating efficiently, a vital factor in defeating the Japanese. There is no question that the United States was in Panama's debt—an obligation that was recognized decades later when President Jimmy Carter influenced the U.S. Congress to turn the canal over to Panama by 2000.

After the war ended in the Pacific, President Arnulfo Arias, a popular leader in Latin America, expressed concern about the many Panama Canal workers who had lost their jobs now that they were no longer needed to handle the locks and steady flow of ships. The city of Colón at the canal's Caribbean entrance was especially hard hit. Thousands of Panamanians in that city were now living in near squalor. Arias's brother, Roberto, a prominent physician confined to a wheelchair, was married to the renowned British ballerina Margot Fontaine, and each time she visited her husband, the president arranged to be photographed with his handicapped brother and the world's greatest ballet dancer. The press coverage he received in this way, especially in the United States, helped Arnulfo Arias cultivate a strong following among North Americans.

Arias's cabinet secretary and key adviser was Eduardo Duque, who came from a respected Panamanian family and had a good relationship with Truman. Knowing this fact, Arias sent him to Washington to look for help in developing a free trade zone (FTZ). Arias believed that a customs-free zone was the solution to unemployment in Colón, where some twelve thousand people were unemployed. In 1948, in the Panamanian Congress, Arias had pushed through an ordinance authorizing a free trade zone in Panama. This statute was the first such ordinance in any developing country and set the pattern for the hundreds that followed. There had been zones like these in Europe for centuries, but they had been created as transshipment enclaves; in contrast, the zone in Panama would emphasize the processing of raw materials and the manufacture of end products where goods and equipment could be imported into a zone without payment of burdensome customs duties on the components used in producing exports.

Duque arrived in Washington to look for assistance and was stonewalled at every government agency he visited. Finally, an official in the Commerce Department remembered reading a study on investment incentives that I had prepared for the Federal Reserve Bank of New York's *Annual Report* several years earlier. That report had discussed the benefits of operating in a free trade zone.

So Duque came to New York to see if I could help Panama establish and run an FTZ. I quickly told him that I was not an expert in them and had gathered my basic research from the *Congressional Record*, in which could be found strong warnings from Emanuel Celler, U.S. congressman from Brooklyn. Celler was the real "father" of FTZs, having cautioned a congressional committee that this country needed to "take steps to prevent the relatively new Soviet Union from stealing our foreign markets."

Celler was certain that American importers would need support in order to maintain sufficient inflows of raw materials to keep their factories going. He believed that the communists would be a strong obstacle to this plan and that they had every intention of competing with the United States in finding markets for their exports. Celler's answer to this impending problem was for Congress to pass a law offering incentives to help prepare American importers and exporters to survive the communist threat. This is how FTZs were born in the United States.

The smooth-talking Duque stayed on as manager and marketing director of the Colón Free Zone, opening up offices in Washington, D.C., and New York. To help promote the zone, the New York office asked me to prepare a booklet, *Advantages of Incorporating and Operating in Panama's Colón Free Zone*. This book was distributed to subscribers to *Foreign Tax and Trade Briefs*, Matthew Bender's first international book and a best-seller regarded as the "bible" for companies operating abroad. It covered all the foreign tax rates that I had assembled while serving as a national bank examiner liquidating alien banks during the war.

With Arias's active support and Duque's perseverance, and with my contributions as the zone's adviser, the Colón FTZ began to take shape in the early 1950s. But it was not until the Torrejos regime, from 1968 to 1978 that the Colón FTZ began to blossom into what it was meant to be. President Omar Herrera Torrejos made several visits to the United States looking for advice about developing his country and negotiating for financial assistance to implement those ideas. In my two meetings with him, the second of these shortly before he lost his life in a plane crash in Colombia, he emphasized that the Colón Free Zone needed to be extended to include France Field, which at one time had been an important U.S. air base.

As he would have hoped, the zone was expanded soon after to include France Field. It now covers 242 acres—room enough for more than 900 international companies and 650 foreign representative businesses. Combined exports and imports passing through the zone now exceed $20 billion; some 16,000 companies around the world make use of the zone every year; 10,000 Panamanians work there. All of these factors make it the second-largest FTZ in the world after Taiwan's Kao-hsiung industrial park.

In 1951, my Panamanian booklet and Matthew Bender extensive international tax coverage attracted the attention of the foreign arm of the influential American Bankers Association known as the Bankers Association for Foreign Trade. The chairman of the association's International Tax Program was Milton Strong, vice president of Chicago's American Foreign Bank, the leading international bank in the Windy City. That year, he invited me to join the faculty of the University of Illinois's Annual International Tax Program. Held in Monticello, Illinois, on the Robert Allerton estate, this seven-day seminar drew top-level executives in domestic business and trained them on how to operate abroad.

When Robert Allerton was a boy working on his father's farm, he had his heart set on attending the University of Illinois. He was stopped by a lack of funds; at that time in the 1920s and for long afterward, there were no university grants or loans available to deserving students. FDR's National Youth Program was a godsend for thousands of undergraduate students in the 1930s (including me), who would never have finished college without it.

In the 1930s, because of severe drought conditions, and with consumer spending at an all-time low, most farmers were in debt and barely surviving. Allerton was determined to show the world that farmers could escape from pitching hay, feeding cattle, and turning soil. He went to work seeking better plant hybrids and by crossing two strains of corn came up with one that was far superior to the existing midwestern product. Allerton made a fortune from it and used it to assemble vast landholdings in the Monticello area.

At the center of the Allerton estate was a converted mansion, now used for meetings and as living quarters for faculty and students. The real attraction, though, was the hundreds of acres of wooded gardens, where Allerton displayed one of the world's great collections of European sculpture. Whenever I was not on the podium lecturing students, I was wandering through the sculpture garden admiring the original works by the famous Swedish sculptor Carl Milles. Allerton had arranged to have these masterpieces transported to his estate in Monticello from the historic "Milles Gardens" on the outskirts of Stockholm, where exact replicas of the original works are now standing in their place.

Years later, in 1962, I was visiting Stockholm as editor of the *United States Investor*. Dorothy and I had the privilege of being shepherded around Milles Gardens by our host, Sven Svenson, president of the Swedish Banking Association and former head of the Stockholm Town Council. He was delighted to learn that I had seen the original Milles sculptures; he told me it was the first time he had guided anyone around the "fake statues who had experienced the pleasure of viewing the originals in Monticello."

As a faculty member for the Allerton seminars, my task each year was to lecture American business leaders on the latest developments in operating abroad. While I was describing the advantages of using Panama as an offshore trading hub, one of the students, Russell Baker Sr. — founder of the law firm Baker, Hightower, and McKenzie — questioned whether doing so was worthwhile. At that point, Baker's former partner, Andrew Brainard, a brilliant young Chicago attorney known for his skill in negotiating foreign licensing agreements, sprang to his feet and declared: "Diamond is right. This procedure is legal and in line with the Internal Revenue Code."

Brainard was a licensing specialist, a principal attorney, and legal adviser for the Pritkin family hotels and other interests. That day he told the students that the foremost international licensing expert in the country, Joseph Cardinale of Monsen and Cardinale (a New York law firm with a Latin American client base), made it a practice to establish offshore trading companies for American multinationals, especially in Panama, in order to increase exports while cutting costs and taxes.

Liberia

My presentation at this first Monticello gathering of internationally minded American businessmen caught the attention of two students in particular. One was Ted Hubbell, for many years managing director of Liberian Services, the official representative of the Liberian government in the United States. He listened closely to my description of how Panama was working with U.S. companies, and the encouraging results, and passed on what he learned that day to Liberia's farsighted president, William Tubman.

Tubman was a good friend of this country and had supported the Allies during the war. In turn the United States backed him. Tubman gave Hubbell the go-ahead to market Liberia as an important world center for shipping registration. Many of the world's most important shipping companies would soon be using tax-free Liberia with its low wage scale as their address of registration. Hubbell consulted with me and later recommended that Liberia invest heavily in port facilities at the capital, Monrovia. Soon, its harbor was among the finest and busiest on the west coast of Africa. Hubbell set as one of his goals the creation of an FTZ in Monrovia, although on a smaller scale than the one in Colón, and asked me to prepare a booklet similar to the one I had made for Panama, namely, *Advantages of Incorporating and Operating in Liberia.* These pamphlets were printed by Matthew Bender and Company, publishers of *Foreign Tax and Trade Briefs*, as a gesture of goodwill on their part and were distributed to subscribers as a complimentary bonus.

The second of these middle-aged business students who was especially interested in "going abroad" was William Woolworth Jr., chairman and president of F. W. Woolworth and Company. He was also a roommate of mine: we survived together for a week in the eighteen-bunk master bedroom at Allerton. He took advantage of the situation by soliciting my advice—he was trying to decide whether Woolworth five-and-ten-cent stores, so popular in this country, would be profitable overseas. In 1951, Woolworth had two hundred stores in the United States and little competition from similar ones. Except for a few outlets in Canada, Woolworth's sole foreign venture was in Mexico. Another student, and roommate, was Bill Wrigley Jr., who was considering establishment of a plant abroad for the company's chewing gum products.

Milton Strong was delighted when the University of Illinois announced it would be holding a repeat performance of the trade seminar in the summer of

1952. The university believed that foreign operations were a burgeoning sector in the U.S. economy, and it was determined to add courses on foreign trade to its existing business school curriculum. Today, it offers one of the finest curricula in the country on that subject, just a notch below that of the leading American foreign trade institution, the Thunderbird American Foreign Trade School at Scottsdale, Arizona.

At my appearance the following year at Monticello, I selected Liberia as one example of how developing nations were making economic strides by welcoming foreign investment. Once again, Russ Baker of Baker Hightower (not yet renamed Baker and McKenzie) objected to my thesis, and of course Andrew Brainard was there to support my finding that emerging nations would make little progress without guidance and financial assistance from the industrialized countries.

To my surprise, the third year of the Illinois program, Russ Baker—no longer a neophyte in international taxation—appeared as a speaker, and lauded Venezuela as a location for foreign operations abroad. He now realized that U.S. companies had a golden opportunity to reduce their tax obligations legally. He reported that he had opened an office in Venezuela, which by now was known as an attractive place for headquarters of American multinationals because of its policy of not levying income or withholding taxes on profits earned outside its borders.

Shortly after this seminar, in the fall of 1953, the *New York Times* business section carried this headline: "John Deere & Company Pays $275,000 Tax Penalty." John Deere had taken the advice of its attorney, Baker Hightower, and established a subsidiary trading company in Venezuela. Unfortunately, its lawyers there—Baker Hightower of Caracas, headed by Russ Baker Jr., the managing partner—had forgotten to advise John Deere that title to the goods (in this case, farming machinery) had to change ownership outside U.S. territory in order to qualify for the trading income tax exemption under the Internal Revenue Code at that time. Russ Baker Sr. himself was courageous enough to report this blunder at a monthly meeting of the influential International Executives Association, on which I served as an international trade consultant for more than twenty years. Baker and McKenzie, as it was later renamed after Hightower left the firm, learned quickly: within two years it had established more than twenty overseas offices. Today, the firm has more employees and foreign affiliates than any other American legal or accounting entity.

Partly because the Panamanian and Liberian promotion campaigns suc-

16. Walter Diamond lecturing at the International Executives Association, for which he prepared a monthly newsletter on international business trends similar to the ones written for the Syracuse University School of Management's Kiebach Center for sixteen years, the Overseas Automotive Club, and the Motor and Equipment Manufacturers Association's Export Managers Club where he also served as a trade consultant for thirty years, 1953. Courtesy Matar Studio.

ceeded so well at attracting foreign investors, other developing countries—especially in Latin America—began to realize that to shake off postwar hard times, they would need outside help from the industrialized nations. Many of the leaders of the poorer countries realized that their countries were deteriorating economically, and these officials could not understand why the United States was focusing so hard on rebuilding Western Europe and meanwhile "slighting" them.

Honduras

After my booklets on Panama and Liberia were disseminated, word spread among governments of developing countries that an American economist was available to help them attract U.S. investments. The first person to contact me in this regard was Juan Funes, the Honduran consul general in New York, who was also his country's UN representative. When I explained to him that one of the three most important incentives a country could offer potential investors was an income tax treaty that allowed them to avoid double taxation, he lost no time in convincing Julio Lozano Diaz, the country's president, that this route was the one to take.

At that time the United States did not have a single income tax treaty with a Latin country, so this step was indeed a challenge. However, our first discussions in Washington went surprisingly well, and a convention was signed and made effective in September 1956—a first for the United States, and one that set the pattern for the future.

After this success, from which both countries benefited, Julio came to me about a problem that had been hanging over Honduras for some three centuries. The border between Honduras and Nicaragua, through what is known as the "Mosquito Territory," had been a source of irritation to both republics for several centuries. It had never been drawn precisely. Relations between the two nations had soured to such an extent that sporadic gunfire and incursions into each other's claimed territory were now almost a daily occurrence. Villages were often invaded, sacked, and burned.

At that time, John Holland was the assistant secretary of state for Latin American affairs, and I suggested to Funes that the two of us visit him for advice. This suggestion turned out to be a wise idea—without an instant's hesitation, Holland said: "Take it to The Hague." Less than a year later, the Court of Justice in The Hague awarded the territory to Honduras. To the surprise of many, the decision was accepted graciously by Nicaragua's Samoza government. The border dispute has been dormant almost continuously since then.

Mexico

To show his nation's gratitude, President Julio Lozano awarded me the Honduran Medal of Honor at a ceremony in the office of his consul in Mexico City. The weird circumstances that took me to Mexico began when I arrived at Miami Airport to change planes for Tegucigalpa, capital of Honduras. There I was paged to report immediately to the Honduran Airlines desk, where the Honduran government notified me that because of "a revolution in the streets of Tegucigalpa," I was to immediately proceed to Mexico City, where the ceremony would take place.

I found the airline representative, who told me there were no scheduled flights from Miami to Mexico City but that they had arranged a one-engine vintage biplane to get me there in time to meet the Honduran delegation coming from Tegucigalpa. The plane did have a steward. Since the route was entirely over the Gulf of Mexico, I asked the Spanish steward where the life jackets were. He quickly replied: "Life jacket no good—all shark below."

I arrived in Mexico City at two in the morning. In the nearly deserted airport, I finally found a local taxi driver. After I pleaded with him and waved a fistful of dollar bills, he consented to drive me to the Hotel Reforma in his broken-down car. There I found a communiqué from President Lozano's office apologizing for the awkward situation and instructing me to await directions from the official delegation, which was on its way to Mexico City.

More alarming than any of these events was the jolt I felt when the front desk told me at three that morning that my wife "is out for the evening." Dorothy, by that time a well-known syndicated columnist and women's consumer advocate for *Printer's Ink*, had been invited to be the first woman speaker at the Atlanta Advertising Club. After receiving my changed directions at the Miami Airport, I had telephoned her to meet me at the Reforma in Mexico City instead of returning to New York. At the same time I called Rudy Fauchey, the obliging McGraw-Hill Mexican correspondent for the *American Letter*, of which I was editor, and asked him to meet Dorothy at the Mexico City airport. Of course, Dorothy was overjoyed to see Rudy after eleven hours in the air, which included three airline changes—not uncommon in the early 1950s, when direct flights even between major cities were relatively unknown.

After checking in at the Reforma in the early morning, she went to breakfast at Sanfords, a hangout for American journalists. There she ran into a U.S. government official she knew in Washington. On learning that she was at the Reforma but not in the new modern wing, he took her back to the hotel and arranged for a room change. Thus the clerk's message: "Mrs. Diamond is out for the evening." They had forgotten to adjust the hotel register and did not discover it for several hours after my arrival.

After being presented with a citation by the Honduran delegation for my contributions to the nation's foreign investment program, I was invited to the palace for a meeting with Carrillo Flores, Mexico's leading financial policy maker.

Flores was an extraordinarily accomplished and universally respected finance minister. Mainly through his efforts, the needs and problems of the poorer countries had been spelled out clearly at Bretton Woods and other conferences.

EL UNIVERSAL
EL GRAN DIARIO DE MEXICO

● Premiado por la Universidad de Missouri con la Medalla de Honor, por su labor en el Campo del Periodismo Mundial.
● Trofeo "María Moors Cabot", 1949, por su esfuerzo en pro del acercamiento de todas las Naciones de América.
● Circulación certificada por el Audit Bureau of Circulation (A. B. C.).
● Miembro de la Sociedad Interamericana de Prensa.

Y GERENTE: LANZ DURET	MEXICO, D. F., SABADO 19 DE MAYO DE 1956	AÑO XL - TOMO CLXIV

Sábado 19 de mayo de 195

Pro Tratados Bilaterales

Señor Walter H. Diamond, Director de la famosa revista financiera norteamericana, "McGraw-Hill American Letter", que visitó ayer nuestra redacción con el objeto de informarnos sobre los proyectos que se estudian para obtener Tratados Bilaterales entre México y Estados Unidos y otras naciones, para evitar que los inversionistas norteamericanos paguen dobles impuestos en las empresas que con capital norteamericano establecen en otros países.

COMO SE EVITARA LA DOBLE TRIBUTACION

Estudio del Dr. Walter D. Diamond, que actualmente visita nuestro país

El hecho de que la economía de México se esté cimentando día a día, no obstante la difícil situación que confrontó nuestro país, tras de la desvaluación de nuestra moneda, ha provocado

SIGUE EN LA PAGINA SIETE

Cómo se Evitará la Doble

VIENE DE LA PRIMERA PAGINA

una magnífica impresión, entre los inversionistas de los Estados Unidos de Norte América, ya que, por las estadísticas proporcionadas en el vecino país del norte, se sabe que México mejora constantemente en el campo de las finanzas.

Tal aseveración se desprende de las optimistas declaraciones que nos hizo ayer el señor Walter H. Diamond, Director de la conocida revista norteamericana de finanzas, McGraw Hill American Letter, cuyos comentarios son considerados en el mundo de las finanzas, como de los más autorizados.

El señor Diamond vino a México con objeto de conocer los adelantos que se han obtenido en nuestra Patria, para llegar a la terminación de los estudios para procurar un tratado entre México y los Estados Unidos mediante el cual los industriales y comerciantes norteamericanos, paguen solamente una vez el income-tax, y no dos, como acontece desde hace tiempo.

"Actualmente, nos dijo el señor Diamond, los comerciantes e industriales norteamericanos pagan sus impuestos en el país en donde tienen establecidos sus negocios y cuando envían sus utilidades a los Estados Unidos tienen que pagar allá un nuevo impuesto".

Hace mucho tiempo que se trata de establecer una ley, mediante la cual todos los capitalistas que en plan de comerciantes e industriales invierten en otros países sus capitales, paguen los impuestos que indican las leyes de los países en donde tienen sus negocios y no tengan que pagar otra vez un impuesto en los Estados Unidos, pero no ha sido posible implantarla".

17. Walter Diamond's arrival in Mexico City in 1956 for talks with Minister of Finance Carrillo Flores to help Mexico in planning its economic development, investment guarantees, and tax treaty negotiations, published by Mexico's leading newspaper, *El Universal*, on the front page. Walter is described as one "whose comments are considered by the financial world as among the most authoritative."

Although one of the developing countries, Mexico played a central role in the formation of the International Bank for Reconstruction and the International Monetary Fund. So I very much looked forward to meeting him. I reached his office by walking down a long corridor lined with one hundred or so supplicants, who were sitting patiently in chairs against the walls waiting for a chance to plead for assistance in solving their problems.

Before I met Flores, I had spoken at length to a well-known Mexican businessman, Jose Riochas, a good friend and confidant of Senator James Fulbright. The senator had used his accumulated wealth (from Wurlitzer interests) to establish the Fulbright Scholarships. Fulbright himself had been a Rhodes Scholar. Riochas was the owner of Riochas Wurlitzer and had the exclusive license to sell Wurlitzer instruments in Mexico. With the help of the general manager of Zenith Mexico, Riochas had planted the idea of an income tax treaty in Flores's mind; both Riochas's business and the senator's could benefit from a reduction in withholding tax as well as from relief from double taxation. While we were in Mexico, Riochas arranged for Dorothy and me to call on the Zenith general manager at his mansion in Cuernavaca. Unfortunately, by the time we arrived he was away for an emergency meeting. However, he had thoughtfully arranged for his large staff to entertain us with tortillas prepared on giant hot stones in his luxurious native garden.

In our 1956 discussions, Flores showed little interest in negotiating a taxation treaty with the United States. He himself emphasized the need for foreign investors to take insurance against political and commercial risks. At the time, insurance was available in the United States through the Investment Insurance Division of the International Development Agency (later renamed the Agency for International Development). Mexico and Panama were the only two countries taking advantage of investment insurance, which was providing risk coverage for the publishing operations of McGraw-Hill, the *New York Times*, and the *New York Herald Tribune*.

Flores later became Mexico's foreign minister, and it was during his time in that post that Mexico began negotiating a double-taxation treaty with the United States. It was finally signed in 1996, forty years after Flores and I first discussed it. The Honduras treaty had been abrogated in 1965, nine years after it become effective, so Mexico was the only Latin American nation with an income tax treaty with the United States until the Argentine Income Tax Convention was approved by the U.S. Senate in 2001.

THE HONDURAN TREATY was abrogated at the request of the Hondurans themselves, once the treaty turned out to be a one-way street. With little or no Honduran investment in the United States, but with hundreds of American companies operating in Honduras and taking advantage of the 20 percent exemption from the Honduran dividend withholding tax, Hondurans believed that the country was penalizing itself by not collecting taxes on a good source of income. Even so, the two nations have always remained close. The Honduran people like Americans and respect us deeply. One of my visits to their country coincided with Thanksgiving Day. Our activities that Thanksgiving included a reception for American expatriates at the residence of the U.S. ambassador, which the Honduran president himself attended, a midafternoon dinner provided by the hotel manager, and a midnight Thanksgiving feast on a turkey farm in the hills outside Tegucigalpa that could be reached only by a heavy jeep.

By 1968, when we visited Honduras the last time, the government there had refocused its energies: instead of trying to attract American industry through free trade zones, it was working hard to attract tourists. At the direction of President Lozano, the Ministry of Tourism had launched a campaign to persuade Americans that Honduras's Mayan ruins at Copán were at least as awe inspiring as Mexico's. At the time, Mexico was the number-one destination for American adventure travelers.

Juan Funes, who was still the Honduran consul general in New York and the UN ambassador, arranged a visit to Copán for Dorothy and me. Honduras's national airline, TAN, would fly us from the Tegucigalpa airport, which was still a cow pasture, to the country's second largest city, San Pedro Sula. The Department of Trade and Tourist Development had arranged for a single-engine biplane owned by Del Webb, a prominent American investor in the country, to fly us to Copán from there. On our first attempt to land at Copán, the pilot could not find a hole in the dense clouds after half a dozen tries, so we returned to San Pedro Sula. Only then did the pilot confess that he had never landed at Copán before.

We waited in San Pedro Sula for a week while the weather cleared. By then, the tourism department had chartered a plane from a local airline that was more familiar with the conditions. When we finally landed in a farmer's field at Copán—which did not yet have an airstrip—the pilot jumped out of his seat and ran straight for the nearest church to thank his Savior.

That left Dorothy and me to shift for ourselves. The welcoming committee consisted of the manager of the only hotel in the district, who immediately began to recite all the reasons we should stay overnight there. When our guide appeared half an hour later, and we told him we were there to write articles about the Copán ruins for business magazines, he insisted in broken English that we inspect every nook and cranny of the throngs of the pyramids, stelae, and sculptures. Although beaten down by the ferocious sun, we gathered enough material to please the director of tourism.

Dorothy and I are hardly authorities on pre-Columbian ruins, but we have no doubt that Copán can compete with the better-known Latin American tourist attractions, including Mexico's Mayan ruins and Tikal in Guatemala, but not Machu Picchu in Peru. Moreover, Copán is not in the same league as Persepolis in Iran, Petra in Jordan, Baalbek in Lebanon, Borobudur in Indonesia, or Angkor Wat in Cambodia. Even so, when we returned to the capital we told the tourism authorities, quite honestly, that they were not trumpeting Copán enough. That is still the case.

France

After we returned to New York from Honduras, we received a call from Douglas Egan, the director of the New York office of the Department of Commerce. He told me that President Eisenhower wanted me to join a U.S. trade team that was about to visit France. The French president, Charles de Gaulle, had asked for this visit as a way to help his country lure American capital investment and in that way accelerate its postwar recovery. (France was so ravaged by the Nazi occupation during the war that its economy had deteriorated to such an extent it was rated as a "developing country.") The group would be visiting twenty-six French cities and towns in thirty days, with luncheon meetings sponsored by a different Chamber of Commerce each day. While there, we would be reviewing the French tax structure and recommending changes to it with regard to American companies operating in France. I had to decline the invitation because I could not abandon my post for a month as director of economics for McGraw-Hill International and editor of the *American Letter*. Even so, a meeting was arranged in France between me and the French finance minister, Paul Ramadier.

At that time, there were more American subsidiaries in France than in any other country—around twenty-five hundred of them. (Brazil was ranked second in that regard, with approximately two thousand.) Yet French corporate taxes were 50 percent; when local levies were added, the burden was around 55 percent, which was the highest in Europe. Many American investors were complaining about this "unfair" treatment that continued even after the 1946 Income Tax Convention between the two nations reduced the dividend withholding tax. Ramadier, an ardent conservative and a staunch supporter of the nationalist de Gaulle, was deeply worried that the Socialist Party would sooner or later rule France (which it would). He was certain that the Socialists would soon

18. The Diamond arrival in Paris prior to Walter's meeting with French finance minister Paul Ramadier, de Gaulle's last minister of finance in his "first takeover government," 1957. Photo by Air France, as requested by the government.

be demanding lower taxes, the logic being that corporations could then use the money they saved to pay their workers more, as had been promised.

Time has proven Ramadier correct: the French economy today is being held back mainly by dampened output in several major industries, the consequence of unrestrained demands by workers who are all too ready to go on strike. (The same can be said of many other European countries.) The European economies are in serious need of labor reform, and until that happens, the continent's commercial and industrial hopes will be thwarted. Likewise, Europe's banking and corporate sectors need restructuring.

Ramadier was well aware of these basic economic obstacles in his country. However, in our discussions he focused on the immediate need for U.S. government insurance for American corporations to protect their foreign investments against commercial and political risks. At the time, in the mid-1950s, such coverage was available in the United States under the Insurance Investment Section of the Economic Development Administration (now U.S. AID). However, this type of private investment insurance only covered outlays of funds granted to developing countries through the Overseas Private Investment Corporation, an agency funded jointly by the government and private insurers.

More than once, Ramadier hinted that American companies were sending over too many American managers to direct their French operations. He pointed out that most of these managers were unfamiliar with European customs, tax statutes, and legal channels. His hammering of this point inspired me to prepare a book, *Digest of French Taxes and Business Organization*, published by Matthew Bender in 1957 and the first of that company's many single-country books on foreign taxation.

Costa Rica

Probably the deepest of my relationships with developing countries as a trade or investment adviser was with Costa Rica. Shortly after I returned from France in 1957, I received a phone call from that country's former attorney general, Juan Edgar Picado, who explained that we needed to meet that very day at the Hotel Elysee in New York. A devout Catholic and strong patriot, he had just attended the president's Prayer Breakfast in Washington, D.C. There, his country's UN ambassador suggested he visit me in New York as soon as possible to discuss ways his country might alleviate its severe unemployment problem. Specifically, how could American companies be induced to open factories in Costa Rica?

A close friend and adviser to Costa Rica's president, Jose Figueres Ferrer, Picado had enough clout to authorize me on the spot to prepare a booklet, *Advantages of Incorporating and Operating in Costa Rica*, for distribution to U.S. companies. For this new booklet, I used the Honduran one as a template. But

Picado had other ideas besides that one, many of which would be implemented by his country over the next thirty years.

During the second of my five visits to Costa Rica, Picado and I prepared the ground for the nation's present network of nine FTZs, which together now handle 70 percent of the country's exports. That second visit was in 1957, during Figueres Ferrer's second term as president. At that time the president was launching extensive public works programs as well as sweeping reforms of the education and social security systems.

FTZs were far from being Figueres Ferrer's priority. Picado was unable to convince him that they would provide jobs and alleviate poverty. However, the president did arrange for his private plane to fly us to Puerto Limón, where twelve thousand workers were unemployed. Picado and I saw this deepwater port about a hundred miles east of the capital as the logical place to establish an FTZ, since both plentiful labor and government land were available.

The pilot of the president's plane was a jovial middle-aged Costa Rican with a passion for aerial acrobatics. On our return to the capital, San José, I just assumed it was part of the standard flight plan when he flew us directly into the vol-

19. Walter Diamond advising the Costa Rican superintendent of insurance in his office in San José regarding the need to establish an export credit insurance system to enhance the development of Costa Rica's export market, 1957. *Comunicadores Asociados,* for Ministry of Finance.

20. Walter Diamond advising Costa Rica's minister of finance and director of economic development on establishing a free trade zone, 1957. Comunicadores Asociados.

canic crater of Mount Trazu, where he dipped his wings as if he was greeting the Mayan gods. Fortunately, the volcano was not active in those days, although there have been several eruptions since, one of which recently caused severe damage to the capital's suburbs.

My next visit to Costa Rica came during Figueres Ferrer's third term, 1970–74. As an export trade adviser to the World Trade Institute of the Port Authority of New York and New Jersey, I had been asked by Picado to help prepare an FTZ feasibility study. His insistence that an FTZ program would benefit his country had won the support of Costa Rica's new finance minister, partly because U.S. AID would finance the scheme. During this third visit, Picado arranged for me to open discussions with the Costa Rican government's insurance department to expand its risk coverage to the export field.

The department's officials listened closely to my suggestions and later adopted a more sophisticated insurance system that would cover both political and commercial risks. That system, a product of Picado's foresight, eventually did a great deal to attract American companies to Costa Rica's new FTZs. My discussions relating to export financing involved visiting officials at the Costa Rican Central Bank, a modern building with an entire floor devoted to a display of carefully guarded pre-Columbian gold artifacts.

After preparing a study requested by U.S. AID, I returned to Costa Rica accompanied by the director of the World Trade Institute, Sidney Schachter, a widely admired and congenial trade administrator. When we arrived at the Finance Ministry to discuss my U.S. AID recommendations, which had been sent ahead, Schachter and I were startled to find a room jammed with construction engineers from a number of foreign countries, each grasping a copy of my recommended program.

Following a brief presentation by the minister and his aides, the contractors—hardly any of whom had much experience constructing FTZs—were asked to review my feasibility study and make formal bids based on the plans therein. A Philippine construction company won the bid, probably because it had already constructed a profitable and attractive zone at Baguio, 130 miles north of Manila. The Baguio Export Processing Zone is well known in FTZ circles for its quick and efficient transportation routes to Manila. It is also considered one of the world's most beautifully landscaped FTZs. However, political problems in the Philippines led to delays that forced Costa Rica to withdraw its offer to the Philippine company, and the project was awarded to an Israeli firm.

I was making these visits during the Nixon administration, and all of our instructions from U.S. AID—which was managed by the State Department—came to us by telegram or cable signed "Henry Kissinger, Secretary of State." Needless to say, I questioned this awkward routine, since our assignments were not remotely related to foreign policy. Our activities were highly significant to the nations that welcomed them, but to Washington, at least, they would have been barely a speck on Kissinger's map. I asked about it, and State Department officials told me that Kissinger's specific instructions were for his signature to appear on all communications emanating from the State Department.

I returned to Costa Rica in the late 1980s while Oscar Arias Sanchez was president. This time it was with a colleague, Walter Szykitka, a foreign trade journalist who also is president of the Association for World Free Trade Zones. It was most satisfying to me to visit the country's active FTZs, which were now hosting dozens of American multinationals and employing some sixty thousand Costa Ricans. It had been more than thirty years since Juan Edgar Picado first approached me asking for suggestions about establishing these FTZs. He had died in the interim, but his son, Juan Edgar Jr., was there to serve as our guide around the nine zones. The latter was as elated as I was that these zones—an achievement of two countries working together—were doing so much to raise living standards in his country. Costa Rica's gross domestic product had gone up 300 percent since they were established.

My goal had been to help Costa Ricans solve their unemployment problems, so I was especially touched in 1989 when I attended an Offshore Institute Conference in Vienna. To my surprise, coming to the podium on the first day was Juan Edgar Picado Jr., who was making a special trip to Vienna as an emissary of the Costa Rican president. He was there to tell the delegates, who included seven finance ministers from eastern Europe, that President Oscar Arias Sanchez, a Noble Peace Prize recipient in 1983, had sent him to publicly "extend his gratitude to Walter Diamond for helping his nation for many years."

✻ 7 ✺

Tales of South America

Brazil

*I*N THE EARLY FALL OF 1958, we made the first of a dozen or so trips to
South America with the cooperation of Francisco Megdalia, the gregarious
Brazilian consul general in New York. Megdalia was a close associate of Doug
Egan, the former head of the U.S. Commerce Department's field office in New
York, who was now that department's trade director in Rio de Janeiro. We had
been invited to Brazil as part of President Dwight Eisenhower's efforts to help the
Latin American nations. As editor of the Brazilian edition of the *American Letter*,
my name was familiar in that country's trade and financial circles. The media in
Rio de Janeiro, São Paulo, Pôrto Alegre, Belém, and other Brazilian cities regularly quoted the *Letter* under page 1 headlines, often illustrated with my photo,
when covering American activities and attitudes toward Brazilians.

In 1954 I tried to persuade the Export-Import Bank of Washington, D.C., to
grant a loan of eight hundred million dollars to Brazil in order to bail out U.S. exporters, who had been waiting as long as two years to be paid for the merchandise
they had sold to Brazilian companies. With Brazil's foreign exchange reserves
empty, both the Brazilians and the Americans were clamoring for financial assistance to Brazil. Before paying these debts, to appease their own countrymen, the
Brazilian authorities were insisting that Eximbank publicly acknowledge that
the debts had been incurred as a result of pressure from American exporters. The
Brazilians were blaming those firms for the disaster and maintaining that
the goods had been forced on the Brazilian buyers.

At an early-morning meeting in the Export-Import Bank, I was told that my
efforts to help the Brazilians were impossible to fulfill. I was returning to New
York from that meeting when I heard my name being paged at Washington's
Union Station. Harry Roundtree, the bank's primary negotiator for Latin Ameri-

21. Dorothy and Walter Diamond with Dr. Francisco Megdalia, discussing arrangements for the Diamonds to go to Rio de Janeiro to cut the tape at the opening of the International Trade Exhibition Center where President Kubitschek was scheduled to address the guests at the formal opening, 1958. Photo by Bill Cancellare, News Event Photo Service.

can affairs, was calling to advise me that the bank had changed its mind—Brazil would be getting the eight hundred million dollars. A press release announcing the credit would be accompanied by a statement to the effect that it was "unfortunate" that Brazil's indebtedness had been inspired by "U.S. companies 'overmarketing' their wares." It was later disclosed that the White House and the State Department both played a part in the Eximbank's reversal. Knowledgeable insiders believed that many of Eisenhower's decisions as president were based on loyalty to smaller powers for their military contributions to the Allies in World War II. I was later told that he had interceded in this particular case.

Of course, Brazilian media reports about this episode strengthened my reputation as a friend of Brazil. Moreover, the whitewashing of the lingering debt inspired a strong inflow of American direct investment to Brazil. Because of the overhanging debt, U.S. companies had been cutting back some of their Brazilian subsidiary operations. By 1956 Brazil was the second-largest recipient of American foreign investment after France; some two thousand American firms were active there. All of which meant that my book *Digest of Brazilian Taxes and Business Organization,* published by Matthew Bender, was ripe for the market.

I also became involved in Brazil's wine industry, which was in a bad state. A subscriber to the Brazilian edition of the *American Letter* contacted us for advice about reviving his wine sales in the United States, which had plummeted to rock bottom because his country lacked bottling facilities. We located an importer in Brooklyn who agreed to take an entire tanker load of port wine and bottle it in his warehouse. Brazil's fleet of oil tankers was not in full use at the time, so the resourceful vineyard owner arranged for the ships' holds to be thoroughly scrubbed to satisfy the health inspectors. He then had the compartments redesigned to accommodate hundreds of gallons of port wine. After they were bottled in Brooklyn they became a "best-seller" at eighty-nine cents a bottle.

Dorothy and I arrived in Brazil on a Varig Airlines plane after a refueling stop in the Dominican Republic. This trip was during the thirty-year rule of the notorious dictator General Rafael Trujillo, who despised Americans, especially if they were associated with the U.S. government. For the few minutes we were on his soil, his troops had us covered with loaded rifles, bayonets locked.

We did not realize that the only other passenger in first class was the president of Varig Airlines, whose kitchen in Santo Domingo had prepared a dinner for us—a three-foot-long elaborately decorated fresh salmon. The airplane crew had to remove the partition between coach and first class to force it through the door, and even so part of the coating was smeared.

At the Rio airport we were met by a delegation from the U.S. Embassy and the Brazilian government, who hustled us out to the new International Trade Exhibition Center. Because the funds for the vast structure came from U.S. AID, we had been invited to cut the ribbon after President Kubitschek made a speech. But when we arrived for this assignment, we were met by frantic Brazilian officials, who informed us that the ceremony had been cancelled. It turned out that the structure's glass roof, which had been designed by the great American architect Edward Durell Stone, had sprung several serious leaks and was threatening to collapse on visitors. Stone's first glass covering of this type for the United States Pavilion at the 1958 Brussels World Fair (which we had an opportunity to preview) drew worldwide attention for its daring design. Within days the Russians had taken over the U.S. exhibit building, where they established a grandiose permanent trade center several blocks long that became the gateway for the first So-

22. Walter and Dorothy Diamond are met at Rio de Janeiro airport by Douglas Egan, commercial attaché for the United States, 1958. Courtesy of U.S. Embassy.

viet goods entering Brazil. This move by the Russians was well conceived; soon after the fiasco, they were competing with U.S. exporters for Brazilian business.

On our first evening in Brazil, we were the guests of honor at a reception at the Egan residence. There we were introduced to a number of senior Brazilian government and business leaders, all of whom seemed to have a single issue on their minds: "Where can we get financing to do more business with the Americans?" When I met President Kubitschek the following day, he expressed interest in negotiating an income tax treaty with the United States and asked me whether such a treaty would encourage more American private investment in his country.

During my brief session with Kubitschek, also attended by Oswaldo Pinedo, the cabinet secretary, it struck me that Kubitschek's thoughts were elsewhere than on improving Brazil's climate for capital investment. He was immersed at the time in the controversial project of moving the nation's capital from Rio de Janeiro to the desert hinterlands. At this point—late 1958—he was shuttling between Rio and Brasília and trying to run the government from both.

He invited us to see Brasília, which was then in the end stages of construction, but warned us we would find it difficult to get around because the roads had not yet been paved. Then, as a gesture of goodwill when he learned we were

23. Walter Diamond's arrival in Brazil as reported in one of Rio de Janeiro's leading newspapers indicating that the "editor of the famous *American Letter*" came to their country to recommend ways to improve the Brazilian economy through capital investment and export development programs, 1958. *Ultima Hora.*

going to Argentina next to meet President Frondizi, Kubitschek instructed Pinedo to "personally" fly us to Argentina on the Brazilian president's new Caravel airplane, of which he was enormously proud. As a mark of respect to the Portuguese people, the French had presented Kubitschek with the first Caravel ever built.

Originally, Caravels were lateen-rigged ships conceived in the fifteenth century. The Portuguese had relied on them during their great voyages to explore the coast of Africa and discover sea routes to Asia and the Indies. As brilliantly described in Antonio Lobo Antunes's *Return of the Caravels*, those who sailed the caravels were heroes of Portuguese history.

Before saying good-bye to Kubitschek, I asked him a question that had been on my mind for some time: "Why doesn't your government at least try to end the squalor of the hundreds of thousands of Brazilians living in the slums above Rio?" Even today, 20 percent of *cariocas* (citizens of Rio) live in hundreds of *favelas*, which is the term for the unpoliced slums in the hills ringing the city. A recent account in *U.S. News and World Report* described the *favelas* as a "labyrinth of slums marked by rutted streets and winding alleys, with block after block of gritty concrete tenements filthy with leaky sewers and jerry-rigged electrical wiring." Forty-seven years ago Dorothy and I visited them, and stumbled our way nervously through piles of garbage, stepping over open sewers. Those neighborhoods have barely changed since we first saw them.

The brash question surprised my host. He told me he was eager to help the "poor and needy," but removing the *favelas* would only make matters worse. First, there was no good place to relocate the nearly half-million people. Second, the people who lived in them were "content where they are and cause little harm." Third, if new homes were found for them, it would only anger the 77 million African Brazilians who accounted for almost half the country's population. Brazil at the time had more black people than any other country in the world except Nigeria. Two-thirds of them were living below the poverty line, and only 2 percent of Brazilian college graduates were nonwhite.

We were not able to visit the new capital on our first trip to Brazil, and Oswaldo Pinedo had to cancel arrangements to fly us to Buenos Aires in the president's Caravel. However, we were able to visit Brazil's ultramodern new capital in 1969. Francisco Megdalia, now the Brazilian ambassador to the United States, had asked me to help represent his government in negotiations for a new income tax treaty to avoid double taxation (a topic I had discussed briefly with Kubitschek eleven years before). This request opened the way to our second visit to Brazil.

24. Economist Walter H. Diamond receiving an award from Dr. Francisco Megdalia, Brazilian consul general, later to be ambassador to the United States and minister of finance, for Walter's work in representing Brazil in negotiations with the U.S. for investment guarantees and a tax treaty to avoid double taxation, 1958.

In Brasília, on the colorful veranda of the capitol, we were greeted warmly by the new president, Castillo Branco. The capitol was said to be the most futuristic building in the world at that time. Castillo Branco was not as imposing a figure as his predecessor; he was not as rigid and unyielding as Kubitschek, nor was he as popular. The Brazilian negotiators, led by the finance minister, haggled long and hard over the article of the treaty covering dividend payments. Brazil was stubbornly seeking a complete exemption from withholding tax on dividends; the American delegation, led by the very capable Nat Gordon of the Treasury Department, insisted on a 20 percent levy. Finally, after several strenuous days, the Brazilians accepted to the 20 percent dividend withholding tax, provided the Americans agreed to a 10 percent investment credit for American companies operating in Brazil. Gordon gave the green light, albeit reluctantly, and the treaty was later signed.

I climbed aboard the twin-engine plane bound for Rio de Janeiro, elated that I had been part of the first international tax treaty the Americans had ever signed with a South American nation. A few minutes into the flight, the Varig pilot announced soberly that we were returning to Brasília. Back on the ground, we immediately noticed that the plane's left engine was on fire. The layover gave us another twenty-four hours to explore the new capital's unique architecture. That is how long it usually took a replacement part to arrive from Miami, but since it never did so, we were very fortunate to get two seats on another plane.

Brazil's Congress ratified the treaty quickly. Unfortunately for both countries, the U.S. Senate refused to do so, which dashed many people's hopes for prosperous relations between the two countries. The chairman of the Senate Ways and Means Committee, Albert Gore Sr., pounded his gavel at the treaty hearings and shouted with all his strength that "no foreign subsidiary of a U.S. corporation will get an investment credit while the parent company does not have a comparable incentive." At that point the treaty was doomed in the Senate. Gore's anger had been fanned by the withdrawal of the 7 percent investment credit for domestic companies a few months earlier.

Brazil's pride had been shattered. Officials in Brasília and Rio declared that their country's treatment by the U.S. Senate was an "insult to the nation." To this day, Brazilians have not forgotten this assault on their prestige. Some twenty years later, in the late 1980s, I received a call from Nat Gordon asking me to contact my Brazilian government friends: "Would they consider resuming negotiations for a new treaty?" I did as he asked, and almost immediately got an answer back from the Brazilian finance minister, channeled through the embassy in Washington. No, the Brazilians absolutely would not resume negotiations. "Once insulted as we were," there would never be an international tax treaty between Brazil and the United States. This renewed objective came after Brazil returned to democracy and drafted its 1988 constitution, with 245 articles, one of the world's longest.

Chile

The second leg of my 1958 South American assignment involved a series of discussions with Chile's finance minister, Roberto Vergara, a popular conservative; his deputy, Hernon Briones, one of Chile's most successful businessmen, who owned several industries; and Jose Zabala, the president of Chile's Central Bank and a well-known figure in world financial circles. In the 1950s, reaching Santiago from Rio de Janeiro was not as easy as it looks on a map. This period was before jet travel, and we were advised not to attempt a direct flight over the Andes in a prop plane because of the treacherous weather — in particular, the notorious downdrafts peculiar to the Andes.

So we took a DC-3, a propeller-driven plane, which stopped to refuel in Pôrto Alegre, Brazil. There, while I remained on the plane, Dorothy jumped onto a cargo dolly and rode on it to the far end of the airport to view Varig's kitchen headquarters for a *Tide* column. Varig got her back to the plane just as the engines were warming up again. We had to refuel two more times. One of those times was in Montevideo, Uruguay, which the plane's captain described as one of the most dangerous airports in the Western Hemisphere because of its short runway sandwiched between two mountain peaks.

Uruguay was not on my schedule on that trip. At that time, its economy was in excellent health according to Latin American standards. Beef exports were providing the country with a steady inflow of dollars. It was blessed with a far-sighted financial community that had already established several FTZs in the country, so its government had made no requests to the UN or U.S. AID for assistance in that regard. However, many years after, in the early 1990s, we did visit Uruguay to review the status of its nine FTZs, which handled 80 percent of the country's foreign trade.

Uruguay was one of the first welfare states in the modern world. It established its social security system in 1905. Thirty years later, FDR would use it as a template for the American system. Uruguay saw no need to establish an income tax until 1961. When it finally did, it temporarily lost its appeal to the thousands of European retirees who had been flocking there since the war. During the country's thirteen-year experiment of imposing personal and inheritance taxes, the economy began to slip badly. On top of that, the government found those taxes almost impossible to collect. So it decided to abandon the whole idea of personal taxes, and Uruguay's famous beaches are once again a magnet for foreign retirees.

We arrived in Chile after a turbulent flight over the Andes and were met at the Santiago airport by our McGraw-Hill correspondent, who told us we were not going to Portillo, as had been scheduled. The head ski instructor at that world-famous resort, Othmar Schneider, had "just married a Ford girl and was in Santiago honeymooning." So we grabbed our ski boots, which Dorothy and I usually carried with us during our winter assignments, threw them into the correspondent's jeep, and drove with him to another resort, La Parva. This one was at eleven thousand feet in the Andes and could be reached only by a hairpin dirt road, which ended a thousand feet below the ski slope, at Farraleones, where a derelict army barracks was located.

We did the last thousand feet on foot—a difficult climb over snow and ice, especially for two middle-aged Americans unused to high altitudes. Waiting for us in the *refugio* was our host, the managing director of Mobiloil de Chile, William Litchfield. With him was Briones, who happened to be his next-door neighbor and whom we were going to meet officially in a day or two. Briones, besides being the deputy finance minister, was a member of the Chilean Money and Banking team, ICARE, counterpart of the American Management Association. After a leisurely meal that included several glasses of Chile's best red wines, I decided to test my skis—this, over the warnings from our new friends that the intense midday sun sometimes reached 140 degrees on the slopes. I retreated soon enough to the *refugio* to rest up for the following day's runs on the glacier itself.

We stayed the night at the *refugio*. The following morning, a Sunday, we brushed our teeth using the local champagne, having been warned that the tap water was not pure. As I answered a loud knock on our door, there were Briones and his wife waiting for me with Schneider, the former Olympic gold medalist for Austria, and his bride. They were eager to reach the top of the glacier at La Parva before the early-morning sun touched it. Schneider explained quickly that the skiing was best the one hour before the sun reached this side of the mountain, while the temperature hovered around the freezing point. After skiing down the thousand feet back to Farraleones, where the chairlift began, a few yards from the *refugio* of Emil Allais, another Olympic champion (France, 1952), we took the lift up to thirteen thousand feet, from which height we could view the spectacular monument *Christ of the Andes* in the shadow of Aconcagua, South America's highest mountain. We started our first run exactly one hour before the sun was to touch the glacier's crest. Our plan was to stay an hour ahead of the sun all day in order to take advantage of the best *azucar* (sugar) conditions—conditions I quickly mastered since the cornlike texture of the snow is frequently encountered when skiing in the eastern United States.

At the "stocking-foot hour," from the veranda of the Brioneses' *refugio*, we enjoyed the fabulous Andean sunset reflecting on the glacier. Then we climbed into the jeep, which took us down the mountain to a reception in our honor at the home of Roberto Vergara, the finance minister. Before making our appearance, we had to circle the block several times. The minister had not yet returned from an emergency meeting, and Chilean protocol required that one should never arrive before the host.

In the discussions that followed regarding Chile's credit position—which were why I had been invited to Chile—Vergara emphasized that his goal was to raise Chile's credit rating so as to open the door to development loans from the

U.S. government and the World Bank. He also mentioned that Chilean wines could not be marketed in the United States mainly because of a shortage of suitable bottling plants. Those facilities, centered in Valparaíso, were in a shambles, owing to a discovery in the past of glass fragments in bottled wines that American distributors had imported. Chile now found itself having to ship its highly prized vintages to France in barrels; there, they were mixed with French vintages and sold as French wines. Vergara's mood brightened when I told him about Brazil's success in shipping its port wines to the United States in modified oil tankers. His country soon followed suit and recaptured some of the American market for moderately priced wines.

Vergara also said that he hoped to attract more American and European tourists to Chile. In the 1950s, the demand for Chilean raw materials—famously, copper—was in the doldrums, and he hoped that tourism dollars would help cushion the resulting fall in hard currency revenues. At the time, Dorothy was writing many travel pieces for the *New York Times* and *New York Post* as well as for Pan Am publications. The day before, at Farraleones, she had noticed the empty army barracks at the foot of the ski hill. Now she suggested that the barracks, which were vacant during the southern winter, be converted into temporary quarters for the thousands of young, adventurous American skiers. And that is what the Chileans did. The tourism department had the barracks converted into a skiers' hostel for the many Americans, especially youngsters accustomed to vacationing in summer camps, who were eager to practice their winter sport in Chile during the snowy July and August.

At the reception in his home, Vergara served us huge hot dogs, explaining that he "thought all Americans ate hot dogs as their favorite food." When he learned differently, he and his wife took us out to dinner the following night at the rooftop restaurant of the Santiago Sheraton. Joining us were Hernon Briones; the Central Bank's president, Jose Zabala; and their wives. During our meal, someone bellowed at our table from the far end of the room: "Diamond! Diamond! Will H.R. 5 be approved by Congress?"

Some background is in order here. H.R. 5 was Eisenhower's bill to boost American exports by applying an incentive scheme. Congressman Hal Boggs, chairman of the House Ways and Means Committee, had called me at Ike's suggestion for help in drafting that measure, and I said I would cooperate. Later, Boggs came to New York to meet with me at the Astor Hotel. The bill sailed through the House but was defeated in the Senate because "that new young Sen-

ator from Massachusetts, Kennedy"—to quote a statement made in Congress—
"is obligated to support tariffs and quotas on Massachusetts and North Carolina
textiles and on Utah, Colorado, Nevada, and Montana minerals in exchange for
political backing as arranged by Joe Kennedy, the Senator's father." To my regret,
I repeated this Republican accusation some months later in my annual economic forecast address, made to the New England Bankers Association in Poland
Springs, Maine. As soon as I spoke those words, I was almost booed out of the
hall. A number of delegates later reminded me that I was in Kennedy country
and had touched a raw nerve.

Many economists, including me, believe that Eisenhower should be given
much more credit than he has received for warning about future trade deficits.
He was worried about them even in 1958, when the country was running surpluses. Soon after he gave that warning, the country did in fact begin running
massive trade deficits that ultimately weakened the dollar. Eisenhower had
counted on Democratic support in Congress through his friend Hal Boggs,
whom he admired, and it was a great loss to Ike when the Louisiana congressman
died in a plane crash in Alaska.

Back to the dinner meeting. It turned out that the boor was the director of
Latin American operations for Jones and Laughlan Steel. I did not know him. He
became so obnoxious—he even mocked that evening's entertainer, Harry Belafonte—that Vergara and the women at our table excused themselves and went
home. This event proved to me what I had long believed: the "ugly American"
developing countries resented so much was not usually the American government official; much more often it was the overseas American businessman.
When I returned to the United States, I made a point of emphasizing this fact in
speeches I presented at meetings about foreign trade. My point was that American industrial leaders needed to review the practices of their overseas staffs.

AS AN ADDENDUM, the Chilean political elite strongly suspected that Belafonte was an ardent communist as well as a strong supporter of Salvador Allende.
Allende was the leader of the Chilean leftists in the 1960s and the first communist
ever elected president by a Western country. After three stormy years in power, he
died in 1973 during the coup that brought General Augusto Pinochet to power. It
is well known that Belafonte was high on J. Edgar Hoover's list of suspected communists. Hoover's obsession with the communist threat was so profound that it
was reported the FBI actually compiled an eighteen hundred-page dossier on Al-

bert Einstein, hoping to have him denaturalized and deported as a communist spy. It was quite usual for Hoover to order investigations of celebrities.

Ronald Radosh, in his well-researched book *Commies: A Journey Through the Old Left, the New Left, and the Leftover Left,* wrote that most Americans remember Belafonte as a pathbreaking opponent of segregation and as the first black entertainer to break the color barrier and became an important celebrity: "Few are aware of the political vision he espoused." Radosh notes that Belafonte was the featured speaker at a rally in Castro's Cuba that honored the American Soviet spies Julius and Ethel Rosenberg. There, when he "recalled the pain and humiliation his friend Paul Robeson has been forced to endure" in the 1950s, "tears streamed down his face." According to the *New York Times,* Belafonte "attacked the American invasion of Grenada and criticized NATO for deploying Pershing missiles in West Germany, which Jimmy Carter and Ronald Reagan relied upon to offset the Soviet missile offensive."

During the Chilean presidential election of 1970, Belafonte's prestige contributed immensely to Allende's campaign. My hosts at the Sheraton dinner meeting could not possibly have foreseen that the ballads Belafonte was crooning that night would be a factor in Allende's victory. Nor could they have dreamed Allende's policies would force them into exile in Argentina.

Argentina

After Santiago, we flew to Buenos Aires to meet President Arturo Frondizi. We arrived in the Argentine capital at one o'clock on an unusually cold morning. Our taxi driver initiated us into the mysterious Argentine temperament by stopping suddenly at a desolate farmhouse several miles outside the city. Springing out of the unheated car, which he had parked in a barren cow pasture, he left us waiting nearly an hour before returning, with no apology or explanation. We suspected politics, gambling, or romance, but of course we never found out. We were relieved when he finally he let us out at the Buenos Aires Grand Hotel without further mishap.

Our meeting with Frondizi later that day was a pleasant one. He began by throwing his arms in the air and asking me: "Mr. Diamond, how can I help my poor people?" Frondizi had many political enemies, but he was popular among the common people. He declared himself their friend, someone who would undo all the harm that the Peronists had done to them. At that time in 1958, Argentina's poverty rate was 60 percent and had fallen to 40 percent by 2004. Today, the number of Argentines living in "extreme poverty," as reported by the government's National Statistic Agency, is down to 15 percent.

Frondizi quickly admitted that after many years of Peronism, it was difficult to rule because the Labor Party factions were so deeply divided. He doubted that there would ever be political peace in his country. The problems of his day had been generated by the policies of the Peronist Party, which had preceded his own government. In fact, those same problems dominate Argentina fifty years later. Yet the country survives because it is still has a two-party system—something that has characterized Argentina for one hundred years.

Like most Latin American leaders, Frondizi wanted to attract American investors. He was wary of the German influence over the economy—influence that had been rising since the end of World War II, when Juan Domingo Perón sought out German scientists and technicians to help build the economy. Frondizi permitted American investors to explore for Argentine petroleum for the first time. When I suggested to the president that his country—and especially its capital city—had a great deal to offer American tourists, he immediately instructed an aide to call the ticket office to arrange seats for us in the box of one of the directors of the opera house, the world-famous Teatro Colón, where *Aida* was playing that evening.

By the time we visited Argentina again in the early 1990s, its tourism industry was a major revenue earner. On its own, the Iguazú Falls on the northeastern border with Brazil and Paraguay was attracting a million travelers a year. That area today is home to thousands of Lebanese expatriates, who left their own country during the civil war years to start businesses in this isolated and weakly administered region. It is now suspected that Islamic cells—mainly on the Brazilian and Paraguayan sides of the river—were becoming significantly involved in terrorist activities, including those of al Qaeda.

Before Frondizi ended the interview, he indicated his strong interest in taking advantage of the investment guarantee insurance program available under U.S. AID. I had described this program to him as a strong incentive to American foreign investment. Shortly afterward, the Argentine ambassador in Washington, D.C., approached the Economic Development Administration (now known as the Agency for International Development), and a bilateral investment guarantee treaty was signed. This agreement was one of the first such treaties the United States signed with a Latin American nation.

Frondizi was well aware of the many advantages of FTZs. There are sixteen of them in Argentina. The original one, established in 1943 in Buenos Aires-Rosario, is now one of the busiest on the continent.

Colombia

Few other South American republics have displayed much interest in accepting UN or U.S. AID entitlements to enhance foreign investment or set up FTZs. Most Latin American countries have focused on obtaining loans from the World Bank and the IMF for agricultural, industrial, and mining development. Colombia, for instance, has set its sights mainly on export trade. It has been emphasizing sales of coffee, flowers, precious stones, and woven goods to the United States. The nation has not required assistance in establishing FTZs, because it has had ten of them since the 1960s, which have been quite successful. Nor has it needed much financial guidance, since its Banco Republica de Colombia is one of the strongest in the region. Our three visits to Colombia focused mainly on suggesting ways it could increase its exports.

For instance, I succeeded in finding a liquor importer in Sloatsburg, New York, to promote and distribute Colombia's popular "green bomb," which consists of two parts crème de menthe and one part vodka. The FTZ in Cartegena is unique in that it occupies a series of islands, each with a single factory and accessible only by boat. On one of those islands we found a prominent American petrochemical firm. With World Bank funding, it was processing herbs, chemicals, and agricultural derivatives into a medicine enjoying a strong market in North America.

Paraguay

When we visited Paraguay, it already had five zones operating and three more proposed. One of the existing ones is Ciudad del Este (previously called Ciudad Presidente Stroessner after the former dictator). Located at the junction of Paraguay, Brazil, and Argentina near Iguazú Falls, it hosts more than fifty firms, which use the zone as an entry point to Paraguay, a landlocked country. Nearby is the Itaipu Dam, a monumental hydroelectric dam with a five hundred-square-mile reservoir that is almost one-third larger than the state of Washington's Grand Coulee reservoir. This awesome structure, the biggest such project in

South America and one of the three largest in the world, provides electric power for four countries.

Peru

Peru has eight productive FTZs and did not need my services as a UN industrial economist. However, it did seek our help in promoting one of the world's great historic sites, the lost city of Machu Picchu. Fawcett Airlines tried to land us there three times in ten years, but each time our plane was denied a landing at Cuzco because of dense fog, ground mechanical problems, or inadequate respirators (necessary to survive in the high altitude—airlines were not built with air-compression chambers in the 1950s and 1960s).

Ecuador

When we visited Ecuador, the Finance Ministry officials welcomed my recommendations for establishing FTZs, but the proposal was plagued with obstacles such as protests from the private sector and a general lack of determination. Some twenty years later, the Foreign Trade Zone Act was approved. The site chosen for the first FTZ was in a remote region in northern Ecuador, and little progress was ever made there. However, Ecuador's government was determined to develop an important attraction out of the Galápagos Islands, which are renowned for their unique wildlife and for having been Charles Darwin's natural laboratory. The islands are now a magnet for scientists, nature lovers, and adventure travelers.

Dorothy and I were able to visit the Galápagos as guests of the Ecuadorian government. Our ship, the *Santa Cruz*, visited eight of the thirteen islands. According to the captain, my coauthor, Dorothy, "made history." Six of the islands could be reached only by Zodiac (a rubber raftlike boat). Because she had broken her hip in a fall a few months earlier, she had to be carried onto three of those six. Each time the crew carried her ashore, the captain would warn his passengers: "We carry our guests *off* the islands with broken limbs, not *onto* them." As one can imagine, the rugged volcanic terrain spiked with jagged outcrops and hidden boulders can play havoc with sightseers.

Ecuadorian president Lucio Gutierrez was an ardent promoter of the Galápagos until he was forced to resign in April 2005. During his 2003 visit to the

United States he sought funds to help stabilize his dollarized currency. This maneuver was important if the islands were to continue as an important dollar earner. After he promised that the Ecuadorian economy would be restructured consistent with his dollarization policy, he won financial support from the IMF and the Wall Street banks.

Venezuela

Venezuela's several FTZs provided sufficient returns, and therefore the government had no reason to seek advice from the UN or U.S. AID. As was pointed out to me during discussions with the Finance Ministry, the country's only need was to maintain a good relationship with the United States so that the oil wells could keep pumping. Venezuela is an oil-rich country, and its offshore banking sector is expanding, largely because of its friendly tax system. Officials there made it clear to me that the country did not need outside money in order to develop.

In the boom times of the 1960s and 1970s, after democracy had been established in 1958, the government in Caracas could not possibly have dreamed of the crisis the country would be facing in 2003. President Hugo Chavez now rules with a thinly veiled iron hand. His mismanagement of the economy has led to violence and labor unrest that "threaten Venezuela's core institutions," according to former president Jimmy Carter. Chavez, he continued, must set a date for an "internationally monitored referendum, or resign."

❧ 8 ❦

Winds of the Caribbean

The Bahamas

$\mathcal{D}$URING A VISIT to the Bahamas in 1959 to present my annual trade forecast to the islands' Chamber of Commerce, I received a request from the
managing director of the Arawak Trust Company, John Adams, a great-great-
grandson of John Adams, second president of the United States, who was also the
father of the sixth president, John Quincy Adams. Arawak's John Adams asked if
I would help his bank establish an offshore trading unit. With the approval and
under the guidance of the Bahamian government—whose controversial governor, Sir Stafford Sands, was leader of a clique of hard-boiled politicians, the "Bay
Street Boys"—I accepted the assignment, and stayed involved in it until 1963.

John Adams, who had just retired as vice president of the Portland Trust
Company in Oregon, was filled with energy and was determined for Arawak to
succeed. This was the Bahamas's first offshore banking and management services
operation and its initial entry into the offshore financial world. Arawak had recently been set up by Kleinworts of London, the Canadian Imperial Bank of
Commerce, Goldman Sachs of the United States, and the Bank of Nova Scotia.
It was there to serve the needs of the dozens of American customers and investors
who had just been driven out of Cuba. Their companies had been sequestered by
Castro shortly after he took control of the island in May 1959. I had visited Guan-
tanamo Bay during the war on the *Utahan* to deliver supplies to the U.S. military
base there and had found the Cuban workers very friendly toward the United
States, so it was hard for me to fathom how Castro had gained the support of most
Cubans. But for them at the time, "anything was better than Batista." That perception was shared even in American business circles. Batista's dictatorship had
been both cruel and corrupt, so a majority of Cubans were delighted with Castro
for overthrowing him.

As a welcoming gesture for the bank's new clients and as a chance for them to meet important Bahamians, Sir Stafford hosted a reception on the lawn of his magnificent estate. Considering the lavish setting and the beautiful gardens, the smartly dressed servants and the superb food, we were astonished when one of the cultured ladies with a British accent remarked: "Isn't it wonderful how simply Sir Stafford lives?"

One of the Cuban business refugees whom Castro had expelled was the woman president of the Chicago Great Lakes Feed Company, the largest supplier of animal feed in Latin America. She was living temporarily at the British Colonial Hotel in Nassau. There, she asked me with tears in her eyes: "What should I do now?" She described to me how Castro had sequestered Cuba's companies. As soon as his forces captured Havana, army officers visited her office and handed her a document that stated: "The new government replacing the previous administration will not take over your business operation, but from this date on we will be responsible for all the hiring and discharging of personnel."

Ever since 1948, under the Foreign Assistance Act, the United States had been providing American companies investing in developing countries with insurance against expropriation and nationalization along with protection against war, insurrection, revolt, and currency inconvertibility. Yet not a single American investor had insured any assets in Cuba, which was a tax-haven country with no taxation on income at the time. The Americans' failure to take advantage of that insurance meant that all told, those companies lost around seven billion dollars in assets when Castro nationalized their properties.

I introduced the woman—whose late husband, the former CEO and founder of the business, had passed away a few months earlier—to John Adams. Soon after, Great Lakes Feed became one of the first clients of the bank's offshore trading department. Under the IRS rules in 1959, it was quite legal for American companies to operate through trading subsidiaries established abroad. Those companies were not subject to taxation on their profits unless those monies were transferred back to the United States as dividends or other passive income (royalties, interest, and so on).

This exclusion was practiced by thousands of American entities around the world until it was terminated by the U.S. Revenue Act of 1962 (the so-called Kennedy Amendments). From that time on, "controlled foreign corporations" (that is, those companies whose capital stock was more than 50 percent owned by "U.S. shareholders," meaning individuals holding 10 percent or more of the shares of the subsidiary) became subject to American income tax whether or not the income was transferred back to the parent company. (The American Job Creation Act of 2004 allows part of the accumulated funds to be transferred to the United States at a reduced tax rate.) The Treasury Department referred to this income as "tainted." A typical case of the tax freedom afforded American companies prior to the 1962 Kennedy Amendments involved a Bahamian subsidiary of an American parent that was selling goods manufactured in the United States and shipping them from there directly to a third country. It could do so without being taxed on its profits as long as title to the goods passed outside the American three-mile limit and never touched the shores of the Bahamas.

I had prepared for Adams a booklet titled *Advantages of Incorporating and Operating in the Bahamas*. He made complimentary copies widely available through the press and began making weekly trips to the United States to call personally on investors who had requested a copy. His campaign worked, and today he deserves much of the credit for establishing the islands as a place from which to operate a business. Currently, some 45,000 companies are registered in the Bahamas: 24,500 domestic ones and 20,500 international business companies— IBCs, as they are known.

John Adams and his colleagues from the Canadian Imperial Bank of Commerce and Kleinworts suggested we see how "90 percent of Bahamians lived." Consequently, John escorted us one evening to see a dance program and explore the run-down section of Nassau known as "Over-the-Hill." There we found a wall of discontent and hatred of the "Bay Street Boys." In that neighborhood enough venom was being spouted at the clique to ignite a revolt in an instant. Frustrated by the squalid living conditions, hundreds of destitute Bahamians gathered around our car, some kicking it to vent their anger and declaring that we had no right to invade their turf. Not long afterward, the British called for elections, and Sir Stafford relinquished his hold on the colony. After Stafford lost the election, I was not surprised when the controversial Lyndon O. Pindling assumed the prime ministership. His lopsided election victory meant the end of the "Bay Street Boys" and their business shenanigans.

Cuba

Castro's influence on Latin American politics was much discussed at the time. Specifically, it was said that he was trying to export communism to other countries in the hemisphere. In fact, this rumor was true. Around the U.S. State Department, there was no question that he had close ties to Salvador Allende in Chile. Accordingly, the U.S. Agency for International Development, or U.S. AID, told Castro no when he asked for financial help. However, it was less obvious in Washington that Castro's antidemocratic policies were fostering guerrilla activities in Colombia, the Dominican Republic, Grenada, Guatemala, Peru, and even—more recently—in Venezuela.

For example, there is clear proof that Colombia's savage guerrilla war has been prolonged by guns and ammunition donated by the Castro regime. In the Dominican Republic, the tyrant General Rafael Trujillo, before he was assassinated in 1961, claimed that he had learned some of the "tricks of war" from Castro's repressive policies. President Lyndon Johnson sent in the U.S. Marines after Trujillo was killed, when the political turmoil became so strong that LBJ declared it "his duty" to prevent the Dominican Republic from becoming a second Cuba. Soon after, Joaquin Balaguer became the Dominican president. Balaguer ruled for twenty-two years, winning six straight elections and in between them governing as harshly at times as Trujillo himself.

Castro established guerrilla-training camps in Colombia. Today, guerrillas are operating similar sites in Venezuela and using them to launch incursions into Colombia. Venezuela's president, Hugo Chavez, condones these activities. In the 1960s, Grenada's policies were heavily borrowed from Castro's version of communism, setting the stage in 1979 for the Grenada prime minister, Maurice Bishop, a leading Marxist, to establish relations with Cuba and the Soviet Union. After Bishop was overthrown in a coup in 1983, the United States invaded the island to clean it out politically, and Grenada severed relations with both the communist countries.

It is said that Haiti's two tyrant dictators, François "Papa Doc" Duvalier and his son, Jean-Claude, better known as "Baby Doc," who ruled Haiti with terrible brutality for twenty-nine years, learned their politics from Castro but their torture techniques from Stalin. Human rights groups claim that the two of them murdered between forty thousand and sixty thousand political opponents and embezzled at least five hundred million dollars from state coffers before Baby Doc was overthrown. Their country now has the lowest per capita income in Latin America. During my time with U.S. AID, Haiti was near the top of the State Department's blacklist for financial or economic assistance. My instructions were to ignore any requests for help.

Belize

Belize, once known as British Honduras, has the second-lowest per capita income in the Western Hemisphere. It welcomed as much aid from Washington and London as it could get. My many discussions with that country's finance minister, Rafael Fonseca (who later became prime minister), led to Belize becoming an attractive offshore financial center. Fonseca showed little interest in developing an FTZ to help alleviate the severe unemployment problem. However, some twenty years later the government did establish a small customs-free zone for imported goods, in the San Antonio district, on the Caribbean coast some ten miles south of the Mexican border.

On our first visit to Belize to help establish an offshore financial center for the newly independent nation, Fonseca invited us to lunch at the country's best hotel. He asked if we liked the meat we were being served. When we said we did, he told us we were eating "rodent meat." Naturally, we were puzzled by this description of a Belize delicacy. At least, we were until several years later, when Queen Elizabeth was served the same meat and it was revealed in the media that this delicacy was a member of the muskrat family.

Also during this first visit to Belize, we learned how strongly the government controlled Belizean businesses. We booked a car and guide with a Michigan travel agent, who had an office in the lobby, to visit Belize's most famous Mayan temple, Altan Ha, thirty miles from the capital. Then we were warned that we would have to hire a Belizean vehicle for any travel arranged after arriving in Belize. Otherwise, we were "sure to be stopped by the police and arrested on the spot." It proved to be good advice: a few miles out of Belize City we passed a car whose passengers were standing on the side of the road. Their vehicle had been confiscated.

While in Belize, the government asked me if I could find an American buyer for the country's long-idle Hercules Powder plant. We knew that Belize's mahogany resources were near depletion—mahogany was the country's second-biggest revenue earner after sugar—so I arranged a second visit to Belize. This time, joining me was a vice president of the American Forest Products Company of San Francisco. Having experienced firsthand how much of a backwater Belize was, Dorothy chose not to accompany us. Except for one of two visits to Iran, this trip and a third to Belize were the only times in one hundred overseas assignments that she chose to bow out.

American Forest Products decided not to buy the Hercules plant, because there was not enough mahogany left in the country to justify doing so. On this second visit I did learn how families in underdeveloped regions could survive quite well following their own customs. We were invited to dinner in Belize City at the tax commissioner's home. When we arrived, we found that there was only one door, at the back of the house, and that to enter, we would have to climb two flights of wooden stairs propped on stilts on a muddy foundation.

The stilts were necessary because this part of Belize was all swampland. Houses were built above the waterline in order to keep the reptiles and other local fauna from entering. Also, building on stilts was necessary to stop homes from flooding during the hurricane season, which was always severe in Belize. After climbing the two long flights of splintered wooden staircases and ducking under the family laundry, we were served a delicious rice and chicken dinner by the commissioner's two daughters, both with their hair done up in rollers.

After the British began granting their West Indian colonies more independence, they also started reducing their financial support to them. This meant that each former colony had to find new sources of hard currency. Most of the West Indies islands did not levy income taxes on off-island income, so they resorted to the easiest method available to earn currency: they turned themselves into off-shore financial centers, or tax havens, as they are often called.

Belize took the same route. Its legislators approved a set of laws that were possibly the most enticing of any in the region to attract foreign investors. I had already helped the government restructure its Central Bank. Therefore, I arranged a meeting between Fonseca (now the prime minister) and two retired vice presidents of the Hibernia Bank of New Orleans, who were interested in establishing a financial institution overseas. These two had already visited Barbados with me, but Belize won them over because of its 100 percent tax exemption on bank earnings. At that time, the governor of the Barbados Central Bank, Courtney Blackman, was insisting on a 5 percent tax on bank profits.

By the time of my third visit to Belize, it had built a brand-new capital at Belmopan, some sixty miles east of Belize City. The gravel road to it had been constructed by Venezuelan contractors two years before, although an American firm had originally won the bid. This highway was generally considered a political move on the part of Belize, and it had deteriorated to the point of being dangerous. Even so, Fonseca sent his government jeep and driver to bring us to Belmopan. When we arrived, he greeted us with his usual jocular tone: "How did you like our new roller coaster?"

Two weeks later, we were saddened but not surprised when we learned that

Fonseca and his driver had both been killed when their jeep skidded off the road and turned over. It was also depressing to hear that the tax commissioner had been fired for "inappropriate activities"—the police had arrested him when he was found after working hours in an "indiscrete position with his secretary in the back of his office," according to a local newspaper.

Barbados

In 1977, Barbados wanted advice about establishing an offshore financial center (which would become an extremely successful one). Dorothy and I came down at the government's invitation to address the Caribbean Development Bank Conference, attended by some 350 delegates from around the region. Courtney Blackman, the popular governor of the Barbados Central Bank, was the organizer. An important figure in the Caribbean, Blackman later became the island's ambassador to the United States. He asked me specifically to discuss "the pitfalls as well as the advantages" of an offshore financial center, and when I spoke on the conference's first day, that is exactly what I did.

The following day, Dorothy spoke first. She was introduced by the island's prime minister, Tom Adams, who told the audience this would be a unique experience for them, in that none of them had ever heard a woman speak at a business conference. Dorothy then talked about how Barbados could learn from the experiences of the successful offshore jurisdictions. When she finished, they gave her a standing ovation, and her speech was printed on page 1 of a local newspaper.

During the question session, a secretary at the Barbados Central Bank raised several important issues that revealed her in-depth knowledge of the banking industry. Six months later she was made a vice president of that bank—the first woman official in a Barbados government agency. Later, she would become a prominent figure in her country's government. The Caribbean Development Bank Conference, representing the West Indies central banks, turned out to be one of Tom Adams's last public appearances. Sadly, he died shortly afterward, when his plane crashed in Central America.

Bermuda

Most of my Caribbean assignments were more eventful than that to Bermuda, in the Atlantic Ocean. Government and banking officials in Bermuda showed little enthusiasm for improving the sparingly used FTZ at Freeport, which, when we visited it, turned out to be a single dilapidated warehouse a few miles from Hamilton, the island capital.

For offshore income Bermuda has always been content to depend on its substantial receipts from the eighteen hundred captive insurance companies incorporated there and from its long-established shipping registration service. The latter has made it one of the world's great ocean transportation nations. However, Bermuda is prone to labor problems that can slow down business. While we were there inspecting the FTZ, an islandwide general strike closed down the main road to the airport. Fortunately, the manager of the Stonington Hotel drove us on a little-known back route to the airport, and we caught our flight.

Antigua and Barbuda

Neither did Lester Bird Jr., the chief executive of Antigua (who with his father, "Papa" Bird, ruled the nation for more than thirty years), express much enthusiasm for an FTZ. The UN had suggested to the British Exchequer that it cut back its aid for Antigua and Barbuda (which had been guaranteed when they gained independence). During my two visits with Lester Bird—then acting for his ailing father—and a long session with him in New York, I could not make him change his thinking. Several times during our conversation, he adamantly declared: "Antigua has no customs duties and does not need a free trade zone."

I well knew that Antigua in fact did levy tariffs on certain items that it wished to protect from outside competition. Finally, more than twenty years later, in 1995, Antigua adopted the Free Trade and Processing Zone Act, yielding to competitive pressure from the Dominican Republic, St. Lucia, and other neighbors. The government designated Crabb Island, a peninsula four miles from the V. C. Bird International Airport, as its first FTZ. Construction came to a halt in September of that year after Hurricane Luis devastated the island, damaging or destroying three-quarters of its buildings. The project was eventually finished, but so far it has contributed little to the island's economy. The FTZ has a rum distillery, a canning operation, handicraft workshops, a sportswear factory, and a petroleum refinery. Thus, its revenues have been disappointing.

Anguilla

British aid to Anguilla diminished rapidly after it gained independence in 1981, but the UN was confident this small island had sufficient human resources to make great strides on its own. Two visits there proved to me that, indeed, the Anguillans had enough trained professionals to become a successful offshore servicing center without the usual financial assistance package. My first discussions with two of the cleverest people on the island—Ian Mitchell of Mitchell Chambers, legal adviser to the government, and Victor F. Banks, the finance minister—were the beginning of a warm relationship. Dorothy and I were invited back by the Anguillan Association of Accountants to lecture on other ways the island could supplement its dollar earnings from offshore servicing income. At the time, I emphasized development of the shipping and insurance industries to take advantage of the expanding globalization.

Anguilla gained considerable prestige as a progressive offshore jurisdiction in late 1998, when it began operating the Anguilla Commercial Online Registration Network (ACORN). This state-of-the-art company registration system was developed with financial assistance from the British government and permits all types of entities—including IBCs and limited liability partnerships—to be incorporated and registered electronically within twenty-four hours. Information on all required and permitted documents and activities is also online. ACORN, which works closely with the Anguilla registry, helps practitioners handle trusts by ensuring security and reliability and making sure that regulatory issues are fully addressed. In 1999, the Anguillan Parliament adopted the Companies Registry Act, which provides for electronic-form filing of documents and inspection by the registrar.

Criticism of offshore financial jurisdictions has been growing ever since a series of scathing studies about past abuses. Among the influential reports calling for revised laws have been those of the Bank of England (the Edwards Report), the U.S. Treasury Department, the European Union (EU), the World Bank, and the Organization for Economic Cooperation and Development (OECD). In line with this criticism, my other assignment for the Caribbean region during the 1980s and 1990s involved recommending revisions to laws that would make money laundering and other illegal transactions more difficult.

St. Martin

During a meeting on St. Martin attended by representatives from all the West Indies islands—who were there at the request of the U.S. Treasury Department—I recommended to the delegates that they sign exchange-of-information agreements with the United States as Washington had hoped. This idea was rejected with disdain.

Cayman Islands

Soon after, a series of ethical violations tarnished the Cayman Islands as a financial center. On the heels of that event, I visited the Caymans' finance minister. To the surprise of its neighbors, shortly after my visit, the Caymans signed a pact allowing for exchange of information between it and the United States with respect to fraud, drug trade, and other criminal activities. Within a month of the signing, deposits flowing to the island from overseas jumped by ten billion dollars—apparently, nonresidents were eager to take advantage of a risk-free depository with higher yields and sophisticated banking facilities. The Caymans today is the most important offshore financial center in the Caribbean, with more than five hundred billion dollars of deposits from abroad in 390 banks (reduced from a record 586, the government having clamped down on the unethical practices of small operators). Those banks represent every major financial institution in the world.

Nevis

For Matthew Bender, one of my legal publishers, I prepared booklets on the advantages and pitfalls of incorporating and operating in Nevis, St. Kitts, and the U.S. Virgin Islands. My first visit to Nevis began with a long session with its premier, Dr. Simeone Daniel, who summarized the present poor state of affairs by pointing out that "in 1981 the island of Nevis stood in the Caribbean Sea neglected and without proper direction." Only a few years later, Nevis was boasting of the nickname "the Silicon Valley of the East Caribbean." (Nevis is also the birthplace of Alexander Hamilton, whose many personal effects and relics are proudly displayed at the island museum, a noted tourist attraction.)

That first meeting did not ignite as much enthusiasm as the attorneys in Washington and Charlestown had envisioned. But by the time of my second visit, a year later in 1996, there was a new premier, Vance Amory. My meeting with him was also attended by the managing director of Nevis Services Limited, Mario Novello, and the congenial local manager and the island's historian, Vincent Hubbard. At that meeting, Amory chided them both for their tardiness in getting the island's servicing center off the ground. The government's target of enticing one thousand foreign companies to establish a presence in the first year was far from being achieved.

That second meeting in Nevis took place a few weeks after the American invasion of Panama, during which time the country's president, Manuel Noriega, was captured by U.S. forces for eventual trial in the United States. In the weeks and months leading up to that event, Panama faced public protests, strikes, insurrections, and expropriations of property. As a consequence, many of the American companies operating in Panama had been forced to pull up stakes and move to islands in the Caribbean but bypassed Nevis, which distributed Armory.

British Virgin Islands

Most of those companies chose the British Virgin Islands (BVI). Registrations of foreign companies in the British Virgin Islands skyrocketed in less than a year by twenty-five thousand—mainly from Asia, especially Hong Kong. The BVI's legislation was the most liberal in the Caribbean. Today, more than three hundred thousand foreign companies are registered in the British Virgins, providing 80 percent of the islands' revenue.

In the 1980s, I was invited by the BVI Chamber of Commerce on Tortola to explain to a business group how the United States could help that territory offset some of the income it had lost now that Britain had reduced its financial assistance. Lisa Penn, the registrar of companies, advised me that her government was "well equipped and pleased" to host thousands of foreign companies that relied on the BVI for efficient financial services.

St. Kitts

St. Kitts, the sister island of Nevis in the federation of St. Kitts and Nevis, had watched Nevis's success in developing an offshore servicing center. The number of foreign entities operating on Nevis was approaching twelve thousand. Much of that island's success could be attributed to the persistence of Mario Novello, whose Nevis Services Limited was one of two officially approved servicing companies at that time. Under the guidance of the federation's prime minister, Kenneth A. Simmons, the St. Kitts government sponsored a joint conference of the financial leaders of the Caribbean Development Bank in order to gather insights about other financial centers. The talk I gave at that conference mentioned the pitfalls as well as the benefits of going offshore. Actually, a number of islands were opposed to welcoming foreign operations, fearing that the United States would "colonize" them just as the British had in the past. However, St. Kitts did adopt an attractive program that has paid off with increased revenue from abroad.

St. Kitts has become a popular offshore jurisdiction, mainly because of its efficient Financial Services Department, but it will never gain the worldwide acceptance enjoyed by Nevis. Dr. Simeone Daniel and Vance Amory were farsighted enough to supplement financial services income with tourist revenue as St. Kitts had done, and in doing so have made Nevis an increasingly popular destination for American multinationals. With its luxurious Four Seasons Hotel and its Robert Trent Jones golf course, as well as its less expensive but still delightful Mt. Nevis Hotel, this progressive island is now one of the Caribbean's most attractive tourist resorts.

NOT ALL of the Caribbean islands seeking development assistance from the UN, U.S. AID, or other official agencies were cooperative with us. Some islands actively discouraged our intercession. At other times, obstacles arose that required the cancellation of meetings. For instance, a visit with the Turks and Caicos Islands finance minister had to be cancelled when American Airlines misdirected our luggage. We rescheduled but could not find a plane that would get us there in time for the meeting. And in Grenada, where the plan was to discuss an FTZ, the ministers and company registration officials were impossible to find. It seemed they were literally hiding from us. Grenada to this day is one of the least-stable and least-developed islands in the region.

St. Vincent and the Grenadines

When we visited St. Vincent and the Grenadines, we were received warmly by Linton A. Lewis, representing the Finance Ministry. However, the talks themselves, though lengthy, had little influence. I was there to point out steps that St. Vincent could take to discourage money-laundering schemes. Several years later, the island did adopt ironclad legislation against financial abuses, but only after it had been placed on the "harmful list" of tax sanctuaries, having been fingered by the OECD and the Financial Action Task Force. Both these groups serve as international financial police.

St. Lucia

Carl Pilgrim, director of the St. Lucia National Development Corporation, tried hard to persuade his government to establish an offshore financial center. But while we were in St. Lucia, the officials he had arranged for us to meet evaded all efforts to see us personally. An official of the National Development Office did come to welcome us when we arrived at the airport in Castries, but afterward all of our discussions had to be held by telephone from the other end of the island, where we were staying in the new Hilton Hotel. At breakfast every morning, we had the good fortune to listen to the famous pianist Vladimir Ashkenazy, while he rehearsed for his upcoming recital at Carnegie Hall. Ashkenazy also surprised us by playing two pieces at an eighty-fifth birthday party the hotel manager kindly arranged for me. So the trip was not wasted, especially after two private FTZs—at Grande Cul de Sac on the outskirts of Castries, and at Vieux Fort thirty miles to the south—appreciated our recommendations on finding new tenants and developing marketing expertise.

Jamaica

Visits to Jamaica, the Netherlands Antilles, Trinidad and Tobago, and the U.S. Virgin Islands were fruitful. Jamaica's four customs-free zones at Kingston, Montego Bay, Spanish Town, and Clarendon handle 80 percent of that island's trade and employ more than seventy thousand workers. Impressed by the success of the Colón Free Zone in Panama, the Jamaican government had decided to restore the island to its former role as a redistribution center; to that end, it opened the Kingston FTZ in May 1976. Parliament passed the Jamaica Export Free Zones Act in 1982; that same year, the Kingston Free Zone Company was formed to administer the zone. Its major shareholders are the Port Authority and the Jamaican government. Many American and foreign industrial giants operate out of Jamaica's zones, including Gulf and Western, American Maidenform, Advanced Automation of Boston, Business Methods Services of Maryland, Williamson Dickie Apparel Manufacturing of Fort Worth, Tultex Industries of Virginia, and Global Food Processors of Canada.

Trinidad and Tobago

A short visit to the Port-au-Spain FTZ in Trinidad reminded me of its prominence among Caribbean customs-free areas. In the early 1970s its operations set
the pattern for the rest of the region's zones. With oil Trinidad and Tobago's
major exchange earner, the zone's refineries are busier than ever, and the "up-
side-down" Hilton Hotel (so-called because its first, or ground, floor is on top of
the others) benefits from full capacity most of the time.

Curaçao and Aruba

Likewise, our visit to the Netherlands Antilles showed why the two vast, modern
FTZ complexes at Curaçao and Aruba (and two smaller ones) handle almost all
of those islands' foreign trade. Our inspections of these zones were arranged by
Arrien Schiltkamp, a native of Curaçao, president of U.S. Schiltkamp International Consultants, Inc., and a major partner in the Netherlands' Amsterdam
Trust Corporation. The Schiltkamp operation in Curaçao and Aruba, which
handles some of the worldwide trust operations for AMRO Bank of the Netherlands, is among the largest and most reputable in Curaçao. It is responsible for
the day-to-day financial and trust operations of some ten thousand firms around
the world. Arrien took over the business after the retirement of his father, Jacob
Schiltkamp, a leading notary in Amsterdam and consultant to the Dutch government and International Fiscal Association.

U.S. Virgin Islands

The U.S. Virgin Islands (USVI) qualify as the United States' only offshore jurisdiction (other than the American International Depository and Trust for nonresidents), since they tax their own resident citizens just 10 percent, as permitted
under the 1986 Internal Revenue Code. The USVI also served as a base for
American export operations under the 1962 Domestic International Sales Corporation Act of 1962 (subsequently changed to the Foreign Sales Corporation
Act in 1972). More than four thousand American companies were operating
under this tax-saving device as approved by Congress to bolster U.S. exports until
the law was replaced by the Export Territorial Reduction Act of 2002. Termination of this export incentive also became necessary after the European Union
and the OECD threatened tariff sanctions against the United States. Congress fi-

nally abolished the law in 2004. However, the Treasury Department had assigned me to review the procedures of various entities in the Virgin Islands to make certain the operations were authentic, as demanded by the legislation.

Working closely with Trident Accounting Limited of St. Thomas, we visited a number of "qualifying" offices of American companies, only to find that indeed the Treasury had been right to suspect questionable practices. Code violations of administrative duties required of foreign sales corporations were easy to uncover. An obvious example was found in a tiny ground-floor office in the luxurious Bluebeard's Hotel. Here, in large print on the glass door, were listed the names of four major *Fortune 500* American corporations. Several times during our week's stay at the hotel, we knocked on the locked door. Not once did we find a representative of any of these companies, although the law required a physical presence, the on-site processing of trade documents, and all the other necessities of a going concern.

Many of those Americans who relinquished their U.S. residency and became "qualifying" USVI residents in order to save on their taxes have encountered problems with the IRS. Most of the questions or delays in obtaining a smooth transition have arisen from contretemps between the USVI Treasury and the IRS as to how to allocate tax payments between the two agencies.

Guatemala

On one of our trips to Costa Rica, U.S. AID asked me to stop off in Guatemala City. That country's president, Kjell Laugerud Garcia, and his finance minister were seeking help in reviewing Guatemala's economic zone legislation. My instructions indicated that Secretary of State Henry Kissinger was especially concerned about ending the political and terrorist strife that had been Guatemala's lot for nearly a half century.

In 1954 a coup toppled President Jacobo Arbenz, and the country had barely survived the subsequent years, during which military rulers alternated with weak presidents while other factions terrorized the population. When an American ambassador was assassinated, the United States sent in the military to help the government quell riots and terrorist activities, and a devastating earthquake set the economy back ten years. Not until 1996 did any semblance of peace and stability begin to return.

Juan Edgar Picado Sr., Costa Rica's former attorney general, made a special trip from San José to greet us at the Guatemala City airport. With him he brought Armando Dieguez Pilon, a prominent Guatemalan attorney and legal adviser to the government. It was 1975, and the legislature had just declared the new president to be General Kjell Laugerud Garcia, even though General Efrain Rios Montt, the antigovernment candidate, had won the election. Pilon had been urging past administrations to adopt export incentive legislation with FTZs as the core mechanism.

On that first evening in Guatemala Picado entertained us with a dinner at the country's best hotel, the Camino Real. He had long been an avid admirer of President Richard Nixon, having met him in Washington, D.C., several times—usually at the president's annual Prayer Breakfast—so he thought he was honoring me when he seated me under a huge portrait of him on the restaurant's wall. Needless to say, he was aghast when I explained to him that almost the entire American press corps, including me, had loathed Nixon for years.

As editor of the McGraw-Hill *American Letter,* I used to join other members of the American Business Publishers Association every month for a breakfast meeting with the president of the Senate. The point, of course, was to gather background on congressional issues. For many years, Robert Taft, as president of the Senate, was our guest speaker. Taft would arrive at the appointed time of eight o'clock, mingle with the editors and publishers, brief us at eight thirty on the latest political issues, and take questions at nine. But Senator Taft had passed away, and as the incumbent vice president, Nixon had replaced him. So he was our invited guest.

Nixon did not appear at eight for coffee, as had Taft. Nor did he arrive by eight thirty for breakfast. Instead, he kept the editors and publishers waiting anxiously until nine twenty, when he rushed into the room. Without waiting for an introduction, and giving no explanation for his tardiness, he blurted out: "I'm not going to apologize for being late—I know these Hilton breakfasts." He then went on arrogantly, as if he were doing us a favor: "Furthermore, I'm not going to give a speech but will only answer questions."

The editors and publishers were so stunned by this bullylike approach that a dead silence fell over the room for several minutes. Finally, the senior vice president of McGraw-Hill International, a former *Washington Post* foreign editor, Eugene Warner, summoned the nerve to ask a question: "Mr. Nixon, would you care to speculate on the candidates for the next election?" Quickly, Nixon responded, "If Ike doesn't run, of course the Republicans have no one other than myself," pounding his chest proudly to show his confidence. Then he went on: "As far as the Democrats are concerned, they have no one except that shyster lawyer out in Chicago who just lost his first case." This grotesque blunder—he was deflating Adlai Stevenson, a popular statesman with the American press—was regarded by the editors and publishers as such an intolerable insult to their favorite politician that they never forgave Nixon for it. It is said that this one awkward occasion revealing Nixon's meanness shaped the future attacks on him by the press for years to come. Even the former president's astonishing achievements with China, Russia, and Egypt could never undo the dislike the press held him in after he degraded Stevenson.

Pilon, the aforementioned Guatemalan attorney, had been chosen to work with us in preparing an economic recovery plan for Guatemala. He was confident that sooner or later his country would adopt legislation to establish FTZs for processing the country's natural resources for export. So he arranged to take us to several remote areas of the country to examine their potential as FTZs. On one occasion, we were driving down the national highway toward Chichicastenango—a major tourist attraction because of its old cathedral and colorful Indian markets—when our driver suddenly stomped on the brakes with all his might to stop us from falling into a monstrous pit at least 150 feet deep. He stopped us right at the edge. His four stunned passengers climbed from the car to observe the huge truck that had been a few yards ahead of us and was now lying on its side at the bottom of the hole.

After explaining to us that this sort of thing was not unusual in Guatemala (the highway department could not afford better roadwork), our companions instructed our driver to back up. They had spotted a dirt track a few hundred feet back that would take us to Atitlán, near Antigua, the original capital of Guatemala, founded in 1776. Antigua, a historic city, and Atitlán, on the shore of sparkling turquoise Lake Atitlán, are tourist magnets today. The old capital was destroyed by volcanic eruptions in 1917 and 1976, and magnificent gardens have taken root in the volcanic ash. The bucolic atmosphere of the town and its surroundings indicated that this location was not suitable for an FTZ.

In 1978, Guatemala adopted legislation to establish FTZs. Shortly before it was passed, we made our second visit to Guatemala on behalf of U.S. AID, to review the new law with President Laugerud Garcia and to discuss incentives that might be offered to attract investment and thereby ameliorate the country's growing unemployment problem.

When we arrived at the presidential palace, we were told that the president had been called into an "emergency session" and that we were to meet Mrs. Garcia, an able businesswoman with a keen knowledge of world affairs. She was especially interested in an export credit insurance system to help Guatemalan exports. Near the end of that discussion, the president appeared. His wife had filled a pad with notes, which she handed to him.

Two years later, in 1980, Garcia inaugurated the first FTZ, a few miles from Guatemala City, The formal ceremony included the opening of housing for port workers. Not long afterward, in March 1982, Garcia was deposed and replaced by a military regime headed by Rios Montt. In 1984 his government adopted the Law on Incentives to Export Producing Companies. At that time, this law was considered among the most comprehensive in Latin America; it covered financial subsidies, tax reductions, export insurance, and training programs, all under the supervision of the Ministry of Economy.

Puerto Rico

One of the most perceptive people I ever had the privilege to know was Governor Luis Muñoz Marin of Puerto Rico. He was a pivotal figure in his island's history and a faithful friend of Washington, and Puerto Ricans practically worshiped him. In 1962, as research director of the U.S. Foreign Credit Insurance Association, I was sent to address some five hundred Puerto Rican government and business officials in the main ballroom of the San Juan Condado Hotel. The topic: how to establish a viable export credit insurance system that would protect Puerto Rican exporters from political and commercial risks.

Shortly after I began that presentation, I made the error of referring to Puerto Rico as a colony. As soon as I did, a tall, well-spoken man with a pained expression rose in the audience and interrupted me: "Puerto Rico is a commonwealth, not a colony or territory." That was my introduction to Muñoz Marin, who was already widely viewed as "the George Washington of Puerto Rico."

In my conversation with him after my talk, he told me that export insurance was only one among many trade and investment incentives he had in mind to improve his island's image and attract industry from the mainland. His widely praised "Fomento," the Puerto Rican Economic Development Agency—which reached its zenith in the 1970s—attracted ten billion dollars of direct investment by American companies under Operation Bootstrap. In fact, the list of mainland multinational corporations that eventually established subsidiaries on the island reads like the Fortune 500.

Almost all of these Puerto Rican operations would avail themselves of the popular Section 936 of the U.S. Internal Revenue Code, which allowed up to twenty years' profits from the tax-free earnings accumulated under Operation

25. One of Walter's most rewarding travel experiences was his 1962 meeting with the Commonwealth of Puerto Rico's famed governor Luis Muñoz Marin (his picture is on the U.S. five-cent stamp) at the governor's palace. The late governor of Puerto Rico, whose international airport is named after him, is in the center of the photo, flanked by Walter, on his left, and Jack Merriweather, vice president of the U.S. Export-Import Bank, on his right, with the directors of the Superintendent of Insurance and Fomento. Fotografia de la Fortaleza.

Bootstrap to be reinvested in designated neighboring islands or selected Central American nations without being subject to further taxation. Fomento was a great success in that it raised the average Puerto Rican's annual per capita income and made a huge dent in the unemployment figures. Many undeveloped countries around the world, especially in Africa, would use it as a template.

The U.S. FCIA export insurance system, modeled after Britain's British Export Credits Guarantee Department (established in 1917), was to be the core of Puerto Rico's economic development program. Governor Muñoz Marin played a significant role in getting the FCIA off the ground in Puerto Rico.

After my presentation, the governor suggested that I return with him to the "palace"—El Moro Castle—to discuss the FCIA further with him and his insurance superintendent. He asked my speaking partner to join us. He was Jack Merriweather of Washington's Eximbank, which was a 50 percent partner with FCIA's twenty-odd private insurance companies.

Jack was a scion of the Merriweather clan. His more famous sister, Marjorie Merriweather Post, was a prominent Washington hostess. Jack was one of the three vice presidents of the Eximbank, having been appointed by President John F. Kennedy. The other two were Governor George Docking of Kansas and Jim Bush, the older brother of President George H. W. Bush and uncle of President George W. Bush. Anti-Kennedy Republicans and the press often said that some of the best appointments JFK ever made were to the Eximbank. I often shared duties with the three vice presidents when it came to presentations for business-people at Commerce Department field offices. More than once, when Jim Bush was my speaking partner, he would remind me how promising a talent his kid brother George was. He had enormous respect for him: "Wait till you see my younger brother—he is captain of the Yale baseball team."

As we left the palace after our invigorating discussion with the governor and his insurance superintendent, which included a long session with the palace photographers, Muñoz Marin invited Merriweather and me and our wives to join him and his wife that evening at a concert by Pablo Casals, widely considered the greatest cellist of the century. The enormous university auditorium had long been sold out for that concert. Of course, we went.

I returned three more times to Puerto Rico at the government's invitation, to offer input into economic policies relating to Fomento. I suggested revitalizing the dormant Mayagüez petroleum zone and establishing another zone near San Juan, which would eventually have eleven subzones, each representing a private company. Muñoz Marin, who later became an important president of the Organization of American States, has for many years been revered as the "father of Puerto Rico," and is honored with the naming of Puerto Rico's Muñoz Marin International Airport and a five-cent U.S. stamp. He will always be remembered as a good and useful friend of the United States.

☀ 9 ☀

Images of the Far East

India

SHORTLY AFTER RETURNING from my Latin American assignments in 1959, I received a request from Curtis McGraw, president of McGraw-Hill, to accompany a high-level team of Indian government officials and industrial leaders to the Annual International Monetary Fund and World Bank Conference in Washington, D.C. This group of India's top executives, who shaped their nation's financial policies, included Morarji Desai, the finance minister; J. R. D. Tata, chairman of both the Reserve Bank of India and Tata Industries, which owned the largest steel mills in the British Empire; and G. D. Birla, who controlled much of the country's textile industry as well as numerous other commercial interests. The Birla family was widely esteemed for its philanthropic and religious activities.

Early in the twentieth century, the founder of McGraw-Hill, James McGraw, had cultivated an excellent relationship with Indian leaders, and that mutual respect continued. So on the way to the conference, the Indian delegates stopped in New York for a round-table discussion with McGraw-Hill editors. Chiefly because I was editor of the *American Letter*, which published a bimonthly Indian edition, as well as being the economist for the McGraw-Hill International Corporation, headed by Colonel Willard Chevalier, I had been chosen to guide the Indian delegation around the Washington conference.

Chevalier was prominent in the upper echelons of the international financial community and was on the board of the influential National Foreign Trade Council. Later, after he retired, it would be my good fortune to replace him on the council's Administrative Board.

In Washington, D.C., the first evening, the Organization of American States hosted an elaborate reception in the main ballroom of the Pan American build-

26. Walter Diamond, as director of economics of the
McGraw-Hill International Corporation and editor of the
McGraw-Hill *American Letter*, addressing the other editors
of the company, 1959.

ing. While I was enjoying a conversation with Desai, Tata, and Birla and several
American leaders, I heard someone bellow from the other end of the room: "Diamond! Diamond, you rat!" I stood there aghast as my accuser approached our
group—he was the leading American foreign currency expert at that time, Franz
Pick. Indifferent to the ruckus he had caused and to the delegates' stares, Pick
immediately complained: "Diamond, you cheat me out of my living. You get all
the trade and foreign exchange speech invitations that used to be mine because
you don't ask for an honorarium." Pick, whom I scarcely knew, had been in
steady demand over the years as a luncheon speaker at foreign trade meetings.
McGraw-Hill had long encouraged its editors to accept all possible speaking engagements without receiving compensation—to be paid for them was considered unethical, since many readers and advertisers of McGraw-Hill publications

were usually attending. The point of such speaking engagements was, of course, to provide readers and advertisers with as much information as possible in order to maintain rewarding business relationships.

The opening session of the Annual International Monetary Fund and World Bank Conference featured a speech by President Dwight Eisenhower, who told twenty-five hundred delegates that the U.S. government was optimistic about increasing its financial aid to developing nations, especially in Latin America. Ike was well aware that many Washington politicians thought our neighbors to the south were being neglected.

Next Ike warned that the United States must find new markets if it hoped to avoid future trade deficits. Our country had been surviving on sizable export surpluses every year since the end of the war. The president had the foresight to predict that those healthy trade surpluses could not continue unless our overseas sales rose sharply. More than once during his Rose Garden press conferences, he would repeat the warning that sooner or later America would encounter trade deficits if imports kept increasing. Of course, he was right. Today, this country's trade deficits exceed a half-trillion dollars annually. That is a gigantic drain on the U.S. economy and a main reason the dollar has been tanking against the euro and other major currencies.

I remember well two other significant events at that conference. At a reception hosted by the International Chamber of Commerce—whose executive director, Wilbert Ward, was the retired senior vice president of the National City Bank (now Citibank)—we got our first glimpse of Patrick Moynihan, then a prominent Democratic activist. While we were talking to his younger brother Bob, the council's public relations director, Pat whisked by us. As he vanished into the next room, Bob told us: "You should meet my older brother; he's going places." Patrick Moynihan would soon become an aide to JFK, a senator from New York, and U.S. ambassador to India.

Another special memory of that conference is the black-tie dinner in the Shoreham Hotel ballroom where we found ourselves sharing a table not only with our Indian guests but also with the finance minister of Ceylon (later Sri Lanka) and Andrew Gomery, the international vice president of Manufacturers Trust and their wives. Ceylon's finance minister, S. N. R. Bandaranaike, asked Dorothy to dance, so of course I invited Mrs. Bandaranaike to be my dancing partner. Mr. Bandaranaike eventually became prime minister of Ceylon; when he was assassinated soon after, Mrs. Bandaranaike replaced him. Which means that Dorothy and I enjoyed the unique experience of dancing simultaneously

27. Walter Diamond, director of economics for McGraw-
Hill International Corporation, pointing to the area in
India that seemed most favorable for establishing free trade
zones, 1959.

with two future prime ministers. (For the record, many years later, their daughter
also became prime minister of Sri Lanka.) It was under Mrs. Bandaranaike that
the rebel Tamil Tigers were outlawed.

THE 1959 VISIT by the Indian team set the groundwork for future efforts to lure
American investment to India. In the 1950s there had been almost no foreign investment, and 90 percent of what there was came from the British. After Prime
Minister Jawaharlal Nehru visited the United States in the early 1960s, many
multinationals decided to put their capital in his country, in order to establish a
foothold in the Indian markets. Nehru had devoted much of his life to gaining
freedom for India; now, that goal having been accomplished, he was calling for
his country to industrialize and to reform its society. This move reflected his

study of Marxism. He encouraged his finance minister, Desai, who later became prime minister, to adopt five-year economic development programs.

Nehru's enormous popularity was vital to ending the Hindu-Muslim unrest that immediately followed independence in 1947. He played a key role in the partition of the subcontinent into India and Pakistan. I had the good fortune to interview him after he gave a talk to a small group at the Overseas Press Club. Of the dozens of presidents, kings, princes, prime ministers, finance ministers, and other dignitaries I have had the privilege of meeting, it was Nehru who left the most lasting impression. His compassion for all, rich and poor, the fortunate and underprivileged, was based on a single philosophy—his "Golden Rule." "The roots of peace," he told me, "grow out of respect for your neighbor. One must do unto others as you would want done unto yourself." Sorrowfully, he added: "I have my doubts that there ever will be peace between India and Pakistan because it is impossible to blend two cultures into one."

Following Nehru's brief visit, the Indian government decided to establish an Investment Center in New Delhi and invited the United States to be the backbone of the agency. The center's director was Joseph Budrez, the former executive director of the Netherlands Antilles Industrial Institute, an offshoot of the flourishing Netherlands Industrial Center in New York. Budrez and I had worked together on several projects involving various American investments in the Netherlands. Once he arrived in New Delhi, he sought my help again, with Desai's approval.

MY VISIT TO INDIA in 1965 began in Bombay. I met with economic and legal professors from the university there who were eager to learn how manufacturing incentives might work in India. I pointed out the benefits of tax holidays and industrial grants. Besides that advice, I recommended as always that India consider establishing foreign trade zones to process its raw materials. Today, approximately six hundred foreign companies operate at FTZs in Kandla and Santa Cruz, two of the most successful FTZs in the world. India now has fourteen zones, employing fifty thousand workers and handling 60 percent of India's foreign trade.

Pakistan

After an extended stay in India, Dorothy and I stopped in Pakistan with the same task ahead—to suggest ways to attract American investment. At that stage in the country's short history, the government lacked even basic knowledge of international trade and was depending heavily on academics to suggest legislation. General Mohammad Ayub Khan, who had assumed presidential powers in 1958, had little time for economic development policies; he was occupied mainly with the fighting along the Pakistani-Indian border and with a rebellion in Kashmir as well as Chinese incursions along the border in northwest Pakistan. My discussions with several academics and accountants from the universities in Lahore and Karachi led to adoption by the government of a series of tax holidays and grants as well as a regime of accelerated depreciation, inducements that are still part of Pakistan's revenue code. They did inspire a limited amount of American investment, but it was the FTZ legislation that did the most to stimulate Pakistan's exports.

Like India, Pakistan was proud of its textile industry, which produced imaginative and colorful designs. In their efforts to capture world markets, both countries faced the same problem: not enough output. There was little mechanized weaving equipment. Both nations depended on cloth woven by hand, often by indentured children in rural districts, who toiled away in small makeshift workshops. Some of these children were as young as six. After visiting some of the sweatshops in both countries, Dorothy wrote a column about them for *Modern Floor Covering* magazine that exposed this heartbreaking practice. This exposé increased pressure on both governments to pass child labor laws, which they eventually did.

As a relatively new country, Pakistan in the 1960s was especially backward in its industrial development—so much so that foreign businessmen were seldom seen in the two largest cities, Lahore and Karachi. Even today, two-thirds of Pakistanis survive on less than two dollars a day, and nearly 40 percent of Pakistani children are undernourished. Only 44 percent of all adults (just 29 percent of women) can read.

In Lahore we were guided around the centuries-old Shalimar Gardens by government officials. Dorothy's simple black dress attracted a crowd of Pakistani women, who had never seen Western clothing. There must have been 150 of them. They followed her around in their native shawls and saris while we enjoyed the astonishing gardens and fountains.

One of our hosts involved in the investment planning meetings was a perpetually cheerful tax partner from Touche Ross (now Deloitte and Touche) who had the unusual name of Minoo Minoo. He was located in Karachi and on our last day arranged for us to stay before our 2:00 A.M. flight to Geneva at a client's

Luxury Beach Hotel—whose general manager was proud of the "007" sign over the front entrance, which was there to telegraph his familiarity with Hollywood's James Bond. At that time "Luxury" meant having a bathroom with an open channel of untreated water running alongside the tub.

Japan

The first of our several trips to Japan was in 1968. Dorothy had been asked by *Institutions* magazine to write a preview article about the Osaka World's Fair of 1970, and I had been assigned by the Japan External Trade Organization (JETRO) in New York, in collaboration with the UN, to meet with Finance Ministry officials in Tokyo regarding the future of the Okinawa FTZ. This period was at the peak of the wrangling over the island, which the Americans had captured from the Japanese during World War II after one of the bloodiest battles of the Pacific theater, during which the Japanese lost 103,000 of their 120,000 troops. The return of Okinawa (which finally happened in 1972) was one of the most sensitive subjects between the two countries during the postwar years.

The original Okinawa FTZ was located at Naha, the capital of Okinawa, one of fifty-five islands in the Ryukyu Islands. Three other FTZs had been authorized by the 1974 law but never got off the ground. In our discussions in 1968, the trade minister expressed high hopes of making the entire island of Okinawa a free port, with the goal of replacing Hong Kong as Southeast Asia's leading entrepôt. The extension never happened. Today, Okinawa has the largest American military base in the Pacific. The island is also a leading tourist attraction for the Japanese, who come in part to see the American base.

The Osaka World's Fair was meant to show the world that Japan was once again an industrial power. However, it also emphasized the country's prowess in providing education to its swelling school-age population. We visited Kansai University's exhibit at Osaka and were told it was seeking an exchange program with an American college. They asked us if this was feasible. When I returned to the United States, I put them in touch with Syracuse University, and discussions were held when a delegation visited Syracuse and met with the chancellor, but an agreement never materialized.

The Osaka World's Fair also showcased Japan's cuisine, including its famous Kobe beef. During the 1960s and 1970s, Americans were interested in learning more about international cuisine, so Dorothy's preview article in *Institutions* was well received by readers.

28. Walter Diamond with the president of Kansai University at Osaka, Japan, and Raymond Otani, executive director of the Association for World Free Trade Zones, before they visited the late chancellor Melvin Eggers of Syracuse University to discuss a reciprocal education program as sister universities, 1990.

Our second and third visits to Japan, in the early 1970s, centered on talks with officials of the Ministry of International Trade and Industry (MITI) concerning Japan's potential if it were to establish FTZs. The government was hoping the zones might help absorb the rapidly rising numbers of unemployed. A key factor was American pressure on Tokyo to ease import restrictions. Washington was warning that the United States could not continue running large trade deficits with Japan. American purchases of Japanese goods were mounting, yet the Japanese were restricting imports of American goods. The United States and the European Union were calling for Japan to restructure its commercial and banking mechanisms.

Despite JETRO's prodding, neither round of meetings with successive finance ministers and their advisers made much headway. It was gently indicated to me that MITI had little luck in getting Prime Minister Eisaku Sato's attention.

29. Walter Diamond explaining the Diamond books to representatives of the Japanese delegation visiting the United States for assistance in establishing foreign access zones in their country's thirty-one precincts, 1990.

Sato had been minister of construction, of finance, and of science and technology, but he lacked experience in international affairs.

Sato had signed an agreement with the United States in 1972 that reestablished Japanese sovereignty over Okinawa. That agreement, however, permitted U.S. forces to remain on the island. Having underestimated the public outcry, he was forced to resign as prime minister. His handling of Okinawa generated bitter protests and strikes throughout Japan. Just before he resigned, the main avenues of Tokyo were packed with organized demonstrators chanting: "Don't Go, Sato!" While we were riding in a shuttle bus over a bridge in front of the diet (parliament) building, we came up against one group wielding staves and waving swords and chanting their slogan. They began rocking our vehicle back and forth until it was perched on its two right wheels. It was sheer luck that we were not toppled into the ravine below.

In 1974, two years after he resigned as prime minister, Sato was awarded the Nobel Peace Prize, mainly for his efforts to settle the Okinawa question. How-

ever, the animosity stirred in the blood of Okinawans over the U.S. military presence never diminished, and in 2003 Washington announced it was selling the air
base to Japan to be used as a "tourist spot."

AROUND THIS TIME, Japanese leaders were showing little interest in FTZs as a
means to alleviate their country's severe unemployment problem. However,
Tokyo would eventually involve itself again in customs-free zones. It happened
in a roundabout way. In 1978, New York's mayor, Abraham Beame, was looking
for ways to reverse the deterioration of the Bronx. For suggestions, he called on
Stuart Eisenstadt, his economic development administrator. Eisenstadt was familiar with my work in establishing FTZs while an export trade adviser for the
Port Authority of New York and New Jersey's World Trade Institute, so he called
me to ask for a preliminary study and some recommendations.

With the strong support of the Bronx County executive, Stanley Simon, an
open meeting of Bronx businessmen and political leaders was arranged at the
Bronx County Courthouse. Five hundred attended, so it was standing room
only. Two leading organizations, the Bronx Chamber of Commerce and the
Bronx Rotary Club, were the principal sponsors, and New York state assembly-
man Stanley Friedman was there to carry the ball to Albany. The state assembly
quickly approved a law that gave the Bronx permission to apply for a zone at the
U.S. Foreign Trade Zones Board in Washington.

The Bronx FTZ was going to occupy the vacant warehouse of a planned De-
Lorean plant. (The auto tycoon had intended to build his "car of the future"
there; his plans fell through when he could not raise enough money.) I had gone
so far as to obtain the permission for this planned use from the director of the
FTZ board in Washington, John Daponte. The DeLorean site at Hunts Point
would be qualified as a subzone of General Purpose Foreign Trade Zone no. 49,
for which the grantee was the Port Authority of New York and New Jersey.

By the time the proper documents for the law had been officially approved
by the New York state legislature and applications prepared for presentation to
the FTZ board, New York City had a new mayor, Ed Koch. For reasons of protocol, Koch's approval for a Bronx FTZ was required. Koch asked Governor Hugh
Carey to veto the bill, the reason provided by his staff being that it would give the
Bronx too much uninhibited advantage at the expense of Manhattan. At the next
session of the state assembly, Friedman put forward a similar piece of legislation,
and it was on the governor's desk when I encountered Koch at an Overseas Press
Club reception at the Waldorf-Astoria. Finding myself a seat close to the plat-

form—he was the afternoon's keynote speaker—I asked him point-blank in front of some five hundred guests whether he would advise the governor not to sign the second measure. His answer: "I'm for foreign trade, and of course I support a zone for the Bronx." Nevertheless, the second time around the mayor again discouraged the governor from signing the measure. The project became caught up in New York City politics, and the zone never materialized. There is no doubt that the mayor believed he was acting in the interest of his New York City constituents.

I believe strongly in the saying that "something good often results from a disappointing experience." Although the Bronx never did get an FTZ, my venture led to a close relationship with an enterprising Japanese business leader. After the meeting at the Bronx County Courthouse, it was my good fortune to take a taxi from there back to Manhattan with Eisenstadt; Morris Biederman, Beame's close adviser; and the late Raymond Otani, a Rotary Club executive and a persevering Japanese entrepreneur. Biederman's advice was to keep an eye on "that promising newly elected young congressman from Brooklyn, Charles Schumer. He could be governor of New York someday."

Otani told me that his mission in life was to bring his native country, Japan, and the United States closer together. His loyalty to Japan was evident in his experience arranging export-import trade transactions between the two countries and promoting American direct investment in Japan. He had learned about the advantages of FTZs at the Bronx meeting and was certain that Japan was ripe for similar customs-free areas. As chairman of the Program Committee of the New York City Rotary Club, Otani arranged for Dorothy, coauthor of Matthew Bender Company's *Tax Free Trade Zones of the World*, to be the first woman speaker at a New York Rotary Club luncheon. And he arranged for me to address the City Club of New York on how an FTZ in the Bronx would provide New York businesses with a needed boost in domestic and foreign sales.

After listening to accolades about Congressman Schumer from Biederman, and hearing Otani tell me how much he wanted to bolster Japanese trade with the United States, I selected both to speak at the scheduled Foreign Trade Zone Conference (of which I was chairman) at the World Trade Institute. Schumer followed Dorothy on the first morning's program. He diplomatically stated at the outset that she "was a hard act to follow and he could not fit into her shoes." He then went on to describe how an FTZ could make a substantial contribution to his Brooklyn constituents and presented a general background of how zones had helped many depressed regions around the world.

At lunch, three men sat down at Dorothy's table and told her they were from the Rockefeller Real Estate Corporation (later known as Cushman and Wakefield Realty), one of the largest property developers in the United States. They immediately asked her flatly: "If you were to establish an operation in a U.S. zone, which would be the best place to go?" Without any hesitation, she told them: "Andy Clark and the Mount Olive Foreign Trade Zone no. 44 at Morristown, New Jersey."

Clark was related to the prestigious Clark family that owned a partnership interest in Singer Sewing Machines and that had founded Clark Thread. After serving as a sergeant in the U.S. Army Corps of Engineers during the war, Andy had overhauled his old Model T Ford and scouted for a piece of land that suited his tastes, driving from southern Georgia all the way up through New England to the Canadian border. He chose an "incomparable piece of property of 650 acres in the center of New Jersey [with] fertile farmland intertwined with large wooded sections and small lakes." The price: ten dollars an acre. Clark happily bought the parcel, although he had no idea what he was going to do with it. At this stage in his life, he was a legal adviser for Singer.

Andy had been steered to my office at 74 Trinity Place by a vice president of RCA International—one of the few tenants of Foreign Trade Zone no. 24 at Scranton, for which I had prepared the application to the FTZ board in Washington. The first thing Andy said to me was: "What's a foreign trade zone?" That was the start of Mount Olive Foreign Trade Zone no. 44. Today, in this country, there are more than 260 general-purpose zones with some 550 subzones, and Mount Olive is one of the jewels among them.

Rockefeller Realty made an initial investment of $300 million in Mount Olive. That investment has since grown to $700 million, which makes it the most richly endowed zone in the country. At the zone's opening ceremony in 1980, Juanita Kreps, the commerce secretary, cut the ribbon. Dorothy's recommendation led the Rockefeller firm to invest in FTZs. The success of Mount Olive has inspired Cushman and Wakefield to invest in two more American zones.

The Mount Olive International Trade Center (ITC) was the Rockefeller Group's first industrial venture and the second-largest development it ever undertook, surpassed only by Rockefeller Center. Like the world-famous midtown Manhattan complex, the ITC is a showplace, emanating quality, luxury, and concern for the environment. Only 60 percent of the land is occupied by buildings; the other 40 percent has been landscaped with curved roads, lawns, trees, and shrubbery at a cost of $1.5 million. To prevent the concrete buildings from being stained by rain runoff, the drains are mounted inside the buildings. The runoff water is then piped to the center of a lawn, where it forms an artificial lake with waterfalls. The lawns around the lake serve as picnic areas. Other outdoor recreational facilities include trails for jogging, hiking, and bicycling. Several Rockefeller Group subsidiaries have helped to manage and expand the zone over the years.

Meanwhile, Otani had not abandoned his vision of a series of Japanese FTZs, which would help improve American-Japanese relations by increasing trade. After several fruitless trips to Japan, he mobilized the UN, Japan Export Trade Council, and Association for World Free Trade Zones (AWFTZ), of which he was executive director, to have a delegation of business leaders and district officials, including mayors from thirty-one Japanese precincts, and their aides, visit the United States for a conference at the UN.

In the dramatic setting of the UN Assembly, this group listened carefully to two UN officials, Frank Owarish, training director of the UN Institute for Training and Research, and Karl P. Sauvant, head of research at the Research and Policy Analysis Branch of the UN Transitional Corporations and Management Division. These two men stated that the UN had long been advocating free trade and that the creation of FTZs throughout Japan would have a clear and beneficial impact on economic globalization.

The next four speakers then supported the first two and echoed their recommendations with concise explanations of how FTZs would benefit Japan. These four were Tetsuo Matsufuji, president of JETRO New York; Walter Szykitka, president of AWFTZ; Dorothy; and I, as chairman of AWFTZ. After the well-attended UN conference, our group left for a weeklong fact-finding mission. First stop was the Rockefeller zone at Mount Olive, followed by zones in Washington, D.C., Maryland, Virginia, and San Francisco. Of the thirty-one precincts represented at the conference, only two created Japanese versions of FTZs, which are known there as foreign access zones and are designed to absorb unemployment. Internal politics, municipal wrangling, insufficient budgets, and Japan's deteriorating economy prevented the remaining precincts from ever making use of what they had learned during their mission.

Taiwan

During our third visit to Japan we were asked to stop off in Taipei before continuing on to Malaysia, Thailand, and Indonesia. The U.S. State Department was quietly but clearly leaning toward Taiwan in its dispute with the Chinese communist regime and was working hard to strengthen Taiwan's position. I was visiting Taiwan in large part because Ashland Oil, a leading independent refiner, had shown an interest in drilling for oil in the South China Sea. My assignment from Washington was to investigate the feasibility of a large Ashland investment and to learn the reasons for the success of the Kao-hsiung FTZ on Taiwan's western coast.

The island of Taiwan off the Chinese coast had been an important trade outlet for China before Chiang Kai-shek's Nationalists took possession of it in 1947. In the late 1950s, while the bickering between Taiwan and the People's Republic of China stayed red-hot, the Taiwanese lost no time in developing their economy by seeking markets for their rapidly expanding industries, especially in Central America. Chiang Kai-shek's regime was particularly drawn to Panama because of its canal link to Europe and the eastern United States.

Taiwan had observed the success of Panama's Colón FTZ. Now the Chinese Investment and Trade Board in New York, through Taiwan's Finance Ministry office in Washington, D.C., asked me to conduct a feasibility study for an FTZ at Taiwan's most active port, Kao-hsiung. Within less than a year, miraculously, the world's largest FTZ, employing seventy thousand Taiwanese, was up and running at that port. Soon after Kao-hsiung opened, the Finance Ministry approved two more extensive zones at Nantze and T'ai-chung. Today, there are seven zones in Taiwan handling one hundred billion dollars of exports and fifty billion dollars of imports—roughly 75 percent of the country's foreign trade. At one time, the Taiwan zones were producing 80 percent of the world's microchips. In 1982 the government established the Joint Industrial Investment Service Center in Taipei, which offered prompt one-stop service to foreign investors. The deputy minister in charge of the center was M. T. Wu, known as the "father of the export processing zones." Previously, he had headed the Chinese Investment and Trade Board office in New York.

But all that came later. On my initial visit to Taiwan, arrangements were made for the head tax partner of KPMG Peat Marwick in Tokyo, Tom McVeigh, to meet me in Taipei. There we were to open discussions with the Finance Ministry. As we checked into the Grand Hotel in Taipei, Dorothy and I crept cautiously across the highly polished marble lobby; we had been warned how slippery the floor was by a colleague who had broken a kneecap on it two weeks before. (And two weeks *after* our visit, David Rockefeller would slip on the same floor and break his hip.) We were greeted by a stern-looking Chinese woman with the traditional long braid flowing down her back. When we approached, she silently tossed a cable to us that slid down the length of the long marble reception desk.

The cable was an urgent message from Lou Frumer, the vice chairman of Matthew Bender, one of our law publishers, asking me to do a book on tax havens. This topic was a sensitive one for a Big Eight accounting firm manager to undertake, so I immediately turned it down in my mind. Just a few days before, on the way to Kennedy Airport, I had mailed to Bender a manuscript that had been unusually difficult to assemble: *The International Withholding Tax Treaty Guide.*

It was not the first time I had been asked to write a book about tax havens. Leo Cherne, founder and chairman of the Research Institute of America, had asked me to do one fifteen years before. But now I agreed, after prodding from Dorothy, who had wanted me to write an impartial book on this topic. Interest in tax sanctuaries had been growing rapidly since the 1962 Kennedy Amendments. Two days later, after consulting with officials of the Finance Ministry, and visiting the Chiang Kai-shek Museum, we flew to Hong Kong and from there cabled New York that I would do the book, provided I could set my own deadlines. Bender had set a January 15, 1974, date for the manuscript. It was now December 4, 1973. We finally compromised on a March 1, 1974, deadline.

The contract was waiting for me to sign when I arrived back at my office in New York on December 21, 1973. As soon as we received the first cable in Taipei, Dorothy had told me: "I've wanted you to do a havens book for some time. I'll help you write it." She prepared eighteen of the first thirty chapters and thus became my coauthor. Our partnership since then has produced eighty-one supplemented tax and trade books, published by five legal publishers.

With less than three months to prepare a manuscript, Bender, of course, understood that this load was a tremendous burden. So they "bribed" us with the promise to take us to dinner at the "best restaurant in New York" provided we met the deadline for a June 1 printing. On our anniversary date of June 15, Matthew Bender presented Dorothy and me with the first copy at Lutece, one of the finest restaurants in New York. Only then did we learn why Bender had pressed us so hard. Two other legal publishers, one in Australia and the other in London, were preparing competing books at the same time. The controversial topic was ready to be explored because of the increasing worldwide interest in offshore tax havens.

30. Dorothy B. Diamond and Walter H. Diamond in their office in front of
a bookshelf containing their eighty-one books published on international
taxation, trade, investment incentives, treaties, and capital formation and
free trade zones, 1984.

Hong Kong

The Hong Kong Trade Development Council in New York had suggested that we stop in at the then British colony outpost to review its investment incentive program. The office hoped for recommendations about expanding the colony's export credit insurance system. However, the U.S. State Department nixed the idea. In their view, this matter was a "British issue, and it was not appropriate for an arm [the World Trade Institute] of the State Department to meddle in 10 Downing Street plans." This attitude was understandable because of the sensitive negotiations going on with Beijing concerning the colony's fate. Even so, we met later with Mrs. Anson Chan, the popular administrative secretary of the Hong Kong administrative region. At that meeting she revealed that she was being pressured because of rumors that she believed steadfastly that Beijing was "forcing too strong a hand in the economic affairs of the British territory." Both Mrs. Chan and the former chairman of the Hong Kong Trade Development Council were convinced that even without future aid, Hong Kong would make a visible contribution to the Asian economy in its new role as a pillar of Chinese trade.

Two years later, to compensate for the Hong Kong Trade Development Council's failed efforts, Britain's UN mission in New York arranged for us to call on the operators of the rapidly growing and modernistic special economic zone at Shenzhen. After we reviewed the progress made to date while in Hong Kong, we were invited to go to the Shenzhen zone by means of the company's hydrofoil. Unfortunately, there was not enough time for it.

Macao

However, we did arrange to visit Macao, the former Portuguese colony, which is entirely a free trade zone. Many large factories are operating there in the Arecan Preta Industrial Area and at Concordia Park, an industrial site on land reclaimed from the South China Sea at the mouth of the Pearl River. Macao's two main islands of Taipa and Colôane, where the zones are located, are connected by one of Asia's longest and newest bridges. Unfortunately, our inspection was limited owing to barricades placed around the island to facilitate the running of Macao's major event of the year, the NASCAR international auto race. Since our 1973 visit, Macao has become a formidable rival to Hong Kong in attracting investors seeking an entry point to China's extensive and aggressive special economic zone at Shenzhen.

Back in Hong Kong, at a reception at the Hilton Hotel sponsored by the Hong Kong Trade Development Council, our hosts introduced Dorothy and me to the administrative secretary of the Philippine cabinet. At the time, Ferdinand Marcos was still dictator of the Philippines. With no hesitation, the secretary invited us to visit Malacanang Palace in Manila to discuss ways that her country might attract private American investment. When we asked the State Department for approval, it said no: Marcos's regime was shaky at that time.

Thailand

From Hong Kong we flew to Bangkok—on an official basis—to enter discussions about port development. I found little enthusiasm in the Thai Finance Ministry for expansion of FTZ facilities, despite the availability of UN Industrial Development Organization (UNIDO) funds. Under Thailand's National Economic Council Decree of 1977 (also known as the Investment Promotion Law) and the basic customs legislation passed in 1926 and 1960, technically all of Thailand is an FTZ. Since the 1970s, dozens of leading American electronics firms have been operating in the Lat Krabang export-processing zone. Thailand had been succeeding quite well in drawing American companies, owing to an excellent incentive program for industrial development. Our prearranged meeting focused on new tax incentives for international financing activities, as Thailand was considering development of an offshore banking facility, which it subsequently created in 1992. It has since played a key role in the country's progress.

Indonesia

When I made my first visit to Indonesia on the same trip (there would be two more in later years), my meetings with the finance minister—who took his orders from President Suharto—convinced me that his country had no intention of welcoming American investment. The minister explained that past bitter relations with the Netherlands over Dutch oil exploration had completely turned General Suharto off foreign investment. Suharto's ambition was to develop his country into a tourist magnet, with the focus on the spectacular Hindu ruins at Borobudur, which rivaled Cambodia's Angkor Wat. Today, Borobudur is Asia's third-busiest tourist spot in volume of visitors after Angkor Wat and Bali.

Malaysia

Probably the most promotion-oriented nation in the Far East is Malaysia. Its web of investment incentives shapes almost every industry. A keen understanding of what foreign investors require in order to succeed has marked its programs ever since independence in 1954. Credit must be given to the very aggressive Malaysian Investment Development Authority (MIDA), whose New York office has consistently cooperated with UN and U.S. AID assistance.

My first contact with the strong-willed prime minister, Mahathir Mohamad, was in New York, when as finance minister he addressed a dinner arranged by MIDA. Despite Malaysia's expansive foreign investment incentive program consisting of tax holidays, accelerated depreciation, export credits, and various grants, there was one flaw in the nation's policy: the requirement that, with few exceptions, the Bumiputras (native) Malaysians—who represented a powerful political force—must have at least 30 percent ownership in all investment. When I asked him if the law would ever be changed, he told me his hands were tied and that American capital still would flow into his country despite the many hardships this rule involved. As long as he was finance minister, Mahathir stood his ground.

My only visit to Kuala Lumpur, in 1973, was awe inspiring. There I found a full-fledged commercial hub of the Far East—one that has since grown into a leading Asian financial center. I was able during that trip to look around the city to see how the policy was working.

Some twenty years later, in 1998, the Malaysian Parliament lifted the 30 percent ownership requirement, while retaining a 30 percent Bumiputras limit for foreign capital. By then I had prepared a booklet for MIDA and the Labuan Trust Company, *Advantages of Incorporating and Operating in Labuan,* which pointed out that the requirement was an impediment to American private investment. Mahathir's strong policies continued to be questioned by business interests; meanwhile, political wrangling intensified until his opponents forced him from power in 2003.

Kuala Lumpur, Malaysia's capital, had housed the world's second-tallest building at that time. With great skill, the capital oversees a network of two dozen FTZs and customs-free commercial and industrial processing zones. It also guides the aggressive Labuan International Offshore Financial Centre on Labuan Island off the coast of Sabah, a Malaysian state on the island of Borneo.

Two thousand foreign companies operate on Labuan. Penang, once a flourishing port of call for ships on the India-China run, has built a reputation as the "warehouse of the East." Bayan Lepas, Malaysia's second-largest city, on Penang Island, is considered one of the great free zones in the world, covering 223 acres.

Singapore

Another Far Eastern country on my goodwill itinerary, Singapore, frowned on any UN, U.S. AID, or British assistance. The long-serving prime minister, Lee Kuan Yew, was proud of his strict one-man rule. After Singapore was expelled from the Federation of Malaysia in 1965, he wove together a closely knit anticommunist government and built up his country's armed forces in order to maintain political stability. Lee Kuan Yew and his Socialist People's Action Party governed from 1959 to 1990. Under their rule, Singapore probably experienced less unrest and fewer strikes than other Southeast Asian nations.

Lee Kuan Yew was determined to take credit for Singapore's much acclaimed economic gains and had no intention of welcoming foreign aid. So my short visit consisted of a quick look at one of the world's largest container ports.

In January 1993, the Singapore Parliament under a new prime minister, Goh Chok Tong, passed a law to establish an elected presidency. That person would serve as head of state with the authority to veto bureaucratic appointments as well as any government spending that drew on accumulated reserves. To maintain political stability, the government began paying more attention to public opinion. Singapore's unique political institutions and internal cohesion allowed it to impose significant internal taxes, a large part of which went for housing development. The deputy prime minister, Lee Hien Loong, the son of Lee Kuan Yew, is scheduled to become prime minister when Goh Chok Tong steps down.

Australia

In 1978, at the request of the Australian government and Qantas Airlines, we visited that country's ports to explore the feasibility of establishing FTZs. Australia and New Zealand had never established customs-free zones. This trip was not my first contact with the Australians. In the early 1960s I had been asked to prepare a booklet by a prominent Melbourne investment dealer, Robert Mendes, about how Australia's resources could lure American private capital. The emphasis was on a logical investment incentive program. Prior to that, in 1956, as editor of the *American Letter*, I had the good fortune to interview Robert Gordon Menzies, the Australian prime minister, when he stopped in New York. He was on his way to Cairo (after a brief strategy session in Ottawa with former prime minister and Nobel Peace Prize winner Lester Pearson of Canada) as head of the UN mission to try to solve the Suez crisis. Menzies' arbitration skills, along with Pearson's input, are credited with preventing a full-scale war over the Suez Canal.

Canberra, one of the world's most beautiful capitals, was designed and planned by the American architect Walter Burley Griffin, who based his layout on that of Washington, D.C. A highlight is the National Library, housing a vast collection of educational and commercial books. When Dorothy and I looked at the library's index racks, we found our own publications available there.

While visiting Bali, we had become friendly with another hotel guest, Reginald Myles Ansett, founder and chairman of Australia's domestic airline, Ansett Airways. He was interested in developing the northern and eastern sectors of his country around Darwin and Brisbane. Ansett was a well-known aviator and influential business leader in Australia. It was he who arranged our meeting with the finance minister in Canberra after we had met informally with municipal leaders in Sydney and Melbourne.

We made little headway at convincing our hosts that an FTZ would bolster Australian trade, especially in wool, which was the country's main export. However, some years later, after visiting several American FTZs in 1983, the chief minister of the Northern Territory announced to the legislative assembly that he wanted to establish a trade development zone at Darwin. The assembly quickly passed enabling legislation to create the Northern Territory Zone. Darwin's 494-acre zone, landscaped like a tropical park, was financed by a government outlay of AU$10 million (US$8.2 million). Later, another FTZ was established at Brisbane on the east coast. Neither zone, however, has contributed much to Australia's economy.

New Zealand

In the 1970s, New Zealand showed no interest in creating an FTZ to bolster its trade. Even though discussions were held with the trade minister (also the deputy prime minister), nothing came of them. Today, New Zealand is one of the few major countries on the globe without any FTZs. At the time of the discussions, the trade minister emphasized the need to make broader use of his country's export credit insurance program. He was eager to learn from my experience with the U.S. Foreign Credit Insurance Association. His government's objectives were to increase its revenues from meat exports and to lure more American tourists, especially to Mount Cook and Milford Sound.

In an interview with a New Zealand radio station arranged by a local representative, Dorothy was asked to discuss the potential for New Zealand lamb export sales to the United States. I was interrogated about the advantages of an FTZ for New Zealand. The New Zealand public was fascinated by what she had to say, but there was little reaction to what I had discussed. No one seemed to know or care about FTZs.

We were staying at the cozy Hermitage Hotel at the base of Mount Cook, a 12,300-foot peak that is visible from hundreds of miles out in the Tasman Sea (at which I had marveled during my navy days). The New Zealand Department of Tourism arranged for us to view the spectacular sight close up. A few hundred feet from the Hermitage, four Cessna ski planes operated by Mount Cook Airlines were waiting to carry skiers and tourists to the top of the mountain. The chief pilot, who was also the base director, was anxious to take off on this clear, sunny day, and quickly packed us into his four-seater.

Dorothy sat next to the pilot, and a Japanese engineer was with me in the back. On the Fox Glacier, our first landing site, the Japanese passenger was happy to leave us. The harrowing flight had taken us through a narrow mountain gorge; the pilot had to dodge protruding cliffs for much of the way. Our Japanese passenger turned white each time a wing scraped a wall.

Tasman Glacier, our destination, was somewhat less frightening. The pilot often carried skiers there. It was the starting point of a fairly well-groomed six-mile run back to the airfield. Fox and Tasman are two among several shining glaciers radiating down the flanks of Mount Cook. In the spring, the heavy snows become soft and dangerous for landing. At that time of year a pilot has to make three trial landings before setting down. The first is to inspect the snow's condition; the second skims the top of the snow to observe its texture; the third is a short run of 150 feet or so to see if the surface will hold the plane.

When we arrived back in the United States, Dorothy received a cable from the New Zealand Meat Producers Association requesting her to prepare a study on why many American consumers were not buying New Zealand lamb. She quickly found an answer by asking her butcher. New Zealand lamb shipped by oceangoing transport in refrigerated containers was being unloaded in Los Angeles, San Francisco, and Seattle for transfer by air to the large North American meat-distributing centers. In the few hours it took to make the transfer to airline cargo holds, the lamb defrosted. When it was refrozen again, its taste was spoiled for many consumers. This deficiency was eventually corrected to some extent.

China

My first direct contact with the Chinese leadership came when a message from the executive director of the Port Authority of New York and New Jersey, Guy Tozzoli, asked me to attend a small luncheon in honor of China's first official Government Trade Mission. It was just after Nixon's historic visit to China in 1972. Tozzoli was a visionary in trade circles. At the time I was an export trade adviser for the Port Authority's World Trade Institute, which had a subcontract with U.S. AID. He wanted me to attend so that I could explain the benefits of FTZs, especially when they were coupled with a viable export credit insurance program.

The delegation consisted of the five highest-level ministers in the Teng administration—finance, trade and commerce, economic development, technology, and ports. Several of them had been deputy chairmen in Mao Tse-tung's regime. Their portly frames told me they appreciated the amenities of life and lived in luxury—this, at a time when millions of Chinese were starving. When Tozzoli pointed to the buffet-style lunch, all five headed straight for the huge bowl of scarce golden caviar that the Windows of the World chef had been able to find, which took them no time to demolish.

After a luncheon discussion that required each side of the table to count its words with extreme care to avoid any intimidation, my dissertation on how FTZs in China would likely inspire a flood of private American investment prompted the trade minister to invite me to his country. Of course, U.S. AID was expected to fund such a visit, but it was much too soon after Nixon's own visit for me to make a trip for U.S. AID. The Chinese pointed out that many big American companies were already sending representatives to train Chinese in how to operate a free economy, at the same time offering them technological expertise and generally opening up trade and investment avenues.

This trend toward providing "free" help to China backfired a decade later when hundreds of American multinationals began to realize they were losing foreign sales to the same Chinese companies they had helped at their own expense. A classic example: An American construction giant lost a contract to build a railway across the southern part of Africa from Mozambique to Angola—from the Indian Ocean to the Atlantic. The American bid was undercut by a Chinese entrepreneur who had been trained by the same American construction company.

Low-cost Chinese labor is the reason American imports from China have doubled since 2000 to $110 billion. The American trade deficit with China now exceeds $100 billion a year—the highest in the world—and is 60 percent greater than our deficit with Japan. American manufacturers, who have shed 2.4 million jobs since 2001 (that's 2,600 a day), blame China for this disaster. China's Communist Party is considering a complete overhaul of its commercial laws in order to comply with the membership requirements of the World Trade Organization—a process necessary for a full-fledged free trade economy—but it will take many years to accomplish this goal.

As the Chinese delegation prepared to leave for a helicopter tour of the ports of New York and New Jersey, the finance minister turned to me and said he would instruct the municipal authorities on the island of Xiamen, close to the mainland, to meet with me in Canton. There, under the auspices of the World Trade Institute, I would lay out a program for the island's port to establish a pilot special economic zone for China. He tempted me with the promise that Chairman Teng himself would meet me at the airport when I arrived in Beijing. It was widely known that special economic zones were a pet project of Teng Hsiao-p'ing, who visualized them as a way to modernize Chinese production and trade. The visit never happened. The Chinese officials from Xiamen did not keep their appointment with me in Canton.

We would learn from experience that this incident was not an unusual event in the first two decades of China's swing to a more open economy. Hundreds of American companies can attest that however willing they were to lend the Chinese administrative management and operational secrets and methods developed over the years, they were unable to break through the competition from the dominant state monopolies. In 1984, at China's Third Plenum meetings, the late Teng Hsiao-p'ing, the nation's supreme leader, described his third five-year development plan as a "path for reform and openness." The 1993 plenum confirmed China's transition to a "socialist market economy," but the world still has not witnessed a transparent and orderly system.

U.S. AID made efforts to help China create an FTZ program that would enhance the nation's attractiveness for American private capital. Instead, Beijing established a comprehensive network all on its own, completely rejecting our offers to prepare documented recommendations and on-the-spot inspections. Today, the country has a network of more than fifty high-tech special economic development zones (also known as bonded free trade zones), industrial development area zones, export processing zones, finance zones, and high-tech zones.

The Shenzhen Special Economic Zone, twenty-one miles west of Shenzhen—whose name means "Deep Ditch" in Cantonese—and only five miles from Hong Kong harbor, is one of the five largest FTZs in the world. It produces 40 percent of China's electronics exports. The Xiamen Zone, on the tiny island of Xiamen in the Taiwan Strait, also has become a world leader in high-tech products. The Hainan Island Zone was the first in China to offer political risk insurance to foreign investors, adopting a method of private export credit protection that I had described at the Port Authority luncheon for the visiting Chinese delegation.

Mongolia

In the early 1990s, the UN called to advise me that a delegation from the Mongolian People's Republic, headed by the trade minister and including the ministers of industry, purchase, and transport and communication, would soon be arriving in New York from Ulan Bator. They wanted to meet with me to explore the idea of establishing a special economic zone in their country. Of course, I was curious. Walter Szykitka, the president of the Association for World Free Trade Zones, and I met with the Mongolians, and the two of us explained how their country's economic development could be enhanced by a zone. Just as happened with China, our recommendations were used for political propaganda and internal consumption. Further contacts with the UN regarding FTL's have been avoided.

✢ 10 ✢

Western European Milestones

Ireland

*W*ITH THE ADVENT of the jet age in 1959, most of the traveling world was happy to see flight times reduced by as much as 40 percent. However, the people of Ireland faced some very anxious days, since one of their main dollar earners began to fade away. Shannon International Airport had been the key refueling stop for Constellations and DC-6 propeller planes for North American travel to and from Europe, and many travelers made a point of stopping at Shannon's huge array of customs-free shops. Here they would empty their wallets of unused currencies by purchasing Irish-made clothing, linens, souvenirs, and other articles. With nonstop jet planes, much of that spending was about to vanish.

Faced with this sharp loss of dollar income, the general manager of the Shannon Airport Authority, Jack Lynch, called on Ireland's Industrial Development Authority (IDA) and the national airline, Aer Lingus, for help in solving the problem. At the time, Lynch was also Ireland's minister of industry and commerce.

Realizing that I had contributed to the success of the Colón FTZ in Panama, Aer Lingus and IDA arranged for me to visit Lynch in Shannon. We held several long meetings, and I made a number of area inspections to map Shannon's potential as a processing and manufacturing customs-free trade zone. Soon after, the Shannon Industrial Authority was on its way to becoming one of the three largest and most profitable zones in the world. A few months after Lynch maneuvered legislation through the Irish Parliament to convert Shannon into a full-fledged industrial operation, the first three foreign companies—Standard Press Steel of the United States, a Japanese electronics firm, and a Netherlands piano manufacturer—were operating in the zone.

Lynch, along with Bill Maxwell, Aer Lingus's public relations director, arranged a luncheon for us at the Guinness Brewery. There, it was obvious to me

31. The Diamonds at New York's Idlewild Airport on their way to Ireland, 1960. *Hartsdale New York News.*

how much respect business leaders had for Lynch. He was energetic but also a good man for details, and besides all that, he was a great mediator. In the political arena, his broad smile and flexible style had quickly elevated him to the cabinet as minister of education, then of industry and commerce. Subsequently, he would be named finance minister; later still, he would be elected to two terms as prime minister. In 1973 the troubles in Northern Ireland would cost him a third term as prime minister. Although usually an optimist, he saw little hope that the old conflict between the Catholics and the Protestants would ever be settled.

Lynch will long be remembered as the architect of Shannon, for he gave the site an air of professionalism that it had lacked when it was mainly a shopping mall for travelers. When the Shannon Industrial Free Zone opened, it encountered a number of basic physical handicaps. Lynch was a good listener and knew how to take advice, and was as dedicated a minister as anyone could hope for. When I told him that the zone's biggest bottleneck was its narrow entrance, which trucks would have difficulty getting through, he quickly ordered county officials to widen the road leading to the gates.

At first, merchandise and containers unloaded at the nearby ports of Limerick, Cork, Waterford, Dublin, and Greemore where often they lay paralyzed because of congestion on the narrow, pothole-ridden road from Limerick to Shannon. Lynch persuaded the county to provide a wider and more modern highway between the two ports. Today, Limerick is well known for its capacity to service trucks quickly on their way to Shannon. The zone employs around eight thousand workers and hosts more than half the nearly seven hundred foreign firms in Ireland. The country benefits from the billion dollars' worth of exports that flow out of Shannon each year.

Denmark

Denmark, our second stop on our itinerary, showed its deep appreciation for Truman's Marshall Plan aid by welcoming us warmly. Our host, Dan Hansen, was a well-known Danish journalist as well as McGraw-Hill's *World News* correspondent. His father had been a popular mayor of Copenhagen who was revered for hiding some two hundred Jews from the Nazis during World War II. As general manager of the Richmond Hotel, he had hidden them under the rafters to escape from the German invaders, and thus they avoided being sent to concentration camps.

Hansen had arranged for me to meet with the finance minister, Hans Knudsen, who wanted Denmark to expand its export markets. Our discussions centered on improving Denmark's export credit insurance program, Eksportkreditxpaadet. Both Knudsen and the trade minister, Hilmar Baumsgaard, were eager for American private investment, as they were certain it was the best way to diversify their nation's production economy, which centered on fish processing (Denmark had more than eight thousand fishing vessels) and the manufacture of woolen goods and shipping paraphernalia. They wanted their country to attract American companies, especially ones that would produce consumer goods for the European market. Denmark's government realized that American multinationals were not in a hurry to invest at that time and was certain that for the country to reach its goals, it would have to establish an insurance scheme to cover export credit risks.

The trade minister was eager for us to inspect Copenhagen's port, which in the early postwar era was home to the third-largest merchant marine in the world as well as being one of the oldest and largest free ports on the globe. The Copenhagen Free Port had been built between 1891 and 1894, conforming to a prizewinning design selected from a public competition. It had been rushed to completion to offset the advantage Hamburg would gain from the opening of the Kiel Canal.

By 1916 the original port works had been fully utilized. Since then they have been expanded several times until now they cover 161 acres. About three thousand ships call at the free port every year. The ministers of finance, trade, and public works (the Copenhagen Free Port operates under the latter's control) felt no need for any assistance from the U.S. Economic Development Administration or European Economic Administration (formerly the Marshall Plan) for the port and shipping industry. Denmark had great expertise in operating free ports, and the government made it clear that it would be happy to offer any assistance in this field to developing countries.

While we were inspecting the Copenhagen port facilities—Dan Hansen had arranged this tour through the public works minister, Kai Lindberg—England's Queen Elizabeth greeted us with a broad smile as she disembarked from the royal yacht, the *Britannia*, just as we were arriving at the dock adjacent to Copenhagen's famous landmark, the Little Mermaid. Her majesty was making an official visit to Denmark's King Frederick IX at Fredericksberg Castle, a mammoth structure that had little security when we visited it. The British monarch's youthful appearance at that time, just eight years after her reign began, drew headlines in the press. Many Danes were indignant that the media had debased the queen's youth by contrasting it with the reigning monarchs of Denmark, Norway, and Sweden, who ruled as elderly and experienced kings.

ONE OF THE MOST GRUESOME SIGHTS I have ever seen on my travels occurred when Hansen and I were returning from a Sunday morning meeting in Copenhagen. We were approaching the street where he lived when we saw an object tumbling down a hill toward us. To our horror, it was a human head. Hansen explained nonchalantly that there must have been another drunken-driving accident at the top of the hill—a frequent weekend occurrence. Explaining further, he told me that many Swedes regularly took the short ferry ride across the Kattegat to Copenhagen (where alcoholic beverages were available) for the sake of a weekend bender. Denmark had very few liquor laws, whereas Sweden's were draconian. The next day's paper confirmed that the head was in fact Swedish.

Norway

On my first visit to Norway, in 1960, I was deeply impressed by the respect the nation's bankers and businesspeople had for their king, Olaf V. He seldom appeared at business events; even so, his ideals were very much in the thoughts of political and business leaders in their dealings with one another, and their king returned this respect. In fact, all three Scandinavian monarchs—Frederick IX of Denmark, Gustav VI Adolph of Sweden, and Haakon VII of Norway—radiated confidence in their respective political and business leaders.

Norway's three thousand merchant ships had made a great contribution to the Allies during World War II, serving under Allied command, since that country had been conquered early in the war. For this service to the Allies, Norway received a generous Economic Coorperation Administration (ECA) allocation after the war to reconstruct itself. Trondheim and other ports had been practically destroyed by Nazi warplanes. My assignment when I visited Norway was to attend conferences with Central Bank officials, including the bank's noted governor, Erik Brofass, who kept a close watch on the nation's financial affairs.

I also met many other leading bankers. We explored various avenues for accelerating the use of ECA funds through commercial lines of credit. The finance minister, Peter Bjerve, was not interested in establishing an FTZ, and today Norway is the only major European country without the facilities of a free port. To bolster hard-currency earnings, the government emphasizes the shipping and travel industries. Oslo is ranked as the most expensive city in the world in which to live. Even so, every year Norway lures some five million tourists, who are attracted mainly by its magnificent fjords and by various facets of its seagoing heritage.

Sweden

We flew to Stockholm from the Norwegian port of Bergen, and were greeted by Sven Svenson, the chairman of the town council and president of the Swedish

Bankers Association. After several sessions with member banks of the association, arranged by Svenson, I recommended to the Swedish Riksbank—one of the world's most sophisticated and successful Central Banks—that it place more emphasis on guarantees for the rapidly expanding insurance market covering export credit risks. I also suggested that credit terms be eased for importers in developing countries.

Discussions with Sweden's bankers were quite friendly. They reflected intense loyalty to their country and placed great importance on protecting Swedish sovereignty. Their antipathy to NATO and the European Community (later renamed the European Union) was rooted in their history. Economics was secondary to politics, they pointed out. Sovereignty must come before industrial power, they maintained. This strong nationalism reared its head again forty-three years later, when Swedish voters overwhelmingly rejected the euro in a referendum.

Like Denmark, the Swedish commercial sector, led by Gunnar String, the finance minister, and Gunnar Lange, the commerce minister, was deaf to offers of assistance in fostering free trade. Sweden already had three free ports—Göteborg, Malmö, and Stockholm—and they were contributing heavily to this seafaring nation's economy. The first of them—Stockholm—had been established in 1919.

Italy

Foreign investors, especially Americans, ignored Italy for many years after the war. They preferred France and the Low Countries—Belgium, Luxembourg, and the Netherlands. So when I arrived in Italy on our second trip in the fall of 1960 as the guest of the government and Alitalia, our discussions with Finance Minister Giuseppe Tremellant and his staff as well as with private bankers focused on how to attract foreign private investment.

The Treaty of Rome, which created the European Community, was signed in 1957, the year of our first visit to Italy. At the time, Italy was one of its weakest signatories. It had been battered by the war, and its postwar recovery was encountering one bottleneck after another. Its inflation rate was the highest in Western Europe, its currency was weakening daily, and the government was changing hands as frequently as two or three times a year. Its political parties and leaders clashed so often and so bitterly that there had been twenty-six separate governments during the first twenty years of peace (by 2005 the government had changed hands fifty-eight times).

These were difficult days for the Italian people, and I was struck by how unnaturally glum they seemed. Muggings were all too common in that period, and we were warned that we must be especially on the watch for speeding motor scooters, from which purse snatchers used to rob pedestrians. Security was extremely tight at government buildings. No one except those with hard-to-arrange passes was allowed on the side of the street where Clare Boothe Luce resided as U.S. ambassador. The embassy was heavily guarded by U.S. Marines stationed around a strong fence.

Italy already had on its books the well-publicized Mezzogiorno (southern Italy) legislation. It provided, among other things, a ten-year tax holiday of 100 percent on state and local income taxes for reinvested profits, financial subsidies of up to 60 percent, up to 45 percent accelerated depreciation, and a 50 percent deduction for outlays on research and development. However, the broken economy and political infighting overshadowed any benefits the Mezzogiorno law might have offered overseas producers. When I called on the Banca Nazionale del Lavoro—the leading commercial bank at the time—I found several assertive but open-minded officials who were eager to cooperate with the government in the areas of trade financing and export risk insurance.

Our second mission to Italy in 1960 was cosponsored by the Italian government tourist board and Alitalia. The guide assigned to us for this visit to Italy (there would be a half-dozen more) was Mario Bruno, the airline's assistant director of public relations, a good-natured and highly cosmopolitan man. (His boss was a niece of Pope Pius XII.) Almost everyone we met in Rome knew Mario, and when he spoke, his admirers listened. He insisted we visit the Dolomites, where he arranged a few days' skiing for us at Cortina d'Ampezzo, the site of the 1956 Winter Olympics noted for its terrifying moguls, some as high as sixty feet. This trip was our introduction to Italian skiing; in later years, we would also try Sestriere near Turin (site of the 2006 Olympics) and Monte Cervenia on the Italian side of the Matterhorn. Our host was also eager for us to visit the luxurious villa, which Mussolini had built for his mistress on a hill just outside Rome. It was then one of the capital's best restaurants.

Germany

While serving as trade consultant to the New York office of the Port of Hamburg, Germany's main seaport and second-largest city, I was asked to prepare a booklet: *Advantages of Operating in the Port of Hamburg*. It involved an on-the-spot inspection arranged by Senator Henry Kearns, a powerful legislator in the

Bundestag. All in all I would visit five of Germany's six free trade zones: Bremen, Bremerhaven, Cuxhaven, Emden, and Hamburg. It was a rough but fascinating journey by boat along the Elbe and Weser Rivers and through the North Sea.

The Hamburg FTZ is Europe's largest warehousing facility. The port is at the crossroads of Europe's key transportation routes. Its personnel turn around more than eighteen thousand vessels every year, of which eight thousand are regularly scheduled cargo liners, and they do so in record time. Founded in 1888, the Hamburg FTZ is one of the world's ten largest container ports. It has expanded at an unprecedented rate since the European Union was established in 1957. Of all the zones, it handles the largest volume of foreign trade—roughly 10 percent of Germany's more than one trillion dollars of annual exports and imports. Hamburg's economic viability is demonstrated by the fact that 800,000 of the city's 1.6 million people have jobs related to the port.

The Port of Hamburg has benefited greatly from the unification of Germany and handles all of the former East Germany's container traffic. In fact, its harbor and modern-equipped facilities were greatly responsible for Germany's rapid recovery from the destruction of World War II. (Germany recovered much more quickly from the war than other European countries.)

I had first visited Germany the year before, in 1959. When I called on various German multinationals, including Metalgaschaft Fabrick, Bayer, Bosch, and Mercedes Benz, and on the German executives of some of the three hundred big American firms in the Hamburg area. I had been struck by the deep interest in the American people expressed by German business leaders and government officials. I asked an aide of Chancellor Konrad Adenauer why the Germans followed political events in the United States so attentively and mimicked Americans' habits, customs, and even clothing. He quickly replied: "Your military had the gall to kill us, and then your government resurrected us with financial aid and confidence." Of course, there was a thread of truth in his accusation; witness subsequent U.S. military interventions in Guatemala, Haiti, Grenada, Vietnam, Afghanistan, and Iraq, regardless of who was in the White House.

While in Frankfurt in 1959, our discussions centered on the second-largest export credit insurance system in the world, HERMES. The knowledge gained from these sessions served me well later when I became research director for the U.S. Foreign Credit Insurance Association, which Eximbank had established in 1961. In Frankfurt, I again mentioned to Herman Voltz, a foreign credit expert, my observation that the German people had a notable desire to learn more about America. He told me that the average German yearned for a prosperous economy like the Americans had, after so many decades of economic upheaval.

At the same time, many politicians in the Bundestag, including its president, Eugene Gerstunmaier, and Adenauer himself, cautioned the German people never to forget the hardships of the past. Voltz pointed out as a poignant reminder that the ruins of the Frankfurt opera house adjacent to the German headquarters of the Chase Bank had not been touched since the end of the war in 1945. It was now fourteen years later, and it would be several more before the rubble was finally cleared.

Voltz was an associate of Nelson Rockefeller during World War II, when the latter headed FDR's Office of Inter-American Affairs. I learned a great deal from Voltz about foreign credit. During my six years as the economist at the Public National Bank in New York, I was able to visit Voltz several times while he was the chief foreign credit officer at the Chase Bank. He taught me the intricacies of international credit operations. With that training, I was better equipped to make credit recommendations for overseas loans to correspondent banks and to write a foreign credit column for the *Financial Times of London* for more than twenty years.

During the reconstruction years of the early 1960s, Adenauer quietly accepted the positions of Willy Brandt, the popular foreign minister who would become chancellor himself in 1969. Brandt's conciliatory policies generated heated debate among Germans. He was determined for his people to get beyond the ill feelings they held for the Russians, who had treated German prisoners brutally during the war. He was just as determined to end the overbearing attitude of high-level officials in Bonn. In succeeding at both, he did a great deal to scale down the cold war, for which he deserves a prominent place in European history. Brandt won the Nobel Peace Prize for his efforts. He died in 1992, having lived just long enough to watch the Berlin Wall come down and the Soviet Union collapse.

Germans remain curious about American ways. As an example, forty years after I first noticed this trend, Foreign Minister Joschka Fischer of Bavaria placed a bet with me. I was at a tax conference in Munich, and we were having dinner together with the Swedish president of the International Chamber of Commerce. Fischer asked me who would win the 2000 U.S. presidential election, Gore or Bush. I told him I thought Gore would. He declared immediately: "You're wrong. Bush will win. If he does, you will take me to dinner when I come to New York." "If he doesn't," I asked, "then what?" He jovially replied: "You still will take me to dinner."

Turkey

In the fall of 1962, Dorothy and I arrived in Istanbul on an early morning flight from Tel Aviv after a series of conferences in Israel. We were met by our McGraw-Hill correspondent, Ahmet, who had come up from Ankara at the request of the U.S. Embassy there. The new Turkish government had recently deposed President Adnan Menderes after a period of martial law. Menderes was at that time imprisoned in a nearby island fortress. Turkey was not exactly receptive to American investment. The handful of American companies in Turkey was constantly being impeded in their operations. In the early 1960s, Turkey was in an economic crisis after nearly fifteen years of prosperity, which had been buoyed by American financial aid under the Marshall Plan. I was there because the commercial office of the U.S. Embassy wanted recommendations for an industrial incentive program that might encourage a flow of dollars for Turkish development. The Commerce Department suggested they send me.

Ahmet was a popular Turkish journalist, but like all his colleagues in that country, he was closely watched. When we met for lunch that first day, we found a shy, reticent man who hardly struck us as a seasoned reporter. We learned how precarious his situation was when he kept pressing his two fingers to his lips as a signal for us to whisper—he was being closely watched by political adversaries because of some pro-opposition articles he had published. Wherever we went with Ahmet, especially in taxis, he would signal us not to speak by pressing his fingers against his lips and then waving a finger across his throat.

The Democratic Menderes government had been in power since 1950. Tensions had then developed, centered on strong student demonstrations in Istanbul and Ankara. This display brought a political crackdown that incited further violence. Finally, in 1960, General Cemal Gursel took control in a military coup. Menderes was accused of violating the constitution. Many politicians and journalists were imprisoned at that time. The former premier and his close supporters were later executed.

We were dining with Ahmet at a well-regarded fish restaurant on the Black Sea coast. At one point he whispered, "Menderes," pointed to an island in the distance, and made the finger-across-the-throat signal again. A few days later, Menderes was executed on that island by beheading.

On our second day in Istanbul, we were on our way to visit Ahmet's wife in a private maternity hospital, where she had become a mother for the first time the day before. Ahmet was at work. Our taxi driver parked his car against a curb on a steep hill in an outlying district of the city and vanished without a word or a gesture. After a five-minute wait, he returned with a large box of "Turkish bonbons" and handed it to Dorothy, telling her: "This is from the heart of the Turkish people to the American people. We never forget the Truman Doctrine." This act of generosity reassured us that the Turkish people held Americans in high esteem. It was Truman who had made the difficult decision to move American troops to the Soviet border when Russia's military threatened to take over Turkey's bordering Azerbaijan province in 1947. Heavy shipments of American material and substantial Marshall Plan aid forced the Soviets to back away from the border.

Turkey never forgot Truman's rescue effort. It sent several strong regiments to the Korean War, where they fought with distinction. When we visited Izmir on the Aegean coast of Turkey thirty years later on a U.S. AID assignment to plan a possible FTZ, we were always treated with open arms by government and business leaders. However, the World Trade Institute, the vehicle through which U.S. AID funds were allocated for me to prepare a feasibility study, did not receive the contract for actual construction and implementation of the Izmir zone. It was granted to Bechtel, the American construction group headed by former secretary of state George Shultz. Nevertheless, I am convinced that Turkey's decision in 2003 to send ten thousand troops to Iraq to help police was an outgrowth of the indebtedness the nation felt for the aid the United States had given it.

But all those events came much later. We said good-bye to Ahmet and returned to the United States. We never heard from him again. From New York, we made a number of attempts to contact him by letter, cable, and telephone. They all failed; we never solved the mystery. It saddened us deeply when we learned that his fears had been justified as it appeared he had been executed the same way as Menderes.

Greece

Of all the ministers and public officials I encountered on my assignments, none was more cooperative than the widely admired Xenafon Zolotas, governor of the Bank of Greece, later to become finance minister and finally (for a short time) prime minister. When I visited him in his office at the Central Bank to discuss ways to facilitate bank transfers between countries, he immediately picked up the telephone to contact private bankers for their contributions. When he learned we were having difficulty obtaining hotel rooms at Iraklion in Crete to visit the ruined city of Knossos, he grabbed the telephone again and arranged a reservation for us at the best hotel in Crete. Knossos was an essential stop for us: Dorothy was updating the Greek chapter for the *Pan Am's World Guide*.

I learned later that Zolotas was also president of the National Insurance Company, a quasi-public entity, and was more popular than Prime Minister Constantine Caramanlis and his chief opponent, George Papandreau, who later become prime minister. Zolotas's large, muscular frame reminded one of a Greek wrestler, and his prowess as a swimmer was well known. Long after he retired from politics, while in his seventies, he was often seen churning up the frigid waters of the Aegean while young athletes in their teens were withdrawing because of the cold.

For many centuries, Greece had been a leader in making good use of FTZs, having discovered their benefits centuries earlier from the Phoenicians. Two of Europe's most successful entrepôts were Thessaloníki and Piraeus. Therefore, I was surprised when the UN suggested I look at the island of Corfu as a possible replacement for the inoperative FTZ at Bar, Yugoslavia. Prior to the Yugoslavian civil war in the late 1990s, Bar had done much to channel merchandise and light industrial equipment to Western Europe from the Eastern Europe nations recently liberated from the Soviet Union.

Yugoslavia's railways had been badly damaged during the war and its ports virtually shut down. It was thought that Corfu might be an ideal location for warehousing Eastern European goods and shipping them to EU countries and vice versa. After a lengthy meeting, Corfu's mayor, Chrissanthos Sarlis, was convinced that Corfu should have an FTZ to enhance its place in world trade. But the idea never came to fruition because the government in Athens chose not to fund it.

The Netherlands

Between 1962 and 1965 my overseas assignments focused mainly on the Netherlands and Switzerland. I spent time in both countries to review the tax treaty issues facing both as well as their strategies for luring foreign tourists.

The Netherlands was blessed with talented officials in its Finance Ministry, most of whom had been drawn from its highly experienced financial community, with several others from the academic world. The harmony within that country was the envy of other EU members. J. E. de Awaz was the prime minister as well as the "general affairs" minister, the foreign minister was J. M. A. H. Luns, and the finance minister the widely recognized financial expert J. Zijlstrd. The latter was my contact when it came to arranging meetings with the taxation director, Jan van Dermeer.

At that time, in the 1960s, Holland's normal serenity was being severely tested by student protests and riots, which were characteristic of that era around the world. From our hotel window, day and night, we could see crowds of hostile students in front of the parliament building and the palace as they vented their anger at the government. When I asked the tax director why the ministry personnel and security guards stationed around buildings simply stood at attention, never moving an inch or saying a word, he told me: "Students of today must be allowed an outlet for their anger."

KLM and the Netherlands Tourist Board were our official hosts. The latter's public relations director, Peter van den Brogen, was our guide. Peter was a highly cultured young man whose classmate in kindergarten had been Princess Beatrix. More than once he told us that from kindergarten days they did not "take to each other." When Peter arranged a tour of KLM's kitchens for us, the chefs at their stations were delighted to show us the freshly prepared lobster entrée that we anticipated enjoying on our flight that day. However, when lunch came, the lobster was missing. When we asked the stewardess what had happened to it, she told us: "Oh, that was only for the crew."

During later visits to the Netherlands for U.S. AID, we inspected Rotterdam's free port, which handles more cargo than any other port in the world and is Europe's largest customs-free bonded area. As is well known, Schiphol Airport is the largest retail customs-bonded area on earth. The rest of the Netherlands is open for merchant-controlled, public-bonded, and private-bonded warehouses, which are spotted around the country according to approved specifications. Rotterdam was chartered in 1328 but did not emerge as a shipping center until 1872, after completion of the "New Waterway" to the North Sea. At that point it began to thrive as a free port.

Switzerland

Switzerland has seven entrepôt areas, which it calls "federal warehouses," as well as eight cold-storage free zones. We visited several of them in the early 1960s. My discussions with the Swiss were confined to bank financing and the promotion of tourism. We found time on weekends on various trips to test the snow-blanketed ski slopes at Davos, Klosters, St. Moritz, St. Gervais, Megeve, Gstaad, and Mount Blanc.

Monaco

In 1956, six months after Grace Kelly married Prince Ranier of Monaco, the retired Hollywood actress visited the United States with him. At an Overseas Press Club luncheon, where the prince was the speaker, Charles Collingwood, the renowned CBS World War II correspondent and one of the "Morrow Boys" who worked with Edward R. Morrow, the leading radio and television anchor of the day, was sitting at the end of the dais. During the question period, he asked Princess Grace how she liked Monegasque men. With a twinkle in her eye, she patted her stomach and told him: "Isn't it obvious?" She was expecting her first child, Caroline. Her reply warmed up the press to no end.

The real surprise of that luncheon was the late Prince Ranier's clairvoyant talk laced with humor, which also captivated the press. His knowledge of current economic and political events of the day was startlingly deep. He made it clear that his relationship with the sometimes wavering French government was actually on a solid footing and that there was no problem with Monaco's status as a tax-free jurisdiction as long as France was paid taxes on income earned in France.

In later visits to Monaco for discussions with various government officials—including the finance minister—and private bankers, I was told in clear terms that Monegasques' loyalty to the prince and the House of Grimaldi would remain strong in the long term. The principal threat to the present regime hinged on a long-standing agreement with France: the dynasty must be carried on by a male descendant. That requirement cast a shadow over the principality while I was there but has since been resolved.

Malta

We spent three months in Malta in 1967 and 1968, spread over two six-week stays. That period was one of the most rewarding of our life. Our work there was a sheer delight. I was preparing in-depth recommendations for an export credit insurance system and "designing" the island nation's future Central Bank. Dorothy was preparing a two-page feature about the island for the *New York*

Times. The Maltese are warmhearted but determined people. The British defense of their island against Luftwaffe bombers during World War II is remembered by military strategists as one of the great defensive achievements of all time. Our official host was the trade and industry minister, Dr. Joseph Spiteri, who on meeting us at the airport said he wanted me to start work immediately and that he would pick me up the next morning at eight o'clock.

I would learn that the son of the leader of the Knights of Malta, Nicolas Laurie, had suggested my name to the Maltese prime minister, Alexander Olivier. Laurie had been pointed my way by Bill Vaughn, the editor of *Institutions Magazine,* who had been a bomber pilot in China during World War II under General Jimmy Doolittle, making regular bombing raids over the dangerous Japanese-held Ho Chi Minh Trail. At that time Vaughn had worked with Laurie, who was then a British major doing counterespionage work in the Pacific theater. Nick Laurie became our social host on Malta.

Vaughn, with his navigator, Dick Cahill, and the bombardier, John Cogswell, will long be remembered by the offshore financial world for being the initial explorers in the industry by establishing the first foreign management servicing company, the Overseas Management Company of Panama. It was created shortly after the end of World War II under the guidance of the late Paul D. Seghers. The latter was the founder of the International Tax Institute, and along with Mitchell T. Carroll, the international tax consultant to the influential National Foreign Trade Council and for many years a learned adviser of the International Fiscal Association, was one of the two leading international tax attorneys in the nation. The Overseas Management Company of Panama, whose first managing director, John Cogswell, was killed in a plane crash in South America, survives today as one of Panama's foremost international management servicing companies.

Our first morning on Malta, just as the trade minister, Dr. Spiteri, was picking me up at the new Hilton, another guest arrived on the island—Her Majesty Queen Elizabeth. As her open Rolls-Royce passed in front of the hotel, taking her to an official welcome at the palace, I handed my camera to Dorothy and asked her to take the queen's picture, which she promptly did while I entered the cabinet minister's official car. Dorothy's photo turned out to be quite in demand—the Maltese never saw the queen's unique lavender bonnet again. That morning, before the queen's scheduled arrival, Dorothy and I had helped the hotel manager and his wife decorate the new Hilton's still barren grounds by tying oranges to the recently planted trees.

The queen had just come from the nearby island of Gozo and was to be guest of honor at a state luncheon at the Hilton. While on the British frigate carrying her from Gozo to the main island, she had been informed that the British cabinet had just decided to devalue the pound sterling, from US$4.03 to US$2.80. The news had unnerved her so badly that when she finally arrived at the Hilton, she was quite disheveled and was escorted to a room next to ours to freshen up. A few minutes later, looking elegant again, the queen reappeared with the prime minister, followed by Prince Charles and a sleek, tall brunette, the Maltese prime minister's daughter. Rumor had it that the queen considered her a suitable daughter-in-law. From our table a few feet from the queen's, we observed little conversation between the two. Naturally, it was a great disappointment to the Maltese guests.

The tiny fishing village of St. Julien was being revitalized by the new Hilton. Its attractions included oranges for five cents apiece and five-cent bus rides to enjoy the picturesque scenery to the capital, Valletta, some five miles distant.

Two days later, on November 17, 1967, after Malta and the other commonwealth countries had debated whether the British cabinet's decision was workable (Malta and several other commonwealth governments wanted a US$2.40 rate), the British pound was officially set at US$2.80.

Among the queen's loyal subjects, an important question was why did her majesty select the Hilton for her lunch and not the century-old traditional British Phoenician Hotel inside the fortress at Valletta? The Phoenician's owner, Mabel Strickland, had abandoned her pedestal in London—where she was a prominent hostess to the British elite—to set up shop in Malta. She wanted to help make sure the thousands of British pensioners and expatriates would retain their loyalty to Britain. However, she set some rules for her hotel that infuriated many of the British expatriates, so she had her share of enemies. Dorothy and I had a taste of her rigid operation: when ordering tea one afternoon, the waiter told us he could not serve it to us unless we paid for it in advance.

The queen's visit to Malta was a great success from the human relations perspective, but it did little to slow down the island's rapidly growing Communist Party. On the other side of our room at the Hilton was the Russian ambassador to Malta. He had been living there quietly for more than a year, plotting a communist takeover of the island. It would in fact happen: soon after, the Soviets established a puppet government headed by Dominic Mintoff, the leader of the "Maltese Liberation Movement." Not long after the queen's visit, the British troops stationed there were asked to leave the island, and the military base was virtually closed down.

Ten days after the queen's visit, the U.S. Navy carrier *Franklin Delano Roo-sevelt* anchored off Valletta with two thousand sailors aboard. By Thanksgiving Day of 1967, almost the entire crew was on one- or two-day passes and was swarming around Valletta and St. Julien. The night before Thanksgiving, one of the Mediterranean's fierce storms arrived with gales up to seventy knots—strong enough to toss one of the largest carriers ever built around like a toy. Of course, it meant that the two thousand sailors on land would have to forego their traditional Thanksgiving dinner.

The problem was quickly solved. The Hilton's new manager, Manfred Matichek, declared that all American sailors unable to return to the *FDR* would be the Hilton's guests for a Thanksgiving dinner. There was only one problem: Malta had no yams. So the hotel sent out a Morse code inquiry to the *FDR's* radio room to explain the yam problem. The captain quickly ordered his skele-ton crew to set up a pulley and to anchor a cable to a concrete pillar onshore. After several attempts, they managed to send bushels of yams from ship to shore in gondola-type baskets usually reserved for rescue operations.

DURING THE FIRST of my two six-week visits to Malta, I focused on designing an export credit insurance system for the island. The Maltese government had told the British that it preferred the American system—namely, the FCIA sys-tem—which was more flexible in covering both commercial and political risks. So I took that sign as my lead.

Thus, I needed to interview fifty or so potential Maltese exporters. Several of them were wine makers, and all of them were shipping their product to Ger-many, where it was mixed with German wines for eventual sale on world mar-kets. I was also asked to make recommendations regarding the viability of an FTZ. Would it attract foreign investors? Would they produce and bottle wines for export? The Maltese told me that a free port like the one in Tangier would be their preference. So while returning to the United States, Dorothy and I stopped in Morocco to inspect the Tangier customs-free zone.

In April 1968, Dorothy and I were about to leave for our second stint in Malta when we received an apologetic cable from the trade secretary. We would have to delay our visit one week because of the Easter holiday. It was too late to change our plane tickets, so we visited Florence briefly and after that Dubrovnik in Yugoslavia, where Dorothy wrote another article for the Sunday *New York Times* travel section, having written one on Malta when we had returned from our initial visit there.

The Maltese people were very proud of the concentration of historic and prehistoric areas outside the ancient city walls of Valletta, the capital, designated as a UNESCO World Heritage Site. Our UN guide made sure that we visited the remarkable subterranean necropolis of Hal Safieni Hypogeum dated back to 2500 B.C. containing the megalithic temple of Tarxien, adorned with carved animals and idols, sacrificial altars, and oracular chambers. Also, another highlight of the island, praised the world over, is Caravaggio's masterpiece, *The Beheading of St. John the Baptist*, housed in Malta's main cathedral.

The second stage of the Maltese assignment I devoted mainly to working sessions with the Bank of England's Sir Hugh McDonald, deputy for overseas operations. The British Exchequer had instructed him to prepare the ground for a Malta Central Bank. My contribution was to develop a private banking export financing program to coordinate with a future Central Bank, should one be authorized. At the request of Paul Favre, head of UNIDO in New York, I was to call on more businesses with export potential that might require financing facilities.

During this second part of our Malta visit, we attended several black-tie dinners honoring Sir Hugh. The hosts were William Lyons, the UN Development Programme (UNDP) director stationed in Malta, and Nick Laurie. These evening gatherings were always held under strict British social protocol: after dinner, the women were directed to a separate room for small talk while the men stayed at the table for brandy and cigars. Dinners at the UN director's modest rented house where his French wife prepared cheese soufflés and beef ragout served by three waitresses contrasted to the meals at the Laurie *palacio* where simple British food was the menu.

It should be noted that Malta did not open an FTZ until twenty years later, or an export credit insurance system until the late 1980s, or a Central Bank until thirty years after I made my recommendations.

Sicily

After leaving Malta a second time, we stopped briefly in Sicily to appraise its potential for an FTZ. The sites we inspected were Taormina in the northeast, Syracuse in the center, and Palermo, the capital. At the time all three were developing as tourism centers: Taormina for its view of Mount Etna, which was still spewing fire and ash (also where D. H. Lawrence wrote his poem "Snake"), Syracuse for its former residential caves of business entrepreneurs who brought the city fame in ancient times as a commercial trading port, and Palermo where

General Eisenhower directed the vital Sicilian campaign during World War II. To our surprise, we were assigned the hotel suite once occupied by Ike.

Finland

In the spring of 1969, at the invitation of the Finnish government, we joined a press junket inaugurating the Finnish airline's Helsinki-New York flight. At the time, Finland had a popular pro-Western president, Urho Kaleva Kekkonen, whose powers were extensive. He was prodding his parliament and urging his people to get out from under Soviet influence. Kekkonen personally took us all on a boat tour of Helsinki's huge port in order to convince us that the new Finland was for real. The Finnish commercial office in Washington, D.C., which knew about my experience in FTZs, arranged for me to meet the finance minister, Osmo Karthunenat, and the trade minister, T. A. Wiberheimo. I met the latter during our harbor excursion with the president.

Helsinki already enjoyed adequate customs-free facilities for FTZ operations; in fact, it had had them for centuries. So the Finns asked us instead to look north to Oulu and Rovaniemi and west to Turku and Tampere. The Oulu airport was an important domestic terminal with plenty of land around it to build warehouses and processing operations. Turku, a thriving city with a charming folk museum, was not suitable as a commercial or trading center. Rovaniemi in the north was the hub of the reindeer industry and the jumping-off point for Finland's vast Arctic wilderness.

Once a year at Rovaniemi, on a designated date, rugged reindeer herders emerged from their isolated settlements to assemble without their wives at the only deluxe hotel. That year we happened to be staying there at the same time. This annual rendezvous was how they celebrated the plentiful supply of reindeer and their year's good luck. The festivities took place in the spacious hotel restaurant. Since there were no other women in the dining hall, Dorothy became a very popular dancing partner for many of the two hundred or so herdsmen in attendance. None of them spoke English, but one of them approached her, kissed her hand, and stumbled over the words: "I no speak English but I luff you."

We enjoyed the Finnish people's lavish and universal hospitality. However, we were also shocked to see former German POWs wandering the streets of Helsinki. The Russians had released them from the gulag, and somehow they had ended up here. On one occasion, Dorothy and I were walking down Helsinki's main street when we were accosted by a tall, blond middle-aged man.

Stopping a few feet in front of us, he suddenly clicked his heels, threw out his right arm, and shouted: "Heil Hitler."

France

My European assignments during the first half of the 1970s were an outgrowth of the slow economic recovery confronting French industry in contrast with the progress of the German and Italian economies. Sporadic strikes in the French banking and shipping sectors—a result of political and labor wrangling, itself a result of socialist advances—were generating disdain among EU commissioners in Brussels. In an effort to revive the French shipping industry, the ports of Marseille and Le Havre-Fos sent their port directors to New York, where they were directed to me by the French Trade Mission. I prepared a booklet titled *Advantages of Operating in the Port of Marseille* for distribution by Matthew Bender, and a year later another one for Le Havre-Fos. Soon after, I was invited to help start up FTZs at both ports. The task involved four visits to France.

Bernard Frederich, the director of the Port of Le Havre-Fos, made several visits to New York. Introverted and hard to talk to at times, he was not a typical Frenchman. He was a liberal who despised the mayor of Paris, who at the time was Jacques Chirac (now the president of France). Like most Frenchmen of the day, Frederich pined for the good old days when de Gaulle was president. It was obvious to us when we attended a reception hosted by Chirac at the city hall that the mayor was an extremely hardened Nationalist. But—as a *New York Times* political analyst once emphasized—"no one ever accused Chirac of being an intellectual or a strategic thinker."

Marseille would never recapture its glory days as a shipping power. In contrast, Le Havre-Fos—long an underachiever among European ports—is beginning to catch up. Jacques Finst, the director of auxiliare maritime, made strenuous efforts to obtain official funds from Promotour, the official government financing agency, to develop Marseille's Port de Bouc. He never received the needed financing.

Working with these two ports had its rewards. The Port of Marseille's marketing director, Pierre Imbert, arranged for us to use his Alpine time-share near Gap, a pioneer real estate development with forty-eight hundred family apartments known as Superdevolay. The skiing was superb. He also saw to it that we spent another weekend at Merlet in the deep snow range of the French Alps, where in the distance we could see Grenoble, the site of the 1968 Winter Olympics. And we

32. Dorothy and Walter Diamond in front of the Carlton Hotel at the beginning of the Cannes Film Festival as they were interviewed by *Offshore Investment Magazine* after addressing the International Tax Planning Association Conference prior to the film festival, before leaving for Izmir, Turkey, to help establish a tax free zone, 1989. Photo by Traverso, Cannes.

spent a day in Lyon, where I skied on the first plastic ski slope. The chairlift there ran from the top of the mountain that overlooks the cathedral all the way down to the Rhone.

After several trips around the Port of Le Havre-Fos, the director arranged for us to be picked up at our hotel in Caen—which was Ike's headquarters during the Allied campaign in France—for a tour of the Normandy beachheads. It was a touching moment for me to look down from the cliffs and see precisely where my once proud ship, the *Kentuckian,* lay at the bottom of the English Channel.

We later revisited France to examine international tax treaty developments and peripheral investments. This trip brought me to a reception at the residence of the U.S. ambassador to France, Arthur Hartman. While we were leaving, he told me: "I will never forget you, Mr. Diamond, because you told me something I didn't know—that France has two free trade zones at Haute-Savoie and Gex." Both are transshipment points near the Swiss border.

A few years before my 1980 assignment in Paris, I had a surprise visitor to my New York office—General de Gaulle's grandson, Charles II, a young Parisian attorney. Unlike his grandfather, he was modest and reserved. He told me he wanted to express the appreciation of the French people for my help over the years in "encouraging U.S. private investment" to his country.

Austria

At the request of the U.S. Commerce Department, I went to Vienna in 1959 to explore new markets for American exporters. Soviet influence was finally waning in Austria; the Russian occupation forces, a thorn in the U.S. State Department's side, were at last withdrawing by then. My assignment involved calling on several of Austria's largest private banks as well as on officials of the Finance and Commerce Ministries. The former was at that time led by Dr. Reinhard Kamity, the latter by Dr. Fritz Bock. It was enlightening that all these contacts were eager to drop their bonds with the Soviet Union and develop American marketing and trading concepts. In particular, that meant developing export credit insurance to cover political and commercial risks.

Austria was well positioned to be the gateway to emerging Central and East European economies. With that in mind, a Vienna bank joined forces with the World Bank to set up a guarantee facility designed to increase trade and investment by encouraging the issuance of letters of credit. Importers, long hampered by Western shippers' lack of faith in documentary credits emanating from institutions in the former Iron Curtain countries, now rely on increased commerce with them. Initially set at sixty million dollars, the export credit guarantee facility is cosponsored by the World Bank's International Finance Corporation and the Raiffeisen Zentralbank Oesterreich.

Until 2000, bank secrecy in Austria was based on strictly enforced laws. Banks that revealed their depositors' identities could be sued or prosecuted. Anonymous investments are no longer possible, but Austria still welcomes foreign depositors, and some investments may qualify for tax exemptions. Records are now required by banks in maintaining savings accounts. Since 2000, bank secrecy can be breached in criminal proceedings before an Austrian court. The

Austrian government had been criticized sharply by the European Union for failing to comply with secrecy directives.

Our guide in Austria during its swing toward the West was a former UN staffer from Australia, Fred Walker. He introduced himself to us in the Frankfurt airport on a cold, bleak early morning when our Swissair flight stopped to refuel. Fred invited us to a reception that same evening at the home of Herbert von Karajan, the world-renowned conductor of the Vienna State Opera. When we arrived, he was already at his post for the evening's performance. In his absence, the official host was the secretary to von Karajan, Endre Mantolli. His musical aptitude and vast charm had lifted him to the top of Viennese society.

After the reception, Fred, Dorothy, and I joined Mantolli as his guests at his favorite buffet restaurant, where he told us several stories about von Karajan. The one that impressed us most was that he had declared Leontyne Price "the best Carmen who ever lived." Mantolli arranged for us to occupy von Karajan's box at the Staatsoper for the following two nights' performances: *Carmen* and *Madame Butterfly*.

We were befriended by the manager of the Hotel Sacher, Paul Meirhoff, a brilliant hotelier who had turned the Sacher into one of the world's great hotels. Honored by his invitation to visit him the following year at his recently acquired property near the famous ski resort of St. Antoine, we looked forward to the trip. We arrived at the newly opened Meirhoff Avalanche Hotel after a slow, winding train journey from Zurich. Meirhoff greeted us warmly and urged us to rest and then take advantage of the beautiful sunshine by going straight out to the ski slopes. Otherwise, we might not get in any skiing at all. A blizzard could develop at any time, and in this part of the Alps, those storms could last for days. We ignored his suggestion in favor of resting from our trip.

Meirhoff's warning had been right: our skiing was impeded by large, blinding-white flakes for the next three days, although I did get a chance to try the famous Kandahar Run. On the recommendation of Hans Schneider Jr., son of the Austrian skiing pioneer who introduced the Arlberg turn to the United States in the early 1930s, we insisted on trying the ski runs at Zeus and Lech, fifty miles northwest of St. Antoine. With Hans Jr., we recalled our days at North Conway, New Hampshire, where Dorothy had taken ski lessons from his father.

Although we were advised that the roads to Zeus and Lech were passable, by the time we reached St. Christophe, halfway there, we were snowbound. A severe whiteout had started and was preventing our driver from proceeding farther. St. Christophe also is a noted ski resort, on the other side of St. Antoine range. So it was advisable to settle down in the St. Christophe hotel for the twenty more hours the whiteout lasted.

Luxembourg

A few years later, during an official luncheon in Luxembourg, one of Europe's most important offshore financial centers, our host was the Chamber of Commerce, which had arranged for the British ambassador to be the speaker. At the reception before we took our places on the dais, the ambassador had told the day's organizer and program chairman, Francis Hoogewerf—a prominent Luxembourg businessman although a native of Britain—that he wished to sit next to my wife. As soon as the ambassador sat down, he turned to Dorothy and asked her: "What do you Americans mean when you say 'Where's the beef?' "

For many years, Luxembourg has been one of the fastest-growing financial centers in the world. It has more than two hundred international banks with assets in excess of $500 billion, even though its once strong banking secrecy laws are being phased out. Luxembourg banks are at the top of the roster in fund management, leveraged investing, and corporate finance services. That tiny country's sophisticated banking facilities are responsible for its meteoric rise—it is now the world's second-largest center for mutual funds, after the United States. Of the nearly $1 trillion in offshore assets invested in Luxembourg mutual funds, Americans hold $220 billion.

In speaking with many of Luxembourg's bankers, I was struck by an anomaly: although a grand duchy for more than two centuries, it has never had a royal family. In 1964 Grand Duke Jean was named symbolic head of state after his mother abdicated.

Liechtenstein

A short trip to Liechtenstein in the mid-1990s to help market the second-largest bank in the principality, the Bank in Liechtenstein (known as BIL), uncovered several questionable activities. When I submitted my recommendations to BIL several months later, the general manager refused to accept them even though he had asked me for them. He arranged for his bank's legal advisers to notify me of the action it was taking and then cancelled our contract, unethical as it was. Much later, the principality brought its ruling dynasty's famous art collection to New York's Metropolitan Museum of Art. During that event's opening reception, our host, Prince Hans Adam II, apologized to me in person for the "misunderstanding."

Under Prince Hans Adam II, Liechtenstein was a leading offshore financial center until the tiny principality was rocked by a money-laundering scandal. Early in 2000, police from Liechtenstein and Austria, led by an Austrian special prosecutor, seized paper and electronic documents from the ruling family's Liechtensteinische Landesbank. The bank's president was Prince Philipp, a brother of Hans Adam, but no evidence has come to light of any direct involvement in wrongdoing by the ruling family. Eight high-level financial managers were arrested. They included the managing director of BIL, who had asked me to prepare the booklet containing my recommendations for reaching a wider market, and the managing directors of Liechtenstein's two other banks, the Bank in Liechtenstein and Verwaltungsund Privatbank AG. They were accused of participating in tens of millions of dollars in illegal transactions involving domestic and foreign firms.

The special prosecutor, Kurt Spitzer, attributed the growth of money laundering in Liechtenstein to "partial deadlock" in the courts caused by long delays in trying cases as well as failure to cooperate with prosecutors in other countries. His final verdict was that Liechtenstein's white-collar crime is no worse than in other parts of Europe and that most assets arriving in the principality for laundering have actually been "prewashed" in other countries.

Liechtenstein's Due Diligence Act of 1996 has gone a long way toward restoring its credibility in the international financial community. Today, the principality is host to more than eighty thousand foreign-bank holding companies.

Portugal

In 1980, the late Guenter Reimann approached me about preparing a preliminary recommendation for an FTZ in Portugal. Reimann, a German economist who came to the United States in the 1930s, was the publisher of *International Reports*, which was acknowledged as providing the most reliable foreign exchange analyses in the country. Reimann's currency skills were why he was now a financial adviser to the Bank of Portugal, that nation's Central Bank.

Reimann had a very good head for business. He got his start in publishing in 1946 when—at a luncheon I attended—he purchased *Textile World* magazine for $500. He quickly converted it into a foreign exchange tabloid called *International Reports*, for which I prepared a foreign credit column. Forty years later, he sold it to *American Heritage* for $2.7 million and after six months bought it back for $2.3 million. London's *Financial Times* then took it over. The *Times* ran my foreign credit column for twenty more years until it was sold to Informa Publishing of London. My credit contribution still appears in it every month. *International Reports* is now published by World Trade Executive of Concord, Massachusetts.

Madeira

After long deliberation, the Portuguese government used my recommendations as the basis for its Decree-Law no. 163 of June 26, 1986, and Regional Regulation Decree 21/87/M. These laws established an industrial free zone on the beautiful resort island of Madeira. That zone was later converted into an all-purpose financial zone to handle trading, banking, insurance, fund management, leasing, factoring, and other financial services. Under the close guidance of Francisco Costa, the ambitious general manager of the Madeira Development Company, the zone was one of the Bank of Portugal's prize ventures until 2000, when a showdown with the EU forced it to restrict its activities and terminate its zero tax rate after 2011.

Madeira is well known to vacationers for its flowers, wine, embroidery, and unique downhill basket ride. Now it is also known as an international business center. It has broadened Madeira's economy and reduced its dependence upon agriculture and tourism. It has also eased the island's unemployment problem and increased foreign exchange revenues. The only possible drawback to using Madeira's financial services zone, which is nineteen mountainous road miles from the capital at Funchal, is the short and hazardous concrete airport runway, resembling a diving board extending over the ocean. This problem is being corrected by a $4.2 million facility arranged by the European Union.

The Channel Islands

When I visited the three Channel Islands of Guernsey, Jersey, and Sark to review their financial services, one common thread stood out. It was clear from discussions with high-level businessmen in the banking, accounting, and financial communities and in government circles that one must show great respect for the British Crown and all the protocol surrounding it and never criticize her majesty. You could rage all you liked against Westminster for its restrictive rules and regulations, but against the queen? Never.

On Guernsey, where I addressed the Accountancy Association in a banquet hall overlooking the beautiful but congested yacht basin—the island's principal revenue earner after financial services—I was bombarded with questions relating to what the audience referred to as America's "strict auditing practices." My official meetings with the chief executives of both Guernsey and Jersey centered around the extension of their financial services to include more emphasis on their captive insurance and export guarantee programs as recommended by the World Trade Institute.

On the unique island of Sark—which is actually two islands, Great Sark and Little Sark, connected by a natural causeway—the dame of Sark reigned as a benevolent dictator. So revered was she for her resistance to the Nazis that she was made the heroine of a London hit play. I could not understand how she was able to control her people, since there was a local government, a holdover from feudal times. She had forbidden automobiles on the island—an edict that exists to this day, long after her death. Visitors to Sark can get around on foot over the narrow paths and broken stone walks or they can hire a horse and buggy. Local residents use heavy-duty agricultural equipment for motorized transportation.

Gibraltar

Unlike most leaders of offshore financial centers, the former chief minister of Gibraltar, Joseph Bossano, worked hard to promote his colony's financial services industry. A former dockworker and trade union leader, he often spoke at conferences and meetings on the Continent, describing the unique attractions of Gibraltar and always urging his listeners to come to "the Rock" and see for themselves. I asked him once why he did not hire a public relations director to promote Gibraltar's attractions, which included a historic naval base, limestone caves full of archaeological finds, and a colony of Europe's only apes. He told me: "Why should I? The public is more likely to believe me than an advertisement in print." In 1996 his Socialist Party lost an election to the Social Democrats, led by Peter Carisano, who won by promising to revitalize the offshore financial program and to cultivate better relations with Spain and Britain.

The Isle of Man

The Isle of Man's chief minister, Charles Walker, was a reserved man with a brilliant mind. In contrast to Bossano, he relied on competent ministers to oversee his island's financial services. The Isle of Man, in the Irish Sea, is a tourist magnet, its biggest attraction being the international motorcycle races that are held each August on the island's coast road lasting the entire month. The races inspire most islanders to leave the island for the duration after renting their homes. I was asked to visit the island after the British government decided to cut back on its aid to the British colonies and to encourage business diversification.

The UN suggested that an FTZ at one of the island's historic ports might be the answer. Soon after, it was decided to establish the first FTZ in this British isle on the outskirts of Castletown. In 1983 and 1984 the necessary legislation for it was passed. However, four years of delays caused by a failure to negotiate satisfactory contracts with British and American developers became a major scandal. So when we visited Walker, he urged me to find a solution to the problem. I remember his spacious office furnished with magnificent carved-oak tables and chairs and decorated with nautical paintings, photographs, and charts.

Reginald Newton, a former tax commissioner, arranged for me to be interviewed on the island's only radio station. Through that outlet, I told the islanders how they would benefit by providing De Beers and other multinationals with a customs-free zone to produce export goods. Meanwhile, Freddie Allen, manager of the local Barclay's bank, was mustering the island's business community to lobby the government for a quick settlement of a conflict with landowners—a battle that was blocking progress toward an FTZ.

But the real key was my persuading De Beers, the huge South African mining combine, to build a factory in the zone to manufacture diamond-cutting tools. A dinner meeting was arranged at the spacious home of Peter Henwood, general manager of European Trust; another guest was De Beers's overseas vice president. I explained the advantages of processing diamond tools in a UK associate locality that qualified for EU marketing benefits. Not long after those discussions, De Beers leased fifty-four acres on the island and invested 2 million pounds (roughly US$3.7 million) to start building a forty thousand-square-foot plant.

Henwood was a prominent entrepreneur on the island and had access to the personal helicopter of Nigel Mansell, the Formula I auto racing star, who was the Isle of Man's most celebrated British-born resident. Henwood had arranged for us to fly back to Castletown in Mansell's helicopter after dinner. The De Beers official was staying at the Henwoods'.

Our pilot could not find a suitable landing spot in Castletown, so he came down in a hay field on the outskirts. The only problem was that the landing area was encircled with a barbed-wire fence with no gate or other outlet. Returning to the helicopter, the pilot came back with a large pair of wire clippers. He cut the bottom strands enough for Dorothy and me to crawl under the fence. This expedition to the De Beers dinner meeting ended with Mansell's pilot holding up the barbed wire with a sheepish grin.

Cyprus

In 1986 we went to Cyprus for two weeks, sponsored by the UN. This visit had been suggested by the Cyprus Investment Center in New York headed by Denis Drushiotis, who wanted to establish two industrial free zones, at Larnaca and Limassol. Our Cypriot host was a prominent attorney and scholar, Christos Demetriades, who was determined to impress us with the many Cypriot attractions. Together, we stood beside the tenuous Turkish-Cypriot cease-fire line, accompanied by the island's tourism director.

Demetriades predicted that the island's Turks and Greeks would eventually solve their differences and that the island would one day be reunited. The line dividing the Greek and Turkish sections of the island has recently been opened so that Cypriots can visit their relatives again. Opening the borderline is an encouraging sign that a settlement could be made in the near future; Demetriades's forecast may yet become a reality.

Accompanied by either Demetriades or the tourism director, George Papas, we saw all of Cyprus's highlights, including the ski slopes of the Cypriot Alps, the perfectly preserved ancient mosaics at Paphos, and the Aphrodite Rock, where the "goddess" was said to appear. At our hotel we learned that the Cypriots celebrate Easter by roasting outdoors a whole lamb on a large spit, a custom observed throughout the country. Our hosts also showed us Neolithic excavations proving that the island had been inhabited six thousand years ago.

In early 2003, the Greek Cypriots voted in a referendum to join the EU. Turkey has been seeking EU membership for more than ten years, and its application is still being reviewed.

In Cyprus, my talks with the Commerce Ministry and business leaders focused on resurrecting the island's export credit insurance system, which at the time was moribund. That situation would have to change if American companies were ever going to establish themselves in the industrial zones. In 1975, a year after the Turkish invasion, the government passed legislation that enabled FTZs, as part of a program to diversify the economy. Cyprus Airways then entered the picture by commissioning a feasibility study for two Cypriot free zones; this analysis was completed in 1981. The zones were to replace the bonded factories for export-oriented industries, which under Order no. 120/76 could be established anywhere on Cyprus.

The bonded factory scheme offered flexibility but had been less attractive than expected, for several reasons. Plant and equipment were not always exempt from import duties (although raw materials for export processing have not been subject to tax), bonded factories lacked the infrastructure normally furnished by the zone, and bonded factories were subject to steep annual fees to defray the government's costs for customs and inspection.

The main reason FTZs in Cyprus took so long to establish was the indifference of customs officials. The government was focusing much more sharply on enhancing the island's status as a financial services center and as a headquarters for managing nonresident companies—especially those businesses that needed a convenient base for trading goods between Eastern Europe and Western Europe.

Unfortunately, Cyprus's location and inducements attracted some shady investors. Russians were using Cypriot banks to launder money, and Serbians were end-running UN sanctions against Yugoslavia by conducting business through Cypriot straw companies. Russian businessmen and a few corrupt managers of state-run businesses owned about two thousand Cypriot subsidiaries, some of which were used to sell weapons to Iraq and for other illegal purposes. Serbians were shipping oil, machinery, trucks, and consumer goods to Bulgaria and Romania; from there, they were moved across the border to Yugoslavia in violation of UN sanctions.

The Cypriot government was well aware of these problems and did a commendable job in cleaning up unsavory situations. In 2002, it abandoned the long-profitable remittance system of taxation and replaced it with worldwide taxes on income of Cypriot residents and on nonresident incomes sourced in Cyprus. Also, the Cypriot Central Bank, which is supposed to monitor offshore banking units, later stopped licensing new Russian-owned bank branches and decreed banks would have to report any cash deposits and transfers of more than ten thousand dollars.

Iceland

In November 1966 I received a communication from David Sch. Thorsteinsson, the energetic director of the Iceland Chamber of Commerce, advising me that the Icelandic government had decided to form a task force for a "special project" that would enhance the marketing of the nation's largest revenue earner, the fishing industry. Specifically, "the only activity would be the sale of fish bought from a foreign country and sold to another country." Its objective was "never to land the fish in Iceland, nor process nor warehouse in Iceland, but to establish a free port as a transitory activity zone."

After a steady exchange of ideas and recommendations by facsimile with Thorsteinsson and a meeting with him in Amsterdam where Dorothy and I were speakers at an Offshore Institute Conference, Iceland adopted two laws in 1999 on formation of international trading companies. Taking its cue from Ireland's successful International Financial Services Centre operation, Iceland granted considerable latitude in the functions that the fishing and seafood industries could perform, among them transshipment of goods through Iceland, trading in marine and agricultural products under their own name or acting as an intermediary in the trade between parties outside of Icelandic jurisdiction, and operating exclusively as a holding company that owns foreign enterprises. Though disappointing to some observers in the number of offshore trading companies that Iceland has been able to attract owing to increased competition, the Iceland Chamber of Commerce considers the law a key element in the nation's financial structure. Yet the government is resorting to an intensive tourist promotion campaign to draw visitors from around the world to supplement its fishing revenues.

Spain

As an old seafaring nation, Spain counted heavily on its eighteen FTZs and free ports, which were spread around the country. All of them had been making substantial contributions to the country's trade since being created in 1929. However, the free port in the Canary Islands never took hold and had become a drain on the national treasury. In 1996, to revitalize the Canary Islands, the Madrid government adopted special Canary Islands regulations. These laws covered the entire archipelago and offered a myriad of incentives to qualifying private companies that wanted to establish FTZs at sites of their own choosing.

Canary Islands

On a preliminary UN assignment to the Canary Islands in 2000, my task was to review the new regulations with a leading construction firm in Santa Cruz de

The Offshore Institute

E. Jerry James, President Elect
The Equitable Building
730 – 17th Street, Suite 350
Denver, Colorado, 802 12-3580 USA
Tel: +1 720 932 7939   Fax   +1 720 932 7951

January 31, 2003

Mr. Walter H. Diamond
Overseas Press and Consultants
9 Old Farm Lane
Hartsdale, New York 10530

Dear Walter:

Please allow me to wish a "VERY HAPPY BITHDAY" to you on the occasion of your 90th birthday! It is an understatement to say that it is a pleasure, privilege, and honor to know you and to consider you and Dorothy as good friends.

Despite your humble and unassuming nature, all of your colleagues, contemporaries, and admirers are well aware of your international standing, importance, and contributions as an author, advisor and advocate for the financial services industry. On your special occasion, you should be remembered by all of us.

Please have a wonderful celebration today and many enjoyable years to come.

Very truly yours,
THE OFFSHORE INSTITUTE

By: _____
E. Jerry James, President Elect

EJJ:sj
date-31-03.ltr

33. Letter from the Offshore Institute marking Walter's ninetieth birthday, 2003.

Tenerife, the capital. The firm's chairman was Miguel Pago, a prominent is-lander who had built and was managing the most luxurious hotel in the Ca-naries. The son of Pago's partner was in charge of trading operations for the giant firm, but discussions with him proved useless. Although an enthusiastic and keen supporter of future commercial progress for the islands, his indifference to

Madrid's and the UN's suggestion for the Canary Islands' industrial development by establishing an FTZ made it clear to me that the islands would make little headway despite what "the politicians in Madrid wanted."

At our final meeting, over dinner in a local restaurant, a loud commotion startled us. Three employees, one of whom was the manager, ran down the staircase directly behind us. "Another child must have been stolen," my host remarked. "It happens every day." He explained further, and it turned out that kidnappers came over every day from Africa, which was only sixty miles away, to steal young boys off the streets. They were transported back to Morocco or the Western Sahara and sold to underground adoption channels, or they were forced into paramilitary service in Liberia, Nigeria, or the Ivory Coast.

United Kingdom

Britain was the world leader in providing export credit insurance, having established the British Export Credits Department in 1918. However, it was a laggard in developing free ports. Not until the Free Zone Regulations of 1984, when Parliament finally succumbed to pressure from the trading community, did it authorize six free ports: Southampton, Cardiff, and Liverpool, and the airports at Prestwick, Belfast, and Birmingham. My visits to the United Kingdom in the early 1960s were aimed at gaining firsthand knowledge of its insurance system. Later, Eximbank would use the knowledge I had gathered when it devised the Foreign Credit Insurance Association. Still later assignments in Britain in the 1970s and 1980s involved collaborating with the British Information Services in New York, which had been delegated to provide background information on American experience with the U.S. Foreign Trade Zones Act of 1934.

On one of my visits to Britain, in 1986, Prince Philip hosted a tax-planning group at the British Museum. Iced bottles of champagne were waiting for us in the main gallery, but someone had forgotten to provide any glasses, so it was a dry evening indeed.

Yugoslavia

In 1986, ten days after the nuclear catastrophe at Chernobyl in northern Ukraine—the worst such accident in history, which eventually took twenty-five thousand lives—I was visited in my New York office by a delegation from the Yugoslavian port of Bar. The group included the president of Bar's town council, the director of the Yugoslav Institute of Economics in Belgrade, and other regional government leaders. They had come from Washington at the suggestion of the Commerce Department, and they were looking for help to resurrect the country's free customs area in the old kingdom of Montenegro at Bar, twenty miles north of the Albanian border.

Situated directly across the Adriatic from Bari, Italy, Bar is one of ten Yugoslavian free trade outposts and is well located to transship goods between Eastern Europe and Western Europe. However, political squabbling between the Serbian-controlled government in Belgrade and the Montenegrins meant that it was receiving little recognition as a trading center. Its twenty warehouses and three large bulk-cargo terminals, set on fifteen hundred acres of commercial and industrial land, were in the doldrums. My visitors were looking for an economist with FTZ experience who could prepare detailed recommendations for rehabilitating the Bar export processing zone. At the time, the Chernobyl nuclear fallout was polluting agricultural land throughout Europe. The director of the Economics Institute, George Leisjic, told me that his country's farmers were facing dim prospects for the foreseeable future.

My colleagues at the accounting firm of O'Connor, Davies, Mums, and Dobbins—of which a managing partner, Joseph Ménages, earlier labeled me as "one of a kind"—as well as UNIDO officials, warned me that it was risky to visit Yugoslavia so soon after Chernobyl. But Dorothy and I went anyway and soon found ourselves in Dubrovnik, which we had visited twenty years earlier. Leisjic turned out to be a kind host. He met us there, accompanied by officials from the Bar export processing zone, and we set out for the port. It was a tedious journey over broken asphalt roads and a forty-five-minute ferry ride.

We settled into a unique hotel resembling a fishing village in Svelte Stefan, a luxurious resort on its own tiny island and accessible only by a footbridge. Every morning of our three-week assignment we were met at eight o'clock by Leisjic and the zone's official representative, Medicinal Novak, a witty French-speaking Montenegrin. Several times after our daily meetings with the mayor of Bar and his sixteen councilors, as well as local business leaders, Dorothy found a vase of fresh red roses waiting for her at the conference table. At three o'clock a hearty buffet lunch would be laid out on the conference table, and usually that ended the day's work. Occasionally, we would reconvene at six at a nearby hotel restaurant for dinner.

Our round-table sessions were dominated by a good-natured businessman from Titograd, the capital of Montenegro some thirty miles north of Bar. Veljko Krstajic, director of Export-Import Titograd, the largest trading firm in the region, peppered us day after day with well-considered questions that reflected his acumen as a foreign trader. Montenegro is a productive grape-growing area and produces highly regarded wines. However, production had been limited and was mainly for local consumption.

The export market for those wines was virtually nonexistent, yet tests by foreign wine distributors had shown that Yugoslav wines were superior to wines shipped by other suppliers in Cyprus, Australia, Malta, and Morocco. Krstajic was certain that Yugoslav wines could even compete with German and Italian ones. To convince us, he arranged a tour of the vineyards in the lake district north of Titograd. He had a summer residence there, deep in the woods on a lake so clear you could see your shadow in it and admire the unique, rose-colored trout.

Before returning to Bar, Krstajic made sure we stopped at Mostar to visit a historic Byzantine church that was famous for its "display of erotic art." Church custodians would not allow Dorothy, a knowledgeable art patron, to enter because of strict rules prohibiting women from viewing the controversial frescoes. She had to wait until she was back in New York, when she saw my photographs of them, which I had taken surreptitiously.

Krstajic's thoughtfulness toward us was rewarded when I returned to New York and found him a wine distributor that would market his vintages.

The warmth displayed by all the Yugoslavs we met was a highlight of our visit. Some of them joked that the average Yugoslav "loved Americans more than Tito," who had made many bitter enemies during his decades of rule. This fact was confirmed to me when our Bar group took us to an American-Yugoslav Chamber of Commerce meeting at Cavtat, a resort near Dubrovnik, where former U.S. ambassador Laurence Eagleberger made a return visit to be honored by the Yugoslavs. "Your ambassador will never be forgotten by the Yugoslav people," in the words of George Leisjic, who arranged one of my most rewarding UN, U.S. AID, or other assignments over a nearly sixty-year period.

⇻ 11 ⇺

Middle Eastern Lairs

Israel

THIRTEEN YEARS after the birth of Israel in 1948, we arrived in Tel Aviv on an assignment primarily to help the newly independent state establish a foreign investment center that would lure American private capital. A second objective was to assist the government in strengthening its newly hatched tourism development program. At that time, in the early stages of independence, Israel faced monumental economic problems, and the government, led by the "lion of Judah," Prime Minister David Ben-Gurion, was desperate for solutions. With millions of refugees from central Europe and northern Africa flooding the nation, unemployment had reached a staggering 40 percent.

When Dorothy and I looked out at the Mediterranean from our Sheraton Hotel window, all we could see for miles along the shore were hundreds of tents lined up housing thousands of new arrivals—Algerian, Libyan, Moroccan, and Tunisian Jews. Most of these unsettled emigrants had fled their African home-lands because of discriminatory laws that often amounted to persecution.

In the 1950s, Ben-Gurion's government had been hard-pressed to handle this human flood, in spite of the hundreds of millions of dollars of financial aid from the U.S. government and from world charitable foundations. The crippling budget deficit was a constant worry to Ben-Gurion (who was also defense minister), especially since the United States had just elected John F. Kennedy and his position on financial aid was still questionable. Truman and Eisenhower had been pro-Israel, but with both out of the White House, Israeli leaders feared that their financial pipeline might be cut off.

Our visit to Israel was inspired by an unusual chain of circumstances. In late 1960, Alitalia Flight 626, a Constellation bound for New York's Idlewild Airport (later renamed John F. Kennedy Airport), was barely off the ground at Ireland's

Shannon International Airport when its two GE engines detached from the wings and fell off the plane. All two hundred-odd passengers died in the resulting crash. We had been scheduled to fly to Rome in the very same plane. As soon as we heard about the crash, we tried to contact the New York office of Alitalia, which of course could not be reached because so many reporters and stricken families were phoning at the same time.

Within a couple of hours, though, we were contacted by the director of Alitalia's PR department in New York, Joe Le Tourneau, who told us that another "Connie" would be replacing the crashed one for Flight 626 and that he would be sending a car—which turned out to be a Rolls-Royce—to pick us up at our house in Hartsdale, New York. Before Joe called, we had been in touch with our travel agent at Bristed Manning, Betty Nuthall, a British Wimbledon women's tennis champion from the 1920s whose husband was Bill Shoemacher, director of the New York office of the Commerce Department. Bill was always ready to help foreign traders find markets. Betty had heard about the Alitalia crash, and now she was trying to soothe Dorothy, who was nervous about flying to Rome in the replacement plane. With typical British confidence, Betty told her: "Take a walk in the woods, breathe in the fresh air. It never happens twice in a row." It should be noted that Alitalia eventually replaced all of its Connies' engines with those of McDonnell Douglas.

When we boarded the substitute plane, we found two passengers already seated placidly in the bulkhead seats on our right. "How come you got the best seats in the house?" they asked us. When I told them about our invitation from the Italian government—that it wanted us to help the nation attract American investors and tourists—one of the two strangers introduced himself as the comptroller of El-Al. It bothered him that we were on a mission to assist Italy and not Israel—a new nation that needed more help than the Western European industrial countries. "Will you come to Israel to help our government?" he asked. He turned to his seatmate, who was E. Ben Artzi, El-Al's president; he graciously invited us to be his guests as soon as possible.

Six months later we arrived in Tel Aviv. Early the next morning we received a visitor, Israel's investment director, Teddy Kollek, who much later would become Tel Aviv's greatly admired mayor. El-Al had informed him by then that Dorothy was a columnist for *Modern Floor Coverings*, and now he advised us that he would arrange for her to visit Mizpeh, a rug-weaving business started by Ruth Dayan, the enterprising wife of General Moshe Dayan. In an effort to absorb some of the growing unemployment, she was hiring North African women immigrants, who had learned to weave carpets in their original countries. Their workmanship was widely admired, and Teddy Kollek was certain this fledgling industry could put Israel on the map as a major carpet producer.

The weaving shop manager insisted that the only time she could see Dorothy was at eight the following morning. It was then or never. When Dorothy arrived on time for her appointment, the manager explained she was "busy right now" and told Dorothy to browse around the shop. After a half hour of exhibiting the arrogance typical of many central Europeans at that time, the manager suddenly apologized by saying that her attitude arose from dealing with overbearing American philanthropists. She brought another chair to her desk and invited Dorothy to sit beside her. From then on, the interview proceeded smoothly.

When Dorothy's column about the rugs appeared in *Modern Floor Coverings*, it drew broad and instant attention. The big department stores in North America and as far away as Australia and South Africa immediately began calling the magazine for information about how to place orders. Calls came in from Saks, Gimbels, Arnold Constable, and Bloomingdales in New York, Filenes in Boston, I. Magnins in Los Angeles, Sakowitz in Houston, and other large outlets in Chicago, Dayton, Dallas, Washington, and New Orleans; all of them wanted to place orders that would help Israel develop its carpet industry. Within thirty days the flood of overseas orders from abroad had compelled Mizpeh to expand its workforce of North African refugees from twenty to two thousand. Dorothy never received any thanks from Dayan, nor did Mizpeh ever thank the magazine for the early boost the article had provided.

My discussions with Teddy Kollek covered ways that Israel might lure American companies to set up factories in Israel. Kollek was a sheer delight to talk with and was enthusiastic when I suggested an FTZ for Haifa, Israel's biggest port. In fact, there would eventually be three: Haifa, Ashdod (the second-largest port), and Elat (on the Red Sea, directly across from Jordan's Aqaba FTZ). Discussions at Ellerns Bank were designed to expedite letter of credit documents with certain American banks.

Kollek arranged a meeting for me with Levi Eshkol, the finance minister. Eshkol would later serve for several years as prime minister. He welcomed us warmly and instructed his staff to give full cooperation to the investment center and me.

Later on, we were having lunch with Kollek at the King David Hotel and saw the Israeli cabinet meeting two tables away. Eshkol recognized us and motioned for Kollek to bring us over. Eshkol introduced us to the defense minister, Shimon

Peres, whom he described as the "lion in sheep's clothing." Peres had been head of Naval Services and deputy defense minister under Ben-Gurion, who was also defense minister and was widely recognized for his political and military leadership in the 1948 war between the new nation and its Arab neighbors.

As a prime minister in 1988 under the Labor Party banner and again in 1995–96, Peres had a stormy time because of his unwavering stance on expanding Israeli settlements. In all our meetings with government and business officials, Israel's president at that time, Itzhak Ben-Zvi, seemed to be a nonentity: not once did his name arise during our discussions.

Unlike the Israeli leaders of the early 1960s—during which time the new nation was beginning to develop economically and industrially—the hundreds of thousands of fresh arrivals from central Europe showed little warmth for American business visitors, tourists, or even the many representatives of American charitable organizations, who were anxious to help Israel. Many of these central Europeans had endured persecution, and now too often they were acting as if the world owed them a debt. To our astonishment, Dorothy and I were treated rudely by these people several times—hardly becoming to those who were benefiting from Israel's Law of Returning 1950, which provided that "every Jew may come to Israel as an immigrant."

One day a young Israeli spun the revolving door at the Sheraton entrance so rapidly that Dorothy was almost knocked over. Another time we were sitting on a picnic bench outside a winery near Tel Aviv when a pack of young Hasidim in traditional garb swarmed us, pushing us off the bench and into a pool of mud so that twelve of them could sit on one bench.

This rough attitude of the central Europeans eventually wore off as they melded with the original Palestine settlers and learned to behave and to follow the laws. We observed this forty years later; people were much more civilized and caring by then. On that trip, after a tax meeting at the port of Elat, we went to Jerusalem, where I paid my respects at Eshkol's grave at the Mount Olive cemetery.

Iran

In early June 1968, when my second assignment in Malta was finished, we stopped at Rome's airport, where I was supposed to pick up prearranged instructions from the UN. But nothing was waiting for me—no cable either from UN headquarters in New York or from Vienna, the UN's European headquarters.

After we arrived back in New York, I found the instructions, which had been mailed to me by mistake at my home. I was to proceed to Iran at once because it was urgently in need of industrial development assistance. My job would be to help the Iranian Export Development Corporation draw up an industrialization plan.

To meet the deadline called for in the UN's contract with Iran, I would have to fly to Tehran immediately. After one day of rest (which gave us a chance to celebrate our anniversary), I left for Tehran after picking up a package at the UN to be delivered to the UNDP office there. Except for my second and thirds visits to Belize, this Iran trip was the only time in more than 120 UN, U.S. AID, and other foreign assignments that Dorothy did not accompany me.

I was met at the Tehran airport by Dr. Khosrow Habibi, services director for the Export Promotion Centre of Iran, and was immediately escorted to a meeting at eight that morning with the center's director, Dr. Abbas Ordoobadi, and his staff. That meeting went on until seven in the evening. Ordoobadi, a ruthless politician obviously trying to make a good impression on his superiors in the ministries, insisted that my preliminary recommendations be on his desk when he returned to his office the next morning. At the Hilton bar, under dim lighting punctuated by complete blackouts, I completed my analysis of his ten-point credit plan around two o'clock in the morning. My recommendations included establishing credit development banks, an export credit insurance system, a way to eliminate present export problems, a new export development corporation, a thirty-point program to attract foreign investment, and the creation of FTZs. Legislation to these ends was later adopted, despite a heated controversy engineered by the Council of Constitutional Guardians, which claimed that FTZs were unconstitutional. A network of ten FTZs was eventually established along the Persian Gulf, Caspian Sea, and Gulf of Oman.

Three days after my arrival, a final conference was held in the board room of the Export Promotion Centre. Ordoobadi chaired the meeting, which was attended by various other senior Iranian officials and UN envoys. One of the latter emphasized that all UN funds for Iran had been budgeted through 1971 and that no further UN money could possibly be allocated to the Export Promotion Centre. What was available to Iran had already been sent to the economics minister two weeks earlier. That minister would be assigning the funds to various projects according to his own priorities.

At this point, a Dr. Habibi took control of the meeting. He told the UN envoys he was sure the Export Promotion Centre and Central Bank could influence the economics minister to shift the funds to export promotion, which in most people's minds was very important to the economy. The envoy replied that "if this was so important, why hadn't the center asked for funds in the past?"

In the end, Habibi and Ordoobadi requested the shift in funds, to no avail. However, on the instructions of Shah Mohammad Reza Pahlavi, the government eventually allocated enough funds to adopt several of the final UN proposals, including an export development corporation, an export credit insurance system, and a broad scheme for attracting foreign investment.

My three days of hectic maneuvering in Tehran were rewarded with a warm send-off by UN and Export Development Centre officials. On the return trip, the Pan Am DC-9 was forced to land in Beirut because of a fire in the right engine. A twelve-hour layover in the hundred-degree non-air-conditioned terminal while we waited for a replacement part to arrive from Paris did not contaminate a kilo of Iranian caviar that I had promised a Hartsdale neighbor. A stewardess was kind enough to move it from under my seat to a refrigerator in the Pan Am kitchen during the delay.

In the 1960s and 1970s, the shah was still in firm control of Iran. He had come to power in the 1950s after the CIA director, Allen Dulles, hatched a successful American plot to oust Iran's Nationalist prime minister, Mohammad Mosaddeq. The prime minister had been swept aside by a mob guided by the CIA chief in Tehran, Kermit Roosevelt, the grandson of former president Theodore Roosevelt. The shah would rule until 1979, when he was overthrown by Islamic revolutionaries under the banner of Ayatollah Ruhollah Khomeini.

For my second visit to Iran, Dorothy came with me on assignment for the *Pan Am's World Guide*. This trip also started with a flight delay: a French passenger with a heart ailment had an attack over the Atlantic, and the pilot made an emergency stop at Brussels. The hospital medics in Brussels were of little help, since the passenger insisted he be taken to Paris; he told them he wanted to die on his home soil. Another stop was arranged at the Paris airport, but the patient died before we landed there. Bleary-eyed, we arrived in Tehran at six in the morning after a twenty-hour flight.

On checking in with the UN office in Tehran and the Export Development Centre, I learned that progress was being made on implementing some of the recommendations of three years earlier. Our main objective on this second visit was for Dorothy to cover the twenty-five hundred anniversary celebrations of Alexander the Great's founding of Persepolis, which centuries earlier had been the ceremonial capital of Persia.

Before traveling to Persepolis, we had time in Tehran to note that criticism of the shah was growing among his people and that Islam had a stronger hold on Iranians than it had three years earlier. People were afraid to express their opposition for fear of reprisals by the shah's secret police. Almost every office and shop displayed a picture of the shah, but the disdain of the owners could be read in their gestures. On one occasion in Tehran, we spotted an intersection that had four palaces, one on each corner. Seasoned journalist that she was, Dorothy whispered to me that the shah's downfall was inevitable. She was even more certain of it after she interviewed residents of Isfahan and Shiraz.

The shah's celebrations at Persepolis brought leaders and celebrities from the four corners of the world. They included royalty, ministers, presidents, and film stars. Each of the two thousand invited guests was brought to Persepolis in a private jet. It is estimated that the luxuries bestowed on these guests during the week's celebrations cost the Iranian treasury one hundred million dollars.

Persepolis is situated in the fertile valley of the Pulvar River and was first settled by Darius I. Its ruins are among the world's most spectacular. The citadel that contained the Persian Empire's vast treasury was looted by Alexander. These ruins stand on gigantic platforms built of limestone from the adjacent mountain. A few hundred feet from the ruins, the shah had raised a series of grandiose tents, which housed his guests in regal style. The tents enclosed huge suites; the bathrooms were of marble; the draperies had been fabricated by Parisian designers. And these were only a few of the indulgences the shah had showered on his guests. Later, the tents were to be converted into a hotel complex to house future tourists.

Before returning to Tehran, we made two brief stops. The first was in Shiraz, thirty miles southwest of Persepolis, a commercial and industrial center known for its wines, carpets, and metalwork. A UN representative in the capital had recommended I call on several banks to review their financing and FTZ activities. Shiraz had been the capital of Iran before it was moved to Tehran by Aga Mohammad Kahn. Hafez and Sadi, two of Persia's greatest poets, are buried in Sharaz in garden-enclosed tombs, which we had the opportunity to visit. Our second stop was at Isfahan, a picturesque city with many elegant structures built during the reign of Shah Abbas, who made it the capital of Persia in 1398. Today, it is universally acclaimed for its imperial mosque, a masterpiece of world architecture.

The final leg of our return to Tehran was disturbing. As we boarded an ancient Fokker aircraft, the airline agent grabbed a plastic bag of medicine I was carrying in my briefcase. After inspecting it, he exclaimed: "You can't take it with you. It will be returned to you in Tehran."

Iran's antidrug laws were the strictest in the Middle East at that time. "Guilty" travelers were being imprisoned without trial or legal aid. In Tehran we waited more than an hour for the medicine to be returned. Finally, after several futile attempts to obtain it from Iran Airways' personnel, Dorothy took the mission in her own hands. Sideswiping a gatekeeper, she dashed onto the tarmac where the plane was still unloading. With the help of an agent, she retrieved the bag of medicine.

Now settled back in Tehran, we took on Dorothy's second project: an article about the national caviar-processing factory at Babol Sar, some 125 miles north of Tehran on the Caspian Sea. Getting there was not easy. Few taxis in the capital were up to negotiating the winding dirt roads extending far up the slopes of 18,934-foot Damavand, the highest peak in the Middle East. After an all-morning trip through a dozen dark tunnels and a brief stop at 12,000 feet on the mountain—where heavy snow had attracted skiers—we arrived at Babol Sar; then in ninety-degree heat we took a quick dip in the Caspian.

We arrived at the factory in time for our two o'clock appointment and were escorted to the offices of a heavily built Russian woman, who introduced herself as the person Dorothy was to interview. To our surprise, all the workers were old-school communists; Iran was allowing them to operate the plant because of their "fishing skills and equipment." Accompanied by an interpreter, the amiable general manager conducted us on a tour of the factory, beginning with the inlet pond, where sturgeon were fed after being diverted from traps placed in the Caspian.

The manager told us that because the sturgeon were spawned in the northern sector of the Caspian but flourished in the warmer waters of the southern portion, close to the Iranian coast, Moscow insisted that Russia had legitimate claims on the caviar output. When we finally left the processing plant, Dorothy was handed a kilo of caviar that cost her $1.60, and the taxi driver was given a four-foot whole sturgeon packed in ice that could barely be squeezed into the trunk of the car. After sampling caviar for nearly a week in her hotel room, Dorothy virtually lost her taste for it. Her enthusiasm for it has never returned.

Lebanon

We left Iran with a sigh of relief. The atmosphere had been tense, and we were sure that sooner or later it would erupt into violence. Our next stop was Beirut, the main objective of my assignment. We were met by a UN representative, who immediately advised us that political conditions were only slightly more stable than in Iran. Bitter feelings between Muslims and Christians were festering, although the UN had arranged a temporary peace settlement (which would last only until the 1975–76 civil war). To demonstrate the unsettled conditions — as a result of which banking operations were on the verge of governmental intervention — our UN guide made a detour on the way to the Phoenicia Hotel to show us the demarcation line that separated the Muslim and Christian sectors. Because both groups were reluctant to leave their respective neighborhoods, about forty new branch banks had been established; several of them were accused of operating illegally. The finance minister was warning that he might have to shut down all banks and was proposing a ten-year moratorium on new banking institutions.

When the UN was called in to help bring the banking industry out of the doldrums, it preferred an American to assist Lebanon because of the enormous prestige the American University of Beirut enjoyed among the Lebanese. At that time it was the largest American overseas university, with an American faculty of the highest caliber. With an absence of exchange controls, unrestricted repatriation of foreign investment and earnings, bank secrecy, and customs-free movement of goods in eight trade zones that were ranked among the most modern and spacious in the world, the Lebanese economy had been thriving for decades. However, these good times were beginning to dissipate as a result of the brewing civil war between Muslims and Christians.

Despite the animosity between Muslims and Christians, American tourists were still welcomed to a large extent. But after we visited the Roman ruins at Baalbek, our taxi was halted by an unruly crowd outside the ruins. Fortunately, we were escorted safely through the mob. On another occasion, we were invited to the famous Casino du Labun, where Egypt's president Gamal Abdel Nasser had allowed his favorite personal belly dancer to present a special performance for a single night as a gesture of goodwill to Lebanon.

Jordan

In the mid-1980s, Jordan was plagued with severe economic problems, including skyrocketing food and fuel costs, which triggered riots throughout the country and forced the prime minister to resign. Jordan could not turn to Egypt, its traditional supporter, since King Hussein had vehemently opposed the Camp David Accords. His government was in dire need of aid. At that time, he still would not relinquish his claims to the West Bank (he finally did so in 1988). To make matters worse, Saudi Arabia and other Arab countries were ganging up on him. With the Carter administration being attacked by anti-Israeli elements because of America's past history of tilting toward excessive aid to Israel, the White House was ready to come to Jordan's assistance.

King Hussein's growing prestige among American politicians prompted U.S. AID to consider raising financial help for him. So when Sidney Schachter, the director of the World Trade Institute (U.S. AID's New York associate for foreign trade), learned that I was leaving for an assignment on Cyprus, he suggested I make a two-hour flight to Jordan to gather information for a potential relief evaluation.

It was only a matter of time before the U.S. Congress, with Carter's blessing, increased its financial allocations to Jordan. However, large amounts of aid from Iraq, Saudi Arabia, and several Western sources also helped Jordan develop various infrastructure projects, including its transportation network. Eventually, Jordan opened four FTZs. One of them, the Aqaba customs-free area on the Gulf of Aqaba, established in 1973, has mushroomed into one of the Middle East's most important entrepôts. It played a pivotal role in the war between Iran and Iraq.

There had been only "minor incidents" of American travelers in Jordan being targeted. Even so, we had been advised not to leave our hotel in Amman without a government aide to accompany us. We were fortunate, then, to be assigned a well-informed Jordanian guide from the Department of Tourism, who made sure we visited Jarash, twenty miles north of Amman. Jarash is one of the most beautifully preserved Greco-Roman cities in the world and has a Triumphal Arch erected in A.D. 129 to welcome Emperor Hadrian as well as an impressive Temple of Artemis with a magnificent stairway and columns.

At Petra, the "rose-red city, half as old as time," also known as the "Lost City of Stone," our guide tried to unravel for us some of the secrets hidden behind the narrow gorge of the Sic, through which we were transported on donkeys. Before passing through the cleft in the dark rocks, we encountered dozens of nuns from around the world riding their mules sidesaddle in their traditional habits. Suddenly, we glimpsed the noble facade of El Kharzmah, the sublime site of the Treasury of Petra, standing erect in the sunshine and carved with delicate precision into the sandstone face of the mountain. Before returning to Amman after an excellent lunch in a cave, our guide, "as a bonus from the government," surprised us with a winding road trip up to the peak of Mount Nebo (near Mount Pisgah), from which Moses viewed the Promised Land before his death and where we had a clear view of the Dead Sea in the distance.

In my discussions with various ministry officials—from communications, economics, and finance and customs—I was struck by their awareness of the dangers of Islamic fundamentalism. Terrorism had not yet become an outgrowth of Islamic doctrine, but the king and his ministers were already condemning radical Islamic elements as impeding the economic and political development not just of Jordan but also of the world.

These officials pointedly avoided mentioning Queen Noor, King Hussein's fourth wife, who was an American, the daughter of a former president of Pan Am. Noor's anti-Semitism was well known in the government's inner circles but was being cloaked on the king's strict orders. In her best-selling autobiography, *Leap of Faith*, she explicitly attacked Israel, Zionism, and Jews in general. "One fact is indisputable," she wrote. "Israel struck the first blow" in the 1967 war. She complained of "Jewish domination of banking, business and media," and she dismissed the rumor that her husband was on "the CIA payroll for decades," even though Jimmy Carter is said to have revealed this fact.

In the early 1990s, Jordan's support for Iraq became a major embarrassment and resulted in the complete cutoff of aid to Jordan during and after the Iraqi invasion of Kuwait and the Gulf War that followed. Following a lengthy period of isolation, Jordan's support for the peace process and its signing of an accord with Israel led the United States to sign an agreement with Jordan in 1995 that wrote off $420 million of that country's debt to the United States. Relieved of this burden, Jordan has been able to apply the funds to much needed infrastructural upgrading. Over the same period, Jordan and Egypt signed a pact aimed at creating an FTZ for the two countries. Financial assistance from Saudi Arabia and Kuwait, which amounted to as much as $600 million in 1983, has been reactivated. Remittances from Jordanian workers abroad and earnings from tourists exceed $1.5 billion annually.

Fortunately for the West, the present monarch, the popular King Abdullah, who ascended the throne on his father's death, is less domineering and more open and informed than Hussein. At the World Economic Forum in Jordan in 2003, the new king encouraged Israeli and Palestinian delegates to carry on friendly and constructive discussions about Arab-Israeli reconciliation.

Abdullah also arranged Jordan's admission to the World Trade Organization and ratified agreements to establish a free trade area with the United States, the European Union, the European Free Trade Association countries, and sixteen Arab countries. He has also worked for national administrative reform, government transparency and accountability, the advancement of civil liberties, and legislation guaranteeing women a full role in Jordan's political, social, and economic life.

United Arab Emirates

As one of the seven federated sheikhdoms of the United Arab Emirates, Dubai already had one of the world's three largest customs-free shops by sales volume. In the mid-1980s at New York's Roosevelt Hotel I met with a delegation of six sheikhs from Dubai, each representing a different government department. This unusual session had been arranged by the marketing vice president of Sea-Land Service, Inc., of New York, the largest investor in the Port of Dubai, with the help of Dubai's New York PR firm, Zatt International. Dubai International Airport's retail shops were important to the sheikhdom's economy; their sales exceeded $10 billion in 2005, which was 48 percent of the entire world's sales in airport shops. (London's Heathrow Airport and Singapore's Changi Airport were the next largest airports by sales volume.)

The head sheikh of Dubai, Maktumbin Reshid al-Maktum, was fully aware of the rising importance of FTZs around the world. As Dubai's ruler, he had declared that the emirate's objective was to raise the status of the relatively new zone at Jebel Ali, which was established in 1980, and make it the "most dominant in the Middle East." The sheikhdom's leader had authorized the construction of Jebel Ali and was determined to put all his resources into making it a success. The mission explained that it had come to New York to learn from my experience as a U.S. AID adviser for the World Trade Institute. Instead of arranging for me to come to Dubai City, the group's chairman indicated they would prefer to visit and inspect zones in New York, New Jersey, and New England. This trip was arranged.

Dubai has long been a commercial entrepôt and smuggling center—at one time it was known as the "Pirate Coast." It was the only emirate to have enjoyed prosperity before oil was discovered in the United Arab Emirates in 1958. Under a laissez-faire trade policy, Dubai today earns about $3 billion annually from trading activities; the reexport of gold, watches, and cigarettes plays a major part in this trade. In fact, its gold shop at the Dubai Duty Free section of the airport is a dynamic display of the precious metal said to be without compare in the Middle East. At present, Dubai handles two-thirds of the United Arab Emirate's imports.

Altogether, some seven hundred companies from more than thirty countries operate in the Jebel Ali zone. The port of Jebel, twenty-one miles from Dubai

City, has emerged as a major industrial city on the Persian Gulf. As the most resourceful of the emirates, Dubai is enjoying a tourism boom; so many visitors are arriving from other Middle Eastern countries and Western Europe that the emirate is running out of beach space. To solve this problem, the emirate is reclaiming land from the Persian Gulf in the form of islands shaped like palm trees. The first island, scheduled to open in 2006, will have forty-nine hotels and more than four thousand luxury homes and apartments.

Dubai is also constructing an ambitious new Dubai International Finance Center (DIFC), which will contain a stock exchange and more than a dozen office buildings suitable for occupancy by financial institutions. According to the DIFC's chief operating officer, "the center will be the wholesale marketplace where the deals are arranged." It will have an interbank system and a reinsurance market that will "challenge Bermuda's dominance in the field." Meanwhile, the chief sheikh's invitation to me to view the realization of his dream has yet to come true.

✻ 12 ✻

African Maelstrom

South Africa

$\mathcal{M}$Y FIRST DIRECT CONTACT with an African nation seeking economic assistance came in 1962 when, as research director of the Foreign Credit Insurance Association, I returned to my office and there found a tall, well-groomed man sprawled out on a chair with his long legs using my desk as a footstool. Not at all embarrassed, he told me: "I'm Harry Guggenheim, chairman of the board of the South African Export Insurance Corporation." Of course, he did not have to add that he also was chairman and president of the giant De Beers Mining combine, the world's largest diamond producer. Moreover, the name was well known in my family circles, since a cousin had married a "South African Guggenheim." Yes, this was the King of Diamonds in person.

He was calling on me at the suggestion of Harry Roundtree, marketing vice president for Eximbank, which was a 50 percent shareholder in the FCIA. Guggenheim had gone to Washington to learn more about export credit insurance coverage; the South African counterpart was encountering difficulties staying out of the red. Eximbank believed that the South African export insurance unit should be familiar with the inner workings of the American system and that I could be of more help to Guggenheim than the bank, since the FCIA was involved in the day-to-day operations. It developed from our discussion that the South African export insurance system leaned heavily toward commercial credit coverage, whereas the relatively few exporters relying on insurance for payment of shipments were more concerned about the absence of sound political risk coverage. The South African users were reluctant to buy political insurance because the cost of premiums was high relative to most of the other countries that were members of the Berne Union.

When we visited South Africa for the first time in 1970 at the invitation of the Department of Information and South African Airways, I was pleased to note that several of our recommendations had been adopted and that the nation's export insurance system was back on the profit side. Our trip had been arranged by Otto Adendorf, director of the government's Information Office in New York, who later headed the Department of Information in Pretoria, and by Reginald Brett, the American general manager of South African Airways.

Both these gentlemen were always a pleasure to be around and were intent on showing us that South Africa was well aware of the criticisms its apartheid policy was generating in the UN and around the world. They insisted that their government and individual white South Africans were trying to mend their practices. More than once it was pointed out to us that South Africa was in "the same situation as the United States in Civil War days. . . . Just give us time!" We were often reminded that it had taken America a century to "grant freedom to all its peoples." This was the message we were asked to carry back to the readers of our publications and to the business community in general, and I did discuss it in many speeches at various meetings and conferences around the United States.

In my round-table discussions at monthly meetings of the Motor and Equipment Manufacturers Association, the Overseas Automotive Club, the International Executives Association, and the Foreign Credit Interchange Bureau—on all of which I served officially as their international trade consultant over a period of thirty years—I found a surprisingly positive reception for my message. Almost all my listeners, representing vice presidents of international operations, combination export managers, and foreign credit officers associated with major multinationals, were eager to see South Africa adopt an integration scheme as soon as possible.

Five years later, in 1975, we made our second visit to South Africa, again at the request of that country's Communications Ministry, headed by J. De Villiers, and with the support of the UN and U.S. AID's subcontractor, the World Trade Institute. These two institutions hoped to find ways to counter the rapid decline in foreign investment and trade, which was a consequence of rising protests over companies doing business with South Africa. Growing disapproval of the South African apartheid laws, whereby the whites controlled the economy but nonwhites were 75 percent of the workforce, had led to the withdrawal of investments by EU members, Japan, and the United States and inevitably the adoption of sanctions. In the United States, dozens of universities and labor organizations were staging strong protests against companies operating in South Africa and demanding that shareholders of these firms unload their holdings unless the country integrated the Afrikaners and the blacks.

Simultaneously, South African black people were being murdered as violent protests against apartheid erupted throughout the country. To make matters worse, Prime Minister Balthazar Johannes Vorster, successor to the tough-minded Nationalist H. F. Verwoerd after the latter was assassinated by a discontented white government employee in 1966, had sent South African forces into Angola in an attempt to subdue the mounting opposition to whites in exile there. Vorster, however, had the foresight to act in a conciliatory manner by starting a dialogue on racial and other issues with neighboring black nations.

When we returned for our second visit in 1975, it was a revelation to us to observe the many improvements in the everyday lives of nonwhites. Integration was finally making progress; everywhere we went we saw Afrikaners mixing with nonwhites with little apparent fanfare. In 1970 we had visited the Cape of Good Hope, where we marveled at the site of the Atlantic and Indian Oceans clashing together; the Kruger, Hluhluwe, Umfolozi, and Cape of Good Hope game reserves; and the diamond mines at Kimberley. In all these places, nonwhites had appeared only as laborers and had kept an arm-length's distance from tourists, business visitors, and the press.

In 1975, the streets were filled with both nonwhites and Afrikaners moving about together. When we interviewed the manager of the lavish Carlton Hotel jewelry shop—shortly after Richard Burton purchased South Africa's second-largest diamond there as an engagement ring for Elizabeth Taylor—we recalled that during our first visit nonwhites had been forbidden to enter this French-owned hotel. Now we had to weave our way slowly through a mixed crowd. We noted a similar change during our visit to South Africa's most luxurious game resort at Mala Mala: now there were nonwhite office staff and guides. Five years earlier there had been none.

De Villiers arranged for us to take a two-day South African Railway bus journey along the historic "Garden Route" from Cape Town to Port Elizabeth. On our first overnight stop, we were assigned to a hotel deep in the woods where on the grounds was the world's smallest Barclay bank, the size of an outhouse. We were pleased to see mixed swimmers on the beach at Pletenberg Bay, one of South Africa's most popular resort hotels. It was said to be the first integration experiment of this nature.

During this same bus journey along 180 miles of scenic coastline, Dorothy and I sat in two front seats, annotating some two hundred of the twelve hundred

League of Nations and UN tax treaties that we were under pressure to complete for an Oceana Publications deadline. They would be published as a UN-sanctioned work: *International Tax Treaties of All Nations*. Today, this monumental undertaking consists of three thousand treaties with authors' annotations, available on Oceana's Web site.

We found that a good start had been made toward peaceable integration by 1975. But it was a far cry from the racial freedom sought by both the UN and the United States. Sporadic violence continued, and fear pervaded white neighborhoods. One day in Johannesburg we were walking into the park across from the President Hotel—the first integrated hotel in the city—to visit a museum when we had to turn back because of the stir created by nonwhites, as if we had no right to enter their sanctuary. When we mentioned this incident to the hotel concierge, he apologized for not warning us in advance. Much the same thing happened at the Nelson House Hotel in Cape Town: we were advised to avoid the beautiful walkway through the park that led to the city center. Five years earlier, we had made that same walk and had seen no signs of disturbance. Another example of the uneasy life: the trains we took between Johannesburg to Pretoria, where our foreign investment and export insurance discussions took place, avoided stopping in Soweto, the scene of strong racial protests and many murders soon after we left South Africa.

Besides appraising the foreign investment crisis that was staining the South African economy, we were there in 1975 to fulfill a request made to the U.S. Commerce Department that had originated with Eximbank. Fidel Castro, during his drive toward Havana in 1959, had sequestered all business properties his armed forces came across. One of the valuable properties he took over was a diamond-mining venture in the west of the island. Its owner and operator, Rafael Gonsalves, was now a commission diamond agent in New York. Gonsalves was aware of my past association with Harry Guggenheim of De Beers. Washington advised Gonsalves to seek my help in arranging for his New York diamond dealer, Lazarus and Company, to be invited to one of De Beers's closed-shop diamond sightings, which were held periodically in London. De Beers controlled the world's distribution of diamonds, which meant it had the sole right to select the handful of traders from around the world to attend the sightings.

Guggenheim introduced me to Robert Kelley, overseas vice president of De Beers, who was in charge of the London sightings. Through him I arranged for Gonsalves to be invited to a sighting in London. Each sighting purchase contains a number of stones; some are of the best available cuts, others are of lower grade.

For this reason Gonsalves refused to contract for the package placed in front of him; his firm dealt only in high-grade diamonds. Needless to say, this action did not please the auctioneers. Soon after, Gonsalves asked for a second chance at the next sighting. He was turned down once and for all.

In 1988, with UN sanctions taking a heavy toll on South Africa's already sinking economy, I received a cable from Pic Botha, the foreign minister (no relation to the controversial Prime Minister Pieter Botha), asking me to prepare recommendations for an FTZ in the still dependent territory of Namibia. The Johannesburg Bankers Association wanted to show the world that the South African business community was hopeful the UN and other nations would soon end the embargo. Bankers hoped that an FTZ in Namibia would help convince South Africa's critics that the business sector very much wanted to help Namibia.

I had known Pic Botha since the 1970s, when we met at the South African Independence Day celebrations in New York. At the annual dinner arranged by the South African consulate, he had enjoyed sharing the dance floor with Dorothy. The two of us and Guggenheim had casually discussed the benefits that an FTZ could bring to South Africa.

After considering the political implications with UNIDO and U.S. AID, and after several cables from the Johannesburg Bankers Association, I signed an agreement to meet their representative in Windhoek, Namibia's capital. There I would prepare detailed recommendations for an FTZ in Namibia. But after all the arrangements had been made, and after I had received plane tickets from the bankers association, forty-eight hours before departure, I received a cable canceling the visit with no explanation given.

Sometime later, I heard from government officials that the cancellation had been necessary because the prime minister was at that moment negotiating with the UN for Namibia's independence, which followed a few months later, in 1990. The Johannesburg Bankers Association had been advised by Pretoria to delay this sort of assistance to Namibia since it might interfere with the negotiations, which were in the final stages. In 1995, Namibia established a successful FTZ at Walvis Bay, without the guidance of the Johannesburg Bankers Association.

It should be noted that not until Nelson Mandela was elected president in 1994 and the UN lifted its embargo on South Africa did foreign investment begin trickling back into the country. Even then, the inflow of private capital was almost stagnant until the government introduced these reforms: it banned the dual-currency system allowing South African and British exchange, devalued the rand, adopted rigid exchange controls, removed import surcharges, and improvised a set of foreign investment inducements reducing tax rates. Since September 1993 the number of American companies with employees or investments in South Africa has jumped by 40 percent, to more than two thousand.

Rhodesia

In the 1970s I was well aware of Washington's stand against Rhodesia's prime minister, Ian Smith, whose enmity toward the predominantly African population closed the door to any UN or U.S. AID assistance. Even so, we took a three-day break to visit his country (later renamed Zimbabwe). The South African Department of Information had suggested that we see for ourselves what total suppression of individuals can do to an economy.

At the time, 98 percent of Rhodesians were African. Almost all of them—the ones who had jobs—were farm laborers. Nearly 100 percent of the prospering agricultural industry was controlled by two hundred thousand whites.

Starvation is now widespread in the country, whereas in 1970 the African families we encountered in their thatch huts were content with their lives even though they hated Smith. The prime minister knew his time was short. Pressure, from the UN and neighboring states, was building daily for him to resign. In an effort to maintain his harsh regime, he made it compulsory for hotels and businesses to display large photos of him. Woe to the person who tried to disfigure or remove them, since his military police would appear instantly.

Smith's relentless efforts to portray himself as a friend of the people did not make much headway with the average African. Yet uprisings were still rare, since the military police maintained a sharp vigil. As an example, when we approached the great suspension bridge over the Zambezi River and Kariba Gorge separating Zimbabwe from Zambia in order to view Victoria Falls, one of the world's greatest wonders, our entry was blocked by the security police until they were certain we were not insurgents. At the halfway point on the bridge marking the border of the two countries, when Dorothy took one step into Zambia, that country's guards immediately rushed from their post on the Zambian side to warn her of the violation.

When we returned to the United States and I reported my findings on the Rhodesian political and economic scene to U.S. AID, there was no lifting of eyebrows. Washington's intelligence unit already had warned the State Department that the situation in Rhodesia was precarious. The hands-off policy of the Americans was an important element in the changes that followed when British rule ended in April 1980. At that point Rhodesia became an independent nation and changed its name to Zimbabwe.

Robert Mugabe was elected Zimbabwe's president after a coalition of the political parties agreed on a national referendum. Twenty-five years later, he is still president, and Zimbabwe is in chaos, with inflation at 600 percent and accelerating. Because of Mugabe's unacceptable record of human rights abuses, Zimbabwe has been expelled from the British Commonwealth.

In recent years, President Mugabe has been carrying out a policy of expropriating farms from their white owners and distributing them to Africans, and only 30 percent of the original farms are still operating. Much of the once rich agricultural nation has been transformed into a wasteland. The resulting cut in production causing a food shortage is at the root of the present unemployment problem, the worst the country has ever faced.

Egypt

Soon after President Richard Nixon made a surprise visit to Egypt in June 1974 in an effort to convince Egyptian president Anwar el-Sadat to commence negotiations with Israel, he called on the U.S. Congress to fund $250 million in financial aid for Egypt. Nixon's promise to increase financial aid to Egypt was part of his plan to woo that country after Sadat had resentfully alluded to America's policy of favoring Israel. In Congress, plans to expedite a large financial package for Egypt broke down over questions about how the $250 million should be spent.

The State Department asked the World Trade Institute to make an inspection of Egypt and prepare a preliminary report. The logical approach for Egypt to take was to expand its export markets by taking advantage of its location. Egypt is on the Mediterranean coast, and the Suez Canal is on its territory; presumably, then, there was potential for Egypt to establish one or more FTZs. As the institute's specialist in customs-free areas, I arrived in Cairo with several letters of introduction to Egyptian government officials.

At the suggestion of the U.S. State Department, I called first on Osman Osman, the construction minister, who was also Sadat's brother-in-law. According to the State Department, he was the second most powerful man in Egypt. Tersely, he told me he knew nothing about FTZs. He steered me to the economics minister, Abdul Kaissony, who in turn shunted me off to other ministries, including the Industry Ministry, headed by Aziz Siddy, and the Departments of

Ports and Transportation. I obtained not a single lead; no one was showing any interest.

In desperation, I turned to the U.S. Embassy in Cairo, which likewise did not have any knowledge of FTZs. By a stroke of luck, the American "roving ambassador" to the Middle East, Donald Hetherington, happened to be at the embassy at the very same time I was there. As soon as I was introduced to him, he showed an interest and told me that FTZs were worth looking at. His subsequent recommendations to Washington opened an entirely new approach in future economic and trade relations with Egypt.

Although Congress did approve the $250 million appropriation for Egypt, Cairo never asked the World Trade Institute to submit a plan for FTZs. Instead, the UN, without the usual bidding procedure, assumed control of the project. It allocated $96 million to the Shannon Industrial Development Corporation in Ireland to prepare a study and eventually supervise construction and operation of six zones in Egypt: Nasr City, Alexandria (also known as Al Ameria), Port Said, Suez, Adabia, and Ismailia.

At that time the Shannon Industrial Development Authority was managed by Brendan O'Regan, a determined politician turned entrepreneur with a long list of ventures under his command. He negotiated directly with Sadat. From the start it was not a friendly relationship; it ended four years later after Sadat, who was not as charismatic as his predecessor, Nasser, clashed with O'Regan for the last time over the lagging operations of Egypt's six FTZs. As reported by the UN representative in Cairo, Sadat almost had to have O'Regan dragged from his office.

Sadat, a "German agent" during World War II, had been imprisoned by the British but escaped after two years. In 1946 he was jailed again for participating in terrorist acts leading up to the bloodless coup that deposed King Farouk. Later, he became leader of the National Union, Egypt's only political party, and president of the National Assembly. Nasser appointed him vice president. On Nasser's death in 1970, he succeeded to the presidency and established himself as Egypt's strongman.

Sadat was determined to place the six FTZs in the profit column and to make them important entrepôts in the Middle East. To further these ends, he again called in the UN for advice. After reviewing the usual four or five curricula vitae of possible candidates presented by the UN Development Programme—a mandatory procedure—he personally chose me to visit Egypt as soon as possible.

As required, I stopped first in Vienna for a briefing on the Egyptian political scene. It included a handout to read detailing Egyptian customs and practices. At a luncheon arranged by the UN representative in Vienna handling Egyptian affairs, it was difficult for me to hear any of his advice. In the gigantic UN cafeteria, more than a thousand staffers from 178 nations were shouting in some three dozen languages at once and drowning out all other conversation.

By this time Sadat had rushed through a presidential decree called the Incorporation for Joint Ventures Law no. 43, which established the General Authority for Arab and Foreign Investment and Free Zones.

Dorothy and I arrived at the Cairo airport at eight in the morning on Sunday, October 4, 1981. We were welcomed by the UN representative, who introduced us to our guide for the month's assignment, Colonel Mostafa Abdel Fattah Mohammed, and Ali, our driver. Without any small talk, we were quickly advised that the UN office had made an appointment for me at the Nasr City FTZ for two o'clock that very day—a working day in Egypt, where Friday is the Holy Day. While reviewing a summary of the Nasr City Zone operation, I had immediately discerned several flaws in the administration that had been established by the Shannon team, which was headed by Paul Quigley, one of Europe's top trade zone specialists.

As we left the meeting, the local UN representative instructed Colonel Mohammed, the economic research officer of the Free Zones Sector, to drive past the adjacent parade grounds to the zone area, near the administration building. He wanted to show me the elaborate platform and huge bleacher capacity for Tuesday's October 6 celebration of Israel's withdrawal in the 1973 war from a strip of Sinai desert land bordering Egypt.

At eight on Monday morning, we found Colonel Mohammed and Ali waiting to drive us to Ismailia, 120 miles east of Cairo. We were going to inspect the site of a new FTZ, which the Shannon group had recently staked out. As we drove for three hours over the sunbaked desert, Mohammed proudly pointed out the new border along the highway. Israeli military forces had been camped there until the Egyptian troops "evicted them" during the Yom Kippur War of 1973.

Ismailia turned out to be a desolate expanse of land enclosed by brick walls. After examining the map and site, I explained that seepage would be a major problem. To solve it would require additional funds not accounted for in the construction budget; the project would be delayed as a result. Quick development of the Ismailia zone was a pet project of Sadat. It was going to require a new airport, which would be built beside existing military runways at Abou Sebur, 12.5 miles from the zone. Sadat's original plan called for this airport to be the largest not only in Egypt but also in the entire Middle East.

The manager of the Ismailia FTZ had arranged a luncheon for us at his club, where alcohol was prohibited. The entire staff stood around our table staring at us as if we were Western enemies. Our new companion insisted on driving us 30 miles south toward Suez to see Egypt's beach resort at Kehl as-Suways. As we passed two more of Sadat's palaces, of nine spotted around the country, Dorothy whispered in my ear: "This looks like another Iran." Sadat's palaces, most of them inherited from King Farouk and his successor, General Nasser, could easily compete with those of the shah of Iran, who had fled his country in 1979.

Sadat was aware of the growing opposition to his regime among Muslim fundamentalists. He was certain he could deal with the turbulent atmosphere through political negotiations, without resorting to strong-arm tactics.

Our host, Mohammed, was not one to hide his feelings, and he often expressed disapproval of Sadat's regime. He told us his government was packed with too many "loose Islamics" and openly praised Hitler, declaring that he was his "favorite leader" and that Egypt should adopt the führer's fascist style of rule. This talk troubled us greatly, but the UN more than once had reminded me to avoid political arguments with our hosts.

Our schedule next called for us to leave the next day for the Al Ameria zone at Alexandria, 150 miles north of Cairo. When Mohammed and Ali did not appear, we assumed something must be wrong. A little later, all the radio stations were taken over by mullahs leading the seventeen million Egyptians in prayer. Not until sundown, at six, were the Egyptian people told through official news broadcasts that their president had been assassinated by a group of Islamic fundamentalists. Three hours later, Hosni Mubarak, who had assumed the presidency, told how the tragedy had occurred: several Islamic soldiers while parading past Sadat had broken ranks to spray his viewing platform with gunfire. The president, some of his aides, and several foreign emissaries had been killed.

At that moment pandemonium erupted throughout Cairo. Thousands of Egyptians flooded the streets to vent themselves, after years of stifling their anger at the Sadat government. Americans and other Westerners had viewed Sadat as a peacemaker; the average Egyptian, however, had detested him for failing to keep his promises, especially to build more housing. It was not unusual for two or three families to be living in one home or apartment with little space for privacy. Their most common complaint, which we heard several times, was that "Camp

David promised us a better life and a home for everyone." At the time of Nixon's visit in 1974 there had been seven million people in Cairo. Now, seven years later, there were eleven million, conditions were worse, and many more Egyptians were homeless and starving. In addition, most Egyptians had disapproved of Sadat's peace overtures with Israel and denounced him for going to Israel to negotiate an agreement.

The jubilation in Cairo at Sadat's death was orderly, although there was dancing in the streets. However, in several small cities and rural areas the news touched off riots. Military police had to be called out to prevent anarchy. From the balcony of our room at the Hilton, which faced the Nile, we watched long lines of Egyptians, many of whom were cramped in their homes with little privacy, waiting all night to rent rowboats to celebrate his death with their wives. The Egyptian government's own statistics show that more Egyptian newborns were registered nine months after October 6, 1981, than at any other time in the nation's history.

To prevent a revolution by Islamic fundamentalists, Mubarak almost immediately declared a tight curfew. Only a handful of people were permitted on the streets without passes or approved IDs. Travel by air or rail was prohibited, and no incoming or outgoing telephone calls or wireless transmissions to or from Egypt were permitted.

The Nile Hilton's general manager could not leave his holiday retreat on the Red Sea for a week because he did not have his passport with him. Dorothy was able to go to the nearby Sheraton for an appointment only after the Hilton's concierge had arranged it with the military police. Her return from the Sheraton prompted a minor disturbance at the Hilton entrance when a "listed" taxi driver gave her the wrong change in Egyptian pounds. When the Hilton doorman learned about it, he called in the military police, who sternly retrieved the correct change for her.

The large majority of Westerners were saddened by the assassination of Sadat; almost all the Muslim countries were quick to show their joy. By offering peace to Israel, Sadat had double-crossed them, and they responded by praising his assassins. Khomeini, the newly installed fundamentalist leader of Iran, declared that "a true son of Islam has acted to rid us of the apostate pharaoh." One of his first acts in 1979 had been to sever all relations with Egypt as "punishment" for the peace agreement with Israel. Now he named a fashionable street in his capital after Khalid Almad Showqi al-Islambouli, the Egyptian army lieutenant who murdered Sadat.

The day after Sadat's murder, we were supposed to attend a meeting two blocks away, at Cairo's other Hilton, which was still under construction. During curfew hours we were hostages in our own hotel. We made that meeting only because we had a military police escort. Journalists from all over the world were flooding the city by then to cover Sadat's funeral. On a still unfinished elevator we ran into Tom Brokaw, the NBC anchor, who had just flown in. Tom told us about the difficulties he and all other journalists were having getting through Egyptian security.

Because moving around the country was so risky and the curfew was so strict, the UN representative in Cairo had advised us to shelve our assignment temporarily and to "remain at the Hilton enjoying the warm sun." Ten days after the assassination, Colonel Mohammed and our driver appeared at our hotel to take us to Alexandria, Egypt's second-largest city. There I would evaluate the special economic zone at Al Ameria.

When we arrived at King Farouk's old stamping ground, we were immediately impressed with the laid-back attitude of Alexandrians, which contrasted with the commercial hustle of the wealthy business executives in Cairo, who were the envy of the millions of underprivileged Egyptians. In Alexandria, the people stared at us everywhere we went. When we stopped briefly on the outskirts of the city to view Cleopatra's Needle, Colonel Mohammed and Ali had to move quickly to stop the many guards from shaking hands with us.

At the Al Ameria zone, the general manager gave us a tour of a textile factory that employed eight hundred women. Many of them were well below the age limit set by world labor standards, and a high proportion were suffering damage to their eyesight because of the twelve-hour shifts required of them to thread needles. Some of them stopped working their vintage sewing machines to stare at Dorothy. Madame Nadia, the marketing manager, told us that these workers, who had never seen a woman in Western clothes, wondered how Dorothy could move in them; their traditional loose-fitting cloth robes allowed much more freedom.

Al Ameria was very likely to become the most productive of Egypt's six FTZs. It was ideally positioned beside an important Mediterranean port, had plenty of room to expand, abutted a railway, and was near three hundred million European consumers. Also, the zone had an excellent staff of economic researchers.

My Egyptian assignment required two more trips on successive days to visit the Port Said and Suez zones on the blazing-hot Sinai Peninsula. As a storage and distribution center, the Port Said zone was becoming an important foreign exchange earner. It was helping offset the loss of foreign exchange that had resulted when tourists and sailors had stopped visiting the city in large numbers after sales of alcohol were restricted. However, the Port Said zone never produced many export goods of the sort that could absorb some of the unemployed. At this zone, like the one at Suez, too many firms were importing consumer goods for distribution in Egypt. Some of them even imported items from FTZs in other countries; they filled their storage areas with these products and then supplied distributors in Egypt instead of reexporting them to other countries. Also, there was no land available for expansion at the Suez zone because the entire area had been assigned to importers.

To my great surprise, I found that most of the merchandise Suez was reexporting had originated in the world's largest zone (based on number of employees)—the FTZ at Kao-hsiung in Taiwan. As a result, the Suez zone was crowded with firms that were providing little income for the zone operators. I would soon recommend that Suez's second site under development, at Adabiya, be devoted exclusively to export processing, which was eventually done. In the end, my recommendations for improving Egypt's FTZs were so extensive that my UN colleagues in Vienna and New York could hardly believe that the original team—the one from Shannon—had overlooked such basic elements.

Among them, it was essential to end the widespread theft and corruption in the zones. This enormous abuse continued until February 2005, when Mubarak finally got tough with customs operations. His prime minister, Ahmed Nazif, won him over with a single stroke. To avoid a lengthy debate in parliament, Prime Minister Nazif convinced Mubarak to implement a presidential decree that eliminated tariffs so that the five thousand customs officers who were supposedly "enforcing" regulations no longer in existence lost their jobs. The customs officials learned about their firing through the media. According to Nazif, it was "a bypass operation," when he announced the surprise action with a "wry smile," as reported in the *Wall Street Journal*.

Today, Mubarak faces the "specter of a fundamentalist takeover," and his grip on the country is in jeopardy. Critics, who have protested by the thousands, want a new constitution that provides for a democratic election by the people rather than the present system of the nomination of the president by a parliament and approval by a referendum. Finally, after fifty years of one-party rule, in February 2005, Mubarak acceded to his opponents' demands and asked parliament to amend the constitution so that multiparty elections could choose a president.

Also, the zones lacked systems for recording and tracking incoming and outgoing shipments. In this regard, I arranged for a plan using the IBM inventory control system designed for American zones, the first of which had been installed at Philadelphia Zone no. 35.

Other significant suggestions contained in my Egyptian report related to an income allocation plan, greatly improved transportation infrastructure, and new laws on foreign investment incentives. Of the hundreds of millions of dollars that U.S. AID was granting Egypt, $23.5 million was allocated to FTZ development and to training those zones' personnel.

During the three-week curfew decreed by Mubarak, security was so tight that even emergency telephone calls into and out of Egypt were forbidden. Neither the UN nor my office in New York could reach me. Finally, on October 31, twenty-five days after the assassination, a call came through to me from London inviting us to present an address on FTZs at the upcoming International Tax Planning Association conference in Spain. The following day, upon returning to Vienna, according to a normal UN orientation procedure, we reported our findings to UNIDO's supervisory board of economists, who were familiar with the region. Our appearance this time drew unexpected attention. Because we were the first industrial economists back from Egypt since Sadat's death, we were asked to tape for the UN's records a chronological dossier of the events directly before, during, and after the assassination. The officers at the meeting were especially disturbed that our UN-selected guide, Colonel Mohammed, incessantly espoused Islamic fundamentalism. Clearly, they admitted, local UN representatives would have to scrutinize such people much more carefully before hiring them. Our interviewers in Vienna found it hard to believe that so many Egyptians hated Sadat even while the West was praising him for trying to make peace with Israel.

Morocco

When the U.S. State Department wanted to cultivate better relations with Morocco, in order to help King Hassan halt the spread of Islamic fundamentalism in his kingdom, it advised U.S. AID to launch a program to assist Morocco in attracting foreign investment. At the suggestion of the World Trade Institute, I made a second visit to that country. (The first had been a quick survey of the Tangier FTZ at the request of the Maltese.) This time the Moroccan ambassador to Washington instructed his consul general in New York to contact me, which he did. My first meeting was with R. H. Issirsi, director of the kingdom's Office for Industrial Development, also in New York. Because of the emergency of helping

Hassan fight his political adversaries without delay, it was decided not to make an official request for aid from the UN.

Soon after, in 1978, we went to Morocco. Our second visit was a disappointment. In fact, we found the Tangier zone had deteriorated so badly that the general manager dissuaded us from inspecting it when we arrived. His excuse was that, because he had no vehicle, we would have to inspect it on foot—this, on a humid day with a hundred-degree temperature. Tangier's brutal and constant heat made us wonder why Doris Duke, the tobacco heiress, maintained an elaborate home in the heart of the old quarter.

Tangier was a cosmopolitan city and, except for its FTZ, was thriving mainly because it is a gateway to the Mediterranean and only ten miles from Europe. Yet its zone had never lured any foreign manufacturers or processors. In fact, almost all the zone users were local distributors. (A second zone at Nador, on the Mediterranean coast near the Spanish enclave of Melilla, would be established in 1997 specifically as an export processing zone; it has yet to advance the government's foreign investment program.)

Despite encouragement from the economics minister, M. Hamed Doiwi, and the public works minister, Mohammed Bewhima, local authorities in Casablanca and Marrakech showed little interest in developing FTZs. A U.S. AID representative guided us around a potential site in Casablanca that would have required extensive land rehabilitation. Casablanca has one of the largest deepwater ports in Africa, and its well-developed infrastructure was already handling 63 percent of Morocco's freight.

The Marrakech airport was pointed out to me as a possible site for an FTZ. The inland city drew many tourists, which made for a thriving retail sector. Marrakech and Casablanca were driving Morocco's recent tourism boom, which was helping resurrect the economy after what the U.S. Commerce Department called "one of the worst droughts in over 35 years."

Moroccans are proud of their Berber heritage. From the end of the second millennium B.C. to the eighth century A.D., the Berber tribes had been a power in the region and had been in constant conflict with the Arabs. The mayor of Marrakech and his aides encouraged us to visit the Berber markets in the city. It was here that I turned down a Berber's offer "to trade my camel for your lady." I later learned that this gesture was not unusual.

The municipal authorities also recommended we visit the traditional Monday-morning grand market in the foothills of the Atlas Mountains. Entire Berber families trekked down from their villages to display and market their wares to tourists from around the globe.

Marrakech had become a popular ski destination for Europeans, and our guide suggested we take a winding mountain road for thirty miles beyond the Berber market to Oukaimeden, a large ski resort in the Upper Atlas.

As we approached the mountains we noticed a long black line slowly moving crossways down the mountain. At the bottom of the hill we encountered a battery of British Army ski troops, who had been packing down twelve inches of fresh powder snow. They told us they were stationed at Gibraltar and that they often practiced at Oukaimeden, the nearest place with sufficient snow for training. The heavy rain that had fallen on Marrakech the night before made for superb snow conditions here.

When our driver took us to the only hotel in the area, at the base of the slope, the manager told us he would not rent us skis without a substantial deposit. We rejected his request that we hand over Dorothy's engagement ring; finally, he accepted our watches and passports as security.

The next challenge was to find someone to start the lifts. At the desolate area five hundred yards from the hotel, our driver sounded his horn for fifteen minutes before two Moroccan guides appeared. After Dorothy spoke to them in French, the T-bar lifts began running. Our new friends insisted on coming with us, and for the entire day the four of us had the deep fresh powder to ourselves—impossible to experience on North America's crowded slopes.

After returning to our room at the Mamoulian hotel—where Winston Churchill spent many months following World War II painting landscapes—we looked out over an orange grove and beyond it at the setting sun reflecting on the mountains where we had skied, the same views that had entranced Churchill and that he put on canvas.

Our final two visits to Morocco, in the early and mid-1980s, were made during a time of struggle between secular modernizers and Islamic fundamentalists. The kingdom's "new economy"—a unique form of capitalism designed by King Hassan II himself and endorsed by the IMF—curbed inflation, slashed the fiscal deficit, and generated economic growth.

Hassan also attempted democratic reforms, a fragile experiment. His opponents claimed that his push for "unbridled capitalism" was widening the gulf between the wealthy minority and the impoverished majority. Burdened by a literacy rate of only 50 percent—30 percent in rural areas—his subjects grew restless, and in the end, the king was forced to revert to police-state tactics. During one of our visits to Rabat, the capital, our driver often had to stop frequently at roadblocks so we could show our IDs, especially in suburb and rural areas.

In order to visit another city, a driver had to appear before a local police court to secure permits. Before leaving Rabat for Ifram, in the Er Rif mountain range where Hassan had a secluded summer palace, and where the minister of tourism had arranged a conference for us, our driver stopped at the Rabat police station for a pass. After a forty-five-minute delay our passports were returned to us. Ifram, a small resort town where Hassan had an attractive ski area built for his pleasure, was scarcely known outside Morocco until 1983.

It was at Ifram that the king met Menachem Begin, the Israeli prime minister and Nobel Peace Prize recipient, who shared the honor with Anwar el-Sadat for the Camp David Accord efforts to negotiate a peace agreement. Hassan had also constructed a beautiful new highway for his personal use cut through the mountain range as a time-saving route from Ifram to Fez. Other travelers required special permits from the Rabat police, which had been arranged for us.

By 1985 the fundamentalists had made distressing headway with their claims that Western capitalism was benefiting only a few and that the kingdom was critically short of hospitals, schools, and roads.

The 1973 Investment Code revitalized the Tangier Commercial Free Zone established in 1967 and prepared the ground for other FTZs at Nador and Casablanca. Almost a decade later the revised 1982 Investment Code opened the way for foreign investors by allowing 100 percent capital ownership by overseas companies in all industries except mining, fisheries, and handicrafts. Yet American corporations remained skeptical. The Moroccan finance minister, Abdelatif Ghissassi, suggested that the skepticism was because "some American companies still regard Morocco as primarily a French preserve" owing to the close economic ties remaining between the two countries since independence. The Moroccan industry minister, Azeddline Guessons, later visited Juanita Kreps, the U.S. secretary of commerce, to review the commercial ties between Washington and Morocco.

My investigation for U.S. AID's subcontractor, the World Trade Institute, found that the Moroccan government was lax in approving foreign investment applications. For instance, the red tape in applying for an operation in the Tangier zone involved submitting an application to the Free Zone Commission, composed of the governor of Tangier, the zone director, and the ministers of public works, communications, finance, and industry. After each had scrutinized the many details requested from the prospective investor, several months passed—sometimes more than a year before a decision was handed down. It was also obvious to us that the king's tilt toward democracy was much less effective than he or the United States had hoped. The result was a retreat from the market revolution the king had sought as the Islamic challenge strengthened.

Moroccans were bursting with resentment at Hassan's market reforms. On one occasion we were leaving the compound of the American Consulate in Tangier after an enlightening interview with the consul, a Carter appointee. In a soft voice, the colonel who was guarding the gate expressed to us his distaste for his government, and spoke of the harm its economic policies were doing to poor Moroccans.

Soon after, the U.S. Commerce Department began promoting American-Moroccan relations, and American firms began investing heavily in Morocco. In 1777, Morocco had been the first country to recognize the United States of America, and Washington has never forgotten it. Morocco also signed a Treaty of Amity and Commerce with the United States in 1786; it was reaffirmed by the Treaty of 1836 and continues into the present.

King Hassan visited Washington, D.C., as a guest of President Clinton in 1995 and signed a new agreement to strengthen the pact between Morocco and the Overseas Private Investment Corporation. The White House then announced the Agreement on Trade and Investment to guide the economic relationship between the United States and Morocco.

After King Hassan died in 1999, his son ascended the throne as Mohammed VI. The new king renewed efforts to turn the country into a democracy; human rights were the cornerstone of this experiment. Not long after, his fundamentalist opponents retaliated with a wave of suicide bombings in Casablanca that killed thirty-three Moroccans. In a somber television address, the new king blamed the bombings on those people "who take advantage of democracy to sew seeds of ostracism, fanaticism and discord."

Tunisia

During the late 1960s I visited Tunisia at the request of UNIDO to lay out a program for an export credit insurance system. That country had a trading history going back for thousands of years, when it was the center of the Carthaginian empire, so it now needed little encouragement to expand its commercial sector. Under President Habib Bourguiba, Tunisia already offered customs exemptions for goods produced solely for export. Also, the government had set aside fourteen areas containing more than forty industrial zones as well as two economic free zones (at Zarzis and Bizerte). Its 1972 Investment Code offered foreign investors many concessions, including a total exemption on exports in the designated zone areas. However, American companies were hesitant to invest as long as European firms were flooding the country with imported goods and locally produced items made by their subsidiaries.

Earlier queries by U.S. AID and the IMF had found that American multinationals were reluctant to invest in Tunisia because they lacked familiarity with African customs and business practices. There was good potential for American companies to produce goods in Tunisia for the local market and for export to Europe and the African and Middle Eastern countries, but a system was required to protect them from losses.

When we arrived in Tunisia we had a pleasant surprise: the UNDP representative there was a former colleague, Lee Nehrt, a director of the World Trade Institute. At that time he was on temporary assignment as the Ford Foundation's economic adviser to the Tunisian Planning Ministry. Nehrt quickly alerted me to the delicate political situation: Bourguiba's pro-Western policies were being undermined by his country's strained relations with France over Algerian independence, which Tunisia supported. Bourguiba had been a national hero even before he became president, having succeeded in ousting several French officials from Tunisia. Despite student uprisings, a French naval attack on Bizerte, a Libyan invasion in the southern mining region, and several attempts on his life, Bourguiba would continue to promote modernization and economic growth until his government fell to a coalition led by Zine El Abidene Ben Ali.

Bourguiba was a leader of a caliber rarely found in Africa and took pride in being a strong and stable president. His efforts to bring American investors to Tunisia were continued by Ben Ali, who was also praised for cracking down on the nation's Islamist movement, which was spawning terrorists. However, President George H. W. Bush rebuked him for violating press freedoms. Ben Ali established an export credit insurance agency, the Tunisian Insurance Society—a private agency along the lines of the FCIA—rather than a public entity of the sort I had proposed. Tunisia's aggressive investment policy has lured more than one hundred leading American multinationals. The present success of American companies in Tunisia is a tribute to the policies Bourguiba established.

One of the highlights of our stop in Tunisia was a visit to the Bardo National Museum, renowned for its ancient mosaics. Set in a lovely garden, this nineteenth-century palace holds splendid artifacts ranging from the Carthaginian through the Arab-Islamic periods and includes one of the world's finest collections of Roman polychrome mosaics.

Kenya

In Tunisia, Bourguiba was practically worshiped by his subjects. By contrast, Daniel Arap Moi was regarded by most of Kenya's thirty million people as a tyrant. I arrived in Nairobi armed with letters of introduction from the commercial counselor of the Kenya Embassy in Washington, D.C., Michael Sergon; the executive director of the Kenya Tourist and Trade Office in New York, Peter K. Muiruri; and a director of UNIDO, and presented them to Kenya's planning minister, Robert Ouko.

The minister was a loyal Kenyan, but it was clear to me he had doubts about both the Kenyan economy and his boss, Arap Moi. He did tell me that his country had a stable economy "in spite of external shocks." At the time, in 1982, Kenya was showing little interest in creating an FTZ at its principal port, Mombasa. Arap Moi's predecessor, Jomo Kenyatta, had been one of Africa's great nationalist leaders. He had been imprisoned by the British for campaigning for land reform. When Kenya achieved independence in 1963, he became the new nation's first president. Unfortunately, his successor, Arap Moi, was a despot who suppressed opposition and imprisoned his political opponents. Protests in the late 1980s led the United States to withhold aid to Kenya. This embargo compelled Arap Moi to restore a multiparty system in 1991. However, the Americans never forgot that he had harbored several of Idi Amin's supporters after the fall of that Ugandan tyrant.

Arap Moi's political wars were hampering Kenya's economic progress, so in 1996 he began encouraging local businesses to shun the United States in favor of Japan. He also made radical changes to Kenya's liberal foreign investment policy, which had been established by Kenyatta, and decreed that Kenyans must hold 51 percent of shares in joint ventures. This move was aimed at placing Kenyans rather than foreigners in charge of the economy and at speeding up what he called "Kenyanization."

The planning minister arranged for us to meet Arap Moi, whose office was on the top floor of the tallest building in Nairobi. To reach his office was a chore. Before we even entered the building, we were interrogated and thoroughly searched by military police. Once inside, we were taken to a ground-floor office, where a woman army captain interviewed us. Having done that, she told us she would be accompanying us to the top floor. Next, the heavily armed guards in the lobby refused to let us board the elevator until they had made several phone calls to assure themselves we were not "political enemies." When the elevator door opened on the fifty-sixth floor, a group of Moi's private military guards refused to let us out. After our escort finally convinced them we were not enemies of the regime, they allowed us to enter a narrow, glassed-in passageway in order to admire the panoramic view of Nairobi. But we never met Arap Moi.

When we reported all of these events to the Planning Ministry, the officials there showed no surprise or remorse. Our offer to help Kenya establish an FTZ was shelved, so we never did go to Mombasa, our original destination. Several years later, in 1995, Arap Moi began to understand that foreign investment was essential to his country and revised his Kenyanization tactics, and Kenya did establish a trade zone at Mombasa. So far, though, it has drawn little foreign capital.

Moi was obsessed with the belief he would be assassinated at any moment. His fear had some basis: guerrillas were everywhere in Kenya, especially in the countryside. The staff at the Nairobi Hilton had recommended we travel by plane rather than by car because the insurgents were notorious for their roadside attacks on tourists and government officials. On one occasion we had just attended a luncheon at the Mount Kenya Safari Club owned by William Holden, the Hollywood celebrity, who visited it regularly. It was located near the foot of Africa's second-highest peak, and surrounded by acres of farmland shielded by thick woods. After leaving Holden's club, our schedule called for us to interview the general manager of a small luxurious hotel hidden in a forest followed by a visit to the adjacent animal sanctuary. Our driver, who was usually fearless, told us he would be taking a back road to bypass a section of the normal route from which a band of guerrillas was known to operate. At the reserve entrance, the police at the gate made several phone calls before lifting the barriers for us to proceed. The guerrillas had learned that the narrow road to the hotel and reserve was a good place to rob passing vehicles, which explains all the precautions.

Our visit to Nairobi and its nearby game reserve was a disappointment, except for our good fortune in meeting Richard Leakey, the world-famous anthropologist, who guided us around Nairobi's unique archaeology museum and showed us live specimens of the animal and reptile world. Sir Richard had spent a good part of his early life at anthropological sites in East Africa. He made one of the greatest discoveries of modern times when he uncovered a skull of *Homo habilis* dating back 1.9 million years. Later, as Kenya's director of wildlife, he advocated conservation. We remember him as a kind scholar; the world in general considers him as one of the greatest anthropologists of the twentieth century.

In December 2003, Arap Moi was crushed in a general election by Mwai Kibaki and his National Rainbow Coalition. Kenya has long been considered one of the world's most corrupt countries. The new president quickly warned that necessary changes were too numerous to be accomplished overnight.

Nevertheless, Kenya stands on the threshold of a new beginning in national governance. By declaring zero tolerance for corruption and announcing plans for new anticorruption laws, Kibaki has signaled his determination to make good on his campaign promises. Only by doing so will he be able to make any headway in tackling poverty and unemployment. Kenya is the dominant commercial center of East Africa; its return to economic health, after nearly forty years of corruption and mismanagement, will have a salutary effect on the entire region.

The Seychelles

The Seychelles, a cluster of ninety-one coral and granite islands a thousand miles east of Kenya, is a remote archipelago in the Indian Ocean often described as a tropical paradise. Many historians have named one of these hilly, wooded islands ringed with double coconut shells as the original Garden of Eden.

The tiny republic was desperate to become an offshore financial center when we arrived there in the fall of 1982. This beautiful chain of islands in the Indian Ocean needed a new source of income; Britain had cut off financial aid, and tourism—its most important source of hard currency—was lagging. I was there on behalf of the UN to explore the potential for an industrial zone; just as in Kenya, though, my recommendations fell on deaf ears. It seemed that no one in the government thought it was in his or her domain. However, the government had contracted two farsighted accountants from KPMG Peat Marwick to prepare the ground for a financial center.

An unusual arrangement was instigated by a well-known Italian entrepreneur who had a franchise from RCA in the United States to manage the American satellite operation in the Seychelles. G. Mario Ricci was an aggressive business executive with worldwide financial interests, and he was eager to use both his contacts and his persuasive powers. As chairman and CEO of the Italian conglomerate Unifinco S.A., he had established the Seychelles Trust Company in Victoria, the islands' capital. He contacted me in New York at the suggestion of the UN.

At a luncheon arranged in New York and attended by RCA executives, who were helping Ricci in his offshore financial activities, we met Mario and his stylish wife, who seemed unusually knowledgeable in American customs and business practices. She was fluent in English, Italian, and French, having studied in Europe and the United States. Her father was Haile Selassie, the Abyssinian king. She had been a girl in the 1930s, when the Italians invaded Ethiopia, and had married Private Ricci of the Italian army. Mario had never learned to speak English; at all meetings, his wife served as interpreter. The booklet I prepared at his request, *Advantages of Incorporating and Operating in Seychelles*, was translated by her into Italian for him to read.

There was no UN office in Seychelles, so my hosts when we arrived were Mario's brother, manager of the Danzilles Hotel on Mahé Island, and my two colleagues from KPMG. At that time, Unifinco's two firms—Seychelles Trust Company and Seychelles Corporate Services, both established in 1974—were taking early advantage of the Seychelles 1978 Non-Resident Bodies Corporate (Special Provision) Decree, which had created a new instrument for international tax planning. Both companies operated out of Zurich using mailbox offices on Mahé.

Under President France Albert René, Seychelles had enjoyed political and economic stability since a coup d'état in June 1977 when he replaced James Mancham, the first president after independence in 1976. René's party suspended the constitution and called together a people's assembly that adopted a new constitution, one that emphasized free markets as well as foreign investment with protection guarantees. When I met René in 1984 he made it clear to me that his new legislation abrogating the 1978 Non-Resident Decree would create an "international finance center rendering Seychelles's investment climate still more conducive and more hospitable to direct foreign investment." This point was reiterated to me by the principal secretary, V. Calixte, speaking for the Finance Ministry. Under the 1994 International Companies Act, foreign investors now regard Seychelles as a pillar of the industry for its freedom from income tax, stamp duties, and capital taxes. The Seychelles today is justly proud of its modern FTZ, one of Africa's largest and most profitable trading enclaves, which is managed efficiently by the Seychelles International Industrial Authority. Meanwhile, more than ten thousand international firms are operating successfully in the small republic.

Mauritius

Another island in the Indian Ocean, Mauritius, was concerned that its export processing zone was losing out to Senegal (a potential African rival in luring American foreign investors) when a high-level team of Mauritian leaders visited the United States in 1987 to promote the advantages of their island's eighty-three export processing areas. Under the auspices of Global Consultants, a division of Global Expeditions of Boston, the Mauritius mission included the industry minister, Dr. Diwa Hur Bundhun; the island's chairman, Michael B. Arouff; and Chand Bhadam, director of the Mauritius Development and Investment Authority. Also attending was the American ambassador to Mauritius, Ronald A. Palmer.

Sir Gaetan Duval, deputy prime minister as well as employment and tourism minister, declared that "the spirit of democracy and free enterprise is deeply ingrained in Mauritius." The mission carried the same theme to its meetings with Harvard University, the MIT Sloan School of Management, and several other leading institutions. While in New York, the group met with leaders of the Stock Exchange, Goldman Sachs, the Port Authority of New York and New Jersey, and numerous other organizations. We also accompanied the group on a tour of FTZs in New York and New Jersey.

Mauritius, the first commonwealth country to be granted associate membership in the European Union, had a disastrous youth unemployment rate, mainly because of the population explosion that had followed after malaria was eradicated during World War II. Many of its young people were leaving school at fifteen. This was the main reason the government had launched the Mauritius Export Processing Zone System. Today, there are eighty-three export processing zones scattered around the island, and the unemployment problem has almost been eliminated.

Having achieved an enviable success with its export processing zones, the far-sighted Mauritian government adopted a set of foreign investment laws designed to transform the country into a financial center. They were patterned after recommendations made to the Mauritian mission in 1987. Their particular goal was to lure private American capital. With twenty thousand registered companies, of which two thousand are international or offshore entities, Mauritius is now Africa's leading financial center.

Mauritius was not listed as a "harmful" tax haven in the OECD survey, nor is it on the money-laundering blacklist compiled by the Financial Action Task Force. However, in the survey conducted by the Financial Stability Forum, it is in the lowest category of countries—those nations accused of "not cooperating with onshore supervision and not adhering to international standards."

Mauritius has been one of the most politically stable countries in Africa for many decades and has enjoyed a high degree of prosperity, which can be attrib- uted mainly to the absence of labor unrest and a literacy rate of 90 percent. Op- position parties are flourishing; even so, the present government is strong. The result has been a steady inflow of foreign investment over the past two decades, especially into the large and profitable export processing zone system. The island has long embraced free enterprise and has been rewarded with growth rates aver- aging 6 percent to 8 percent since the 1980s.

Senegal

Senegal, a former French colony that still uses French currency and maintains its heritage by protecting French customs, has its trade heavily tied to France. Therefore, I was surprised when UNIDO asked me in 1981 to review the opera- tions of its newly established Dakar Industrial Free Zone. In view of a conflict of timing—a second assignment for me to visit Egypt had already been sched- uled—I recommended that UNIDO appoint Andrew W. Weil, managing part- ner of Warren Weil Public Relations, to fill the Senegal post. Weil, the president and a founder of the U.S. Foreign Trade Zone Association, specialized in mar- keting Panama's Colón FTZ and other Latin American trading enclaves.

From the very first day of his arrival in Dakar, Weil, a man with deep sympa- thy for the underprivileged, was startled to see firsthand how the poor Sene- galese, who represented more than 90 percent of the five million inhabitants, were barely surviving. Eighty percent of Senegal's two million workers are subsis- tence agriculturalists, and 90 percent of Senegalese are illiterate, even though education is compulsory for children between the ages of six and nineteen. Their suffering was reflected in Weil's recommendation that a new FTZ be expedited. He was instructed to return for a second visit a few months later.

When the administrator of the Dakar Industrial Free Zone, Famara Ibra- hema Sagna, visited New York in 1981, he admitted that the Senegalese zone in the capital was "struggling" to develop a manufacturing sector. He was in the United States to solicit American businesses to establish factories in the Dakar zone. Sagna emphasized that competition from Senegal's neighbor, the Ivory Coast, was hampering industrial growth and that Mauritius's aggressive com- mercial policies were threatening his country's survival. Sagna's visit followed a previous visit, in 1979, of the Dakar zone's administrator, who had also pleaded with American manufacturers to take advantage of the low-cost labor in the port of Dakar. "Investments in the zone are guaranteed by the World Bank," he added. Not until the mid-1990s under President Abdun Diouf's economic expansion program did the Dakar zone make much of a dent on the manufacturing scene.

Senegal's industrial zone has never produced the accelerated revenues the republic hoped for and is once again resorting to its second hard-currency earner after agriculture—the thriving tourist industry. As described by the government, Senegal is "a land of limitless contrasts and beauty from King Peanut, the nation's leading agricultural crop, to the fabled big-game animals of deepest Africa."

❧ 13 ❧

Eastern European Rebirth

Russia

*F*ROM THE VERY BEGINNING, my assignment to help the Soviet Union regain a foothold in its trade with the West was an enigma. A few weeks after President Richard Nixon visited Russia in 1972 in an effort to open up trade channels, I received a call from the American office of Amtorg, the Russian government's trading agency, which handled all imports and exports for the Soviet Union. This trip to Moscow was Nixon's second. His first had been as Dwight Eisenhower's vice president, following Nikita Khrushchev's stormy tour of the United States. It was during Nixon's first visit that the famous "kitchen debate" with Khrushchev occurred, generating headlines around the world.

As a member of the Administration Committee of the U.S. National Foreign Trade Council, I had met Khrushchev at a luncheon at the Waldorf-Astoria. In the few minutes I had with him, I saw no sign of either his well-publicized good humor or his occasional "uncouth" outbursts. Khrushchev had been described in some official circles as being capable of "alternating belligerence and camaraderie."

In 1972 the Commerce Department's trade director was Emil Schnellbacher, affectionately known as "Mr. Foreign Trade" by the U.S. foreign trade industry. He had suggested to Amtorg that they invite me to Russia. Schnellbacher explained to me that he was acting on the president's instructions to the commerce secretary, Maurice Stans, and the treasury secretary, George Shultz, whose enormous influence on Nixon was largely responsible for Washington's decision to abandon the gold standard in 1972, thus freeing it from the fixed rate set by the IMF in 1944. After a meeting in New York with Amtorg's director, Serguey Frolov—who was obviously taking his cue from the Kremlin's foreign trade minister, Nikolai Patolichev—we arrived in Moscow on a Japanese Airlines flight from London on which we were the only Americans.

256

On duty in the shabby Moscow terminal was a six-foot-tall blonde woman weighing at least two hundred pounds, who was standing on a wooden crate under a large sign that said "Immigration-Health." When Dorothy, who had learned a few words of Russian, greeted her with "Dobry vyecher," she broke into a pleasant smile and waved us on without asking to inspect our passports. The Intourist guide, Lena, from the government's official travel agency, who took us to our hotel, explained that she was to be our escort for as long as we were in Moscow and warned that we were not to explore the city without her. She added that her Intourist colleagues in Kiev and Leningrad (now called St. Petersburg again) would meet us when we arrived in those cities.

We were escorted by the female floor manager to a suite including a dining room with a long oblong table laid with impressive silverware. Even more spectacular was our view of the Kremlin and the shining dome of Saint Basil's Cathedral. At the time we did not realize that this venerable hotel beside the Kremlin was the traditional hangout for the Communist Party hierarchy, who dined every day in a lavish penthouse restaurant from a rich menu with dishes unknown to the average Russian. We were told that we were welcome to make use of the deluxe dining facilities at any time. Needless to say, we took advantage of this gracious offer and were served fine steaks, chicken Kiev, and other delicacies usually available only to the Kremlin top brass.

More surprises followed. The morning after our arrival, we were awakened by a loud knock on our door, whereupon several waiters rushed into our dining room, covered the table with an embroidered tablecloth, and laid out complete breakfast settings for us. Breakfast followed. Soon after, the floor manager called to tell us Lena was waiting with a car and chauffeur to take us to our first meeting with Amtorg officials. The more skeptical I became of this effusive attention, the more often I pointed to the ceiling of the suite, to remind Dorothy that the KGB undoubtedly had us pretty well bugged.

By 1972 almost all the old hard-line Communist leaders—Georgy Malenkov, Nikolay Bulganin, Khrushchev, Georgy Zhukov—had been replaced through political maneuvering. The new Soviet leader, Leonid Brezhnev, although restrained by his party adversaries, could imagine the benefits of freer world markets. It was clear to me that in the aftermath of the Stalin years, Russia very much wanted to improve its trade relations with the United States. Amtorg's officials, taking their orders from the Kremlin, expressed their eagerness to adopt a more Western-style export credit insurance program, even though they would not budge on handing over bureaucratic authority to the private sector. Moreover, their openness to lowering tariffs through negotiations with the United States indicated that Moscow was waiting for Washington to take the first step in suggesting a reciprocal trade agreement that would reduce duties on certain essential goods. Nixon had been advised of the Soviet position during his recent groundbreaking visit as president.

At the same time, the State Department was well aware that Brezhnev was encountering political dissent. Leading intellectuals, including many writers and scientists, were protesting various aspects of Soviet life. They wanted their government to stop controlling the flow of ideas and to clean up the Soviet Union's corruption and inefficiencies. Most of these dissidents were imprisoned or forced into internal exile. They included the Nobel Prize-winning nuclear physicist Andrey Sakharov and the renowned geneticist Zhorgen Medvedev (the latter left the country in 1973 and was never allowed to return).

Meanwhile, our Communist hosts continued to perplex us by receiving us warmly, as if we were royalty or official visitors. Not until our third night in Moscow did we begin to understand. We were waiting at our assigned Intourist table in a reception room jammed with hundreds of raucous tourists, many of them arguing among themselves and with Intourist agents about who would be getting tickets for an upcoming concert at the Congress Hall. The Intourist official we were talking to suddenly jumped from her desk and disappeared into a back room.

She had left open a hardcover notebook on her desk, so I leaned over to glance at the page. There, to my utter dismay, was a photo of me with a caption under it: "Supports Nixon's policy." The photo had been taken ten years earlier, in 1962, and had been printed in the *Chicago Tribune*. It, and a detailed dossier on my background, had run in a newspaper article about an address I had presented at the Palmer House to ten thousand International Rotarians. Needless to say, the KGB had done a thorough job in alerting Intourist of my visit.

My speech to the Rotarians encompassed "Ten Steps to Improve U.S. Foreign Economic Policy"—a hot issue during the Eisenhower-Nixon years in Washington and one that had carried over to the Kennedy administration. The address I made that day would have a greater impact than any of the five hundred others on international trade and investment that I have given around the world. After I finished my talk, a man at the back of the packed ballroom jumped up and shouted: "No one here knows me, but I'm Sam Low, Lyndon Johnson's campaign manager when he first ran for senator from Texas." He then declared that "if Lyndon Johnson ever runs for president, I will recommend Mr. Diamond as his foreign economic adviser."

Bearing in mind that this statement was made less than two years before JFK was assassinated, it indeed left an indelible impression on me. Also in the audience that day—which by coincidence happened to be the day of the Bay of Pigs fiasco—was Emil Schnellbacher. He had created a semiannual foreign trade survey patterned after my forecast of the thirty best export markets, which I had been preparing every year since 1952. The Commerce Department's widely distributed monthly magazine, *Business America*, still published these export market studies until it was discontinued in late 2005.

The Bay of Pigs fiasco and Kennedy's demand that Khrushchev withdraw his Soviet missiles from Cuba had worldwide financial implications. The editor and publisher of the *International Letter*, Guenter Reimann, a native German economist widely regarded in the United States for his foreign exchange expertise, called my office asking for my help in analyzing the consequences of the delicate situation. This request was not unusual; in the past I had often helped him deal with emergencies. When Reimann learned I was in Chicago to address the Rotarians, he immediately ordered Dorothy to come to his office at 200 Park Avenue South in my place. Somewhat reluctantly, she complied and spent a hectic day helping Reimann get to press.

When the Intourist agent in Moscow returned to her desk, we noticed a forced smile on her face. She complimented Dorothy on her dress and then handed us not only two tickets for the Congress Hall concert with the Moscow Symphony for that evening but also two more for the Kirov Ballet in Kiev and two more still for a performance of *Lohengrin* in Leningrad.

At the request of Amtorg, before leaving Moscow for Kiev we tried to call on Nikolai Patolichev, the trade minister. Lena showed her pass to the two military guards at the gate of the ministry, a monstrous redbrick building that took up half a block on a main street. However, the building was closed. We quickly sensed there was a problem. Amtorg's chief, Serguey Frolov, was giving orders to Lena's Intourist boss, who in turn passed them on to Lena. She was now extremely concerned that she would not be able to carry out her instructions. And though Lena repeatedly refused to take *nyet* from the guards as an answer, we never met the trade minister.

By the time we reached Kiev, Dorothy and I were certain the KGB had been watching us closely since the day we arrived. This suspicion was confirmed when we sat down for dinner in the restaurant of our Kiev hotel. Dorothy told me the tall blond man at the table in back of me looked familiar. "Yes," I replied, "he is to me, too. I think he was one of the security agents we had a glimpse of in Moscow." In a whisper, she added: "I think he's reading our lips as we talk." When I turned around, he reacted with a broad smile. From that point on, Dorothy and I did not utter another normal word; we communicated in whispers through partially sealed lips.

Near the end of our visit, when we left Leningrad to return to Moscow, we had a taste of the Soviet airline system, which besides being inefficient was rated the least safe in a survey of all the world's airlines. Our Aeroflot Ilyushian 300 never appeared when we checked in at the Leningrad airport. There being no agent or staff of any kind to explain this distressing situation to the scheduled passengers, we all huddled in an anteroom off the empty main office, waiting for word from someone. Because of Dorothy's self-taught Russian (she was familiar with a few words), an official elected her to lead the group to breakfast. Two hours later, an airline employee arrived to tell us another airplane had arrived to return us to Moscow.

When we landed at the Moscow airport and asked the ground crew about the delay, they told us our scheduled plane had crashed, killing some 306 passengers and crew. As usual, the media and the public were never informed of the "mishap." The Soviets classified this tragedy as a "private affair" for security reasons. It was believed that the outside world—including the World Civil Aeronautical Association—was "better off" if it did not know about the bungling Soviet system.

Since there were no baggage handlers to remove the luggage from the cart on the runway, I had to climb up on the wagon myself to dislodge our two pieces at the bottom of the pile and carry them into the terminal.

Hungary

After our U.S. AID assignment in 1986 to help resurrect the Bar FTZ in Yugoslavia, I was asked to evaluate a possible U.S. AID allocation for Hungary. At the time, after two decades of inefficiencies—a consequence of its Soviet-style economic system—Budapest was turning to the West for trade and assistance. Prime Minister Karoly Grosz was determined to modernize the Hungarian economy. Accordingly, from Belgrade we made a three-day trip to Budapest to review the American position with the local office of the U.S. Commerce Department.

Hungarian Airlines, in an effort to promote its tourism, was luring its passengers with an early-morning champagne breakfast, including a cart of liqueurs. It more than offset the disadvantages of traveling in deteriorating Tupolev planes pawned off by Moscow.

American relations with Hungary had been sour ever since 1968, when Hungary helped the Soviets invade Czechoslovakia. Yet Washington was softening its position, mainly because of Ronald Reagan's optimistic view that the Russians would eventually lose control of their European satellite states. As it developed, three years later Grosz was ousted and the Communist Party voted to dissolve itself.

My talks in Hungary focused on solving that country's twenty-six billion dollar foreign debt. That issue was the main concern of the U.S. Treasury and State Departments. The president of Hungary's Central Bank was Gyorgy Suranyi, a straightforward East European financier with Western tendencies. In his words: "Hungary never rescheduled its debt or asked for any kind of relief. Its impeccable debt servicing performance makes it possible to raise, through voluntary lending, sufficient funds to handle its medium- and long-term loans while the interest payments are covered by the trade and services surpluses."

Hungary was the first East European country to adopt market policies in anticipation of the world's changing political climate. In this regard, it took an early lead in the race to attract Western investors. Foreign businesspeople found Hungary the most attractive Eastern European country for expansion because it was the easiest to invest in. Western experts concur that Hungary has been and still is the most successful of the former Eastern-bloc countries in attracting investment because it is the most stable politically and has had its economic reforms in place longer than its neighbors. In fact, as Suranyi pointed out: "Hungary has been in the forefront of these changes as it was the first among Eastern European countries to introduce a market-oriented reform in 1968." This move transformed the Hungarian economy "more radically" even than the economic reforms implemented after 1989.

A study by the U.S. Commerce Department's Eastern Business Information Center confirms that Hungary is leading the region's economic transformation. This position of prominence is owing to the government's commitment to scrapping its centrally planned economy and replacing it with private ownership and free markets. Hungary's legal framework for privatization and facilitating foreign investment has enabled it to redirect its foreign trade westward, to manage its external debt responsibly, and to attract more than ten thousand joint ventures with private capital from around the world. Among the multitude of incentives drawing foreign investors to Hungary were a reduced 3 percent tax rate available to private and public limited companies if they met strict requirements, tax-free interest on savings accounts up to ten thousand dollars, a ten-year tax holiday, and duty-free trade zones set up like American subzones in their own places of business rather than in a separate location. However, in order to be eligible to join the European Union in May 2004, Hungary had to stop registering offshore companies; it must deregister existing ones by January 1, 2006.

Organized crime has been a problem in Hungary. A number of criminal organizations have taken root there, after being forced out of Russia and other former Eastern-bloc countries. Miscreants had infiltrated Hungary because of its tax-haven advantages, and the government is watching them carefully to make sure they do not penetrate the economy.

Czechoslovakia

While researching a new chapter on Hungary for Matthew Bender's *Tax Havens of the World*, Dorothy noticed some glaring differences in how Eastern European companies are organized relative to companies in the noncommunist world. In June 1989, *Offshore Investment Magazine* was sponsoring a conference at the Cumberland Hotel in London and invited Dorothy to speak on the topic of establishing a company in Eastern Europe. Her talk there generated considerable interest. Subsequently, the late Peter Redmond, the magazine's publisher as well as the first president of the Offshore Institute, today's main organization representing offshore professionals, held the institute's first meeting (in Vienna, October 1989) on doing business in Eastern Europe.

As a cofounder of the institute and a chairman of its program committee, it was my job to invite five finance ministers—from Bulgaria, Czechoslovakia, Hungary, Poland, and Romania—to talk about their countries' capital formation policies. Each minister was a Communist hard-liner and brought along an English-speaking translator; for almost all Communist-trained politicians, English was a taboo language. Needless to say, the translations were a disappointment, and the audience let the conference planners know it.

I was amazed to learn from these ministers that they welcomed Western capital in any venture as long as it was invested through the party's centralized authority. Several of them invited me to visit their country to see for myself how venture capital fitted into their economic schemes. The Czech minister's offer was especially appealing, so the week after the Vienna meeting we visited Prague. Among the Eastern-bloc countries, Hungary had more developed democratic institutions, but Czechoslovakia had the most industrialized economic base.

We arrived in Prague and were met by a government tourist officer, who seemed confused by her instructions from the ministry and began checking us into the wrong hotel. Before we could unpack in the less luxurious correct hotel, she rushed us onto a subway that took us to the Old Town and then to Wenceslas Square, where she pointed out that the Communists had brought "great advances" to their people. The next day our assigned guide appeared to inform us that the finance minister, who had scheduled a meeting with us, was unavailable—in fact, he was not answering his phone. After several attempts to reach him through other channels, it developed that he was just then resigning his post. Other meetings planned for us at the Industry Ministry had also fallen through. Communications were so disrupted that no one could be reached by telephone to confirm the prearranged conferences.

When we visited Wenceslas Square, it was obvious to us that the government was about to lose its grip on the country. More than one hundred thousand Czechs were protesting Communist rule, shouting, "Down with Communists!" and "Give up! You lost!" One could see that the dissident movement was imminent. In mid-October 1989, a few days after we left, the Velvet Revolution took control of the country. Václav Havel, the renowned author and longtime dissident, won the country's first democratic election since 1946. Already when we were there, his image was displayed like an icon in hundreds of shop windows. His political enemies would later accuse him of treating the Communists and the secret police too gently. He preached forgiveness and warned against a witch-hunt. His adversaries eventually won; he was defeated for reelection in 1992.

After the Communists fell, the Czech Parliament adopted a new private enterprise law that planted the seeds for foreign investment. Until this far-reaching measure, Prague had been allowing businesses "to hire only relatives," according to Otto Burean, president of the Slovak Society for Foreign Enterprise. The Czech trade minister, Andrej Barcek, visited the White House in March 1990 to open investment and tax treaty negotiations with President George H. W. Bush, and pledged to abandon the state-run foreign trade organization and the giant conglomerates representing each sector of the Czechoslovak economy. Barcek assured Washington that from now on, foreign entrepreneurs and private businesses would be allowed to deal directly in international trade.

Shortly after that meeting, on April 12, 1990, Barcek and Carla Hills, the U.S. trade representative, signed a trade agreement that could have a broad impact on trade relations between the two countries. Yet two years later, in June 1992, at a symposium in New York cosponsored by the UN and the Tax Institute, an official from the Czech Revenue Ministry admitted that some exchange restrictions still existed that were impeding trade between the two nations. One was the requirement that funds earned from Czech export sales had to be sold to the Central Bank. This requirement made it harder for Czech and Slovak buyers to purchase American goods. Moreover, only banks could trade foreign currencies.

Reducing unemployment was a top priority in Czechoslovakia. First, though, the central government had to address its mounting foreign debt and reorganize its banking structure. Unfortunately, the reorganization impeded economic progress, causing dissent to spread rapidly through the country. So little American investment was flowing into Czechoslovakia that Finance Minister Michael Kocac came to the United States to make his case to American businessmen. He emphasized that introducing free markets and privatizing industries would take time.

In June 1991, Nicholas Brady, the treasury secretary, assigned his deputy, John Robson, to go to Bardejov, Czechoslovakia, which was celebrating its 750th anniversary. There, Robson told the Czechs that "America understands how hard it is to make the transition from an economic system where almost everything is owned and decided by the government, to a system where ownership and economic decisions are in the hands of private citizens in a competitive market." He added that the transition to free markets was "not for the fainthearted."

Poland

Poland's transition to democracy brought record amounts of foreign capital into the economy. It all began in October 1987, when the foreign minister, Handlic Zagranicznego, invited a number of American business leaders to Warsaw for a forum, "Joint Ventures and Financing Participation." Although the forum was frowned on by most officials in the Polish People's Republic, it opened the gates for the election of June 4, 1989, in which the Solidarity movement won a lopsided majority.

Full democratization did not come until January 1990, when the finance minister, Laeszek Balcerowicz, applied so-called "shock therapy" to the economy. That month he introduced reforms outlawing price controls, cutting government subsidies, and floating the currency. After the introduction of a commercial banking system and writing laws to establish a securities exchange and the private ownership of property, Poland entered a new phase of democracy. Balcerowicz declared: "What is important to note is that there is no disagreement on the basic element of the government's economic program."

The transition to a market economy brought many hardships to the Poles. Unemployment rose above 24 percent, and widespread discontent led to political instability. The new president, Lech Walesa, threatened to resign, and the government changed foreign ministers four times between 1990 and 1992. To help support the Solidarity government, Western creditor countries—including the United States—cancelled billions of dollars of Poland's foreign debt, and Western banks washed out 40 percent of its private debt.

On March 21, 1990, President George Bush brought the Polish prime minister, Tadeusz Mazowieicki, to Washington, D.C., to sign the Treaty on Business and Economic Relations. This agreement had been set in motion as early as September 1985, when Robert Mosbacher, U.S. commerce secretary, visited Warsaw for talks with Poland's new foreign economic minister, Mavun Swiecicki. The two had signed an agreement to "foster tourism and private business exchange." The Commerce Department then set aside special funds to conduct investment feasibility studies.

Now, at a Rose Garden gathering, the president talked about "the vital role of the U.S. business community in assisting Poland in its historic transition to a free market democracy." He underscored the great significance to Americans of a prosperous Poland and a stronger partnership between Poland and the United States. The West responded to this signal with $280 million in environmental cleanup loans. Not long after Bush and Mazowieicki signed their treaty, Polish deputy Marek Dabrowski stated that his government was ready to start withdrawing subsidies from unprofitable businesses, with or without privatization.

When we visited Poland in October 1991, it was obvious that although they loved their country, the Poles were suffering catastrophically hard times as a result of the recent economic reforms. We visited a number of proposed special economic zones, including Czestochowa, site of the Abbey of Jana Gore and its priceless Black Madonna; Kraków, with its medieval town center; Swinoujscie on the German border; and Sulwalki across the Russian border from Kaliningrad. Everywhere we went, our guide pointed to hundreds of broken-down vehicles at the borders. Unemployed Poles were starving; to survive they were having to sell or trade their personal possessions to Germans and Russians, who congregated unmolested by the authorities in black-market districts along the borders.

A former television reporter from Long Island, Alma Kadragick, saw an urgent need for Polish Americans to help U.S. companies explore this unknown market. To further the project, she took advantage of her Polish heritage and opened her own consulting office in Warsaw. Encouraged by her parents, Katherine and Alex, economics professors at Adelphi College (Alex was a former economic aide to King Peter II of Yugoslavia, who was forced to abdicate his throne), she quickly became a valuable adviser to the American multinationals that were flocking to Poland to make direct investments or start licensing operations.

By the time we arrived in Warsaw, Alma had deeply impressed the local business community with her success in helping American companies process visas and other documents and link up with Polish entrepreneurs and government officials. Her clients included IBM, Citibank, ITT, and Mobil. At a dinner meeting she hosted at one of Warsaw's leading French restaurants, IBM's international vice president praised her for helping IBM enter the Polish market.

Alma knew I was on a U.S. AID assignment to help Poland establish a system of special economic zones, so the first appointment she arranged for me was with Mieczyslaw Nogaj of the Ministry of Foreign Economic Relations. It was Nogaj, on the instructions of Poland's finance minister, who had prepared legislation to establish seventeen FTZs in Poland. However, operations did not commence immediately following passage of the law, partly because bottlenecks had developed in its implementation, and also because Polish businesses and foreign investors lacked enthusiasm. So my task was to review the law. Line by line for more than a hundred pages, Nogaj read through the legislation, seeking our opinions on every article. It took an entire morning.

The key point I made to Nogaj was that American investors would surely be reluctant to move their manufacturing operations to a foreign economic zone offering only a two-year tax exemption. Since it usually takes three to five years for an offshore subsidiary to start earning a profit. We suggested that the tax holiday be at least five years, but preferably eight, since Poland's competitors in Eastern Europe were providing a minimum of eight years on most profits. When we returned to Poland two years later to review the final draft of the law, Nogaj had extended the tax holiday to ten years. We were pleased to hear the good news.

Between our two visits in 1991 and 1993, the UN had sponsored a symposium in New York, "Taxation and Investment in Central and Eastern Europe." At that venue, Poland's deputy finance minister, Rysgard Michalski, spoke to a gathering of businesspeople representing the principal multinationals of the Fortune 500. In response to questions from the audience, he indicated that his government would soon be providing more liberal investment incentives. When asked whether there were "any tax holidays in your country" for profits earned locally by foreign investors, his answer did not sit well with the audience. He stated that under Polish joint venture laws, a foreign investor could be granted an investment tax credit only up to the share capital value. This discouraging response laid the groundwork for the more liberal incentive: the tax exemption was changed from two to ten years.

One of Alma's many contacts in Poland was an American commercial diplomat named Joan Edwards. At Alma's suggestion, she visited us at our hotel. Knowing how important it was for Poland to reduce its unemployment rate, she asked us to prepare a set of guidelines relating to how the Trade Development Center could help the seventeen proposed special economic zones establish successful operations.

Edwards solicited the cooperation of her ambassador, Arthur Davis. He was especially intrigued by the proposed FTZ for Gdansk, so we were asked to draw up a separate plan for that zone. Davis had indicated that President Bush was disturbed by the chaos in Gdansk, the "spiritual home" of the Solidarity movement.

Solidarity had been born in October 1988 when the Communist authorities closed down Gdansk's historic Lenin Shipyard for "economic" reasons. At that point, Lech Walesa and Barbara Priserka Johnson, a Polish American who had inherited most of the Johnson and Johnson fortune, led 25,000 marchers in protest. When Walesa told her that another 10,000 workers would soon be out of work, adding to the 318,000 already unemployed—a figure he said would rise to 900,000 by the end of the year—Johnson offered to give one hundred million dollars of her reported three hundred million dollar fortune to resurrect the failing shipyard.

Today, Poland has transformed itself into a market-based economy with an annual growth rate of 4 percent. It has attracted eight billion dollars of productive American investment. When Poland entered the European Union in May 2004, it brought with it half the economic output of the ten new members that joined that year. Of the twenty-five nations in the EU, it is the sixth largest in population. Its status as an East European power is rising rapidly.

Lithuania

Three years after the three Baltic states of Estonia, Latvia, and Lithuania freed themselves from Soviet domination, their new political independence was severely tested by rising unemployment. Millions of workers employed by the old Communist government had lost their jobs. Lithuania was facing the most critical situation: unemployment was soaring, and political dissent was brewing over how to reduce it. Meanwhile, street crime was becoming uncontrollable, and the government was too beset with factions to find solutions.

In 1995 I received a phone call from Gediminas Petrauskas, a former Lithuanian senator and national hero as past captain of Lithuania's 1990 Olympic championship soccer team. He was calling from Kaunas, the country's second-largest city after the capital, Vilnius. Speaking through a translator, he told me that the UN had suggested he call. His boss, the director of NOVA (the Kaunas Science and Technology Park), operator of a proposed FTZ, had read my monthly column in *Offshore Investment* in which I had expounded the virtues of FTZs to help reduce unemployment in the far corners of the world.

Petrauskas had taken it upon himself to help Kaunas establish an FTZ that would absorb some of its unemployed. When the Lithuanian government refused to make a formal request for assistance from the UN Industrial Organization because Lithuania's funding allotment was destined for more urgent needs, he invited me to Kaunas as a guest of NOVA.

We arrived in Vilnius after a short stop in Poland and were met by a delegation of NOVA's directors, including Petrauskas. He kept us going nonstop for ten days, during which we conferred with government officials, including the interim president, Vytiutas Landsbergis, Lithuania's first post-Soviet head of state, several ministers, three mayors, the Kaunas region governor, and the general manager of the Kaunas airport, which abutted the NOVA administration building. Each morning Dorothy and I would trudge up the five flights of stairs of the deteriorating former warehouse to meet for hours at a time with NOVA's directors. This energetic group treated us like family, and before long we joined their effort to establish an FTZ at Kaunas.

Landsbergis was Lithuania's modern hero. As a university professor he had faced the open fire of Russian troops sent by Moscow to quell the national revolution. He told us he would do his best to help Kaunas have its zone. However, he added, certain political enemies would surely stand in his way. During a subsequent visit to Washington, D.C., he repeated his support for an FTZ when meeting with President Bill Clinton.

Petrauskas easily gained the full confidence of Landsbergis; Kazys Starkevicious, governor of the Kaunas region; Donatas Jankauskas, mayor of Kaunas; Valdas Adamkas, successor to Landsbergis; Keith Smith, U.S. ambassador to Lithuania; and Ruth R. Harian, president and CEO of the Overseas Private Investment Corporation in Washington, D.C.

The governor of the Kaunas region and three local mayors were so elated at the prospect of creating jobs that they hosted a dinner in our honor. There, they bestowed on me their highest award, "Honorary Citizen of Lithuania." This tribute was especially touching for me since my grandfather had emigrated to the United States from Lithuania in 1883.

When we returned to the United States we immediately began preparing the *Tender of a Business Plan for Kaunas Free Economic Zone,* as requested by the Lithuanian government. With the help of Walter Szykitka, president of the Association for World Free Trade Zones, and the cooperation of UNIDO and the World Trade Institute, we submitted a 148-page document that included maps, diagrams, and detailed marketing channels.

Petrauskas was informed by the Vilnius government that NOVA's tender had no competition and that its approval by the Lithuanian Parliament was certain. He also received promises from the European Bank for Reconstruction and Development and the IMF that the Kaunas Free Economic Zone was in "a strong position to make a substantial contribution toward achieving the government's primary objective to enlarge and develop new productive facilities."

Accompanied by his office manager and translator, Petrauskas went to Washington, D.C., and was reassured there that the Overseas Private Investment Corporation would guarantee American investments in Lithuania. At the same time, he attended the Eastern European Investment Conference in New York to describe the proposed Kaunas zone. Dorothy and I invited him to our fiftieth-anniversary celebration at the Williams Club, where he met some of our associates who would be joining us in establishing the Kaunas Free Economic Zone.

On learning that I had been discussing the possibility of a Chrysler plant in Lithuania with that company's vice president of operations in Detroit, Petrauskas was so certain the Lithuanian government would select his consortium to create the zone that he asked us to meet him in Graz, Austria, the center of Chrysler's

34. At a dinner in our honor in 1995 given by the Kaunas governor and the three regional mayors, Walter was awarded honorary citizenship of Lithuania in appreciation for the Diamonds' assistance. Gediminas Petrauskas was quite proud of his feat, as he made sure we would see Diamond Avenue in Kaunas.

European car and van production. Negotiations I had opened with Chrysler in Michigan, Washington, and Brussels were somewhat encouraging.

Although Graz, the second largest city in Austria, had a prosperous free trade zone, Chrysler did not take advantage of the customs-free facilities because the zone is primarily a transshipment center between western Europe and southeastern and central Europe. The Chrysler plant was located on the outskirts of the city, but to reach it we had to pass by the former home of Governor Arnold Schwarzenegger of California, a native of Austria.

Lithuanian businesses and consumers were eager to have Chrysler produce vehicles in their country. Chrysler was especially interested in operating in Lithuania because of the much lower wage rates there compared to Austria and other Western nations. At that time, the Graz plant's sagging profits were causing concern, and the company's European headquarters was seeking some way to boost them. In light of the interest shown by Chrysler, Petrauskas offered the company a choice parcel of land, for which it would pay no rent. Ultimately, of course, the company ended up making an ill-fated merger with Daimler-Chrysler.

All of Petrauskas's hopes were shattered when a relatively unknown entity, the Belgian Consortium, applied for the right to participate in the tender and was awarded the bid. This situation caused a ruckus in the Lithuanian Parliament. One Lithuanian newspaper called it the "scam of the century" and declared that the project amounted to "dirty games played by the corrupt politicians to pocket the government's money." The director of the Belgian Consortium, which had been successful in other areas but had little experience in developing, organizing, or administering a free economic zone, was described in the article as "the protégé of some political parties."

The governor of the Kaunas region and the mayor of Kaunas tried hard to reverse the decision. But when a delegation of officials from Kaunas visited the new president, Valdas Adamkus, he stated that his "hands were tied by the arrogant and complex workings of parliament." It was said that certain members of the Lithuanian government had strong ties with the Port of Antwerp, with which Lithuania had many trade dealings.

Not long after the tender award was announced, I received a call from the general director of the Belgian Consortium, explaining that he and the managing director wished to meet with me in New York. During our discussion they indicated that no progress had been made in developing the Kaunas zone because of a land dispute. They invited me to join their consortium as a consultant, readily admitting they knew very little about developing and operating a zone.

Six months later, while on our way to Sofia to help the Bulgarian government market its nine FTZs, we stopped in Brussels to meet with the Belgian group. There, I presented a plan that involved NOVA and the Belgian Consortium working together to create the Kaunas free economic zone. Later, I received a letter from Lithuania's vice minister of economics, Gediminas Miskinis, in which he expressed the hope that the Kaunas free economic zone, as designated and originally established by NOVA, "will be able to join the forces of all investors—local and foreign—for its achievement of its joint goal."

A bitter debate between the Belgians and the Kaunas region's government over the cost of land and the amount of space required went on for nearly three years. The Belgian Consortium wanted to buy the land—a transaction prohibited by the Lithuanian Constitution, which forbids the selling of land to foreigners. After the Lithuanian government spent three million litai (one million dollars) to purchase the land from the original owners—the bulk of which came out of the national budget—the Belgian Consortium was dissatisfied and threatened to leave the country. To this date, Lithuania has no FTZ. According to government officials, the area "looks like wasteland." Meanwhile, Petrauskas has changed direction and is working to make Lithuania an offshore financial center. He is also now active in an environmental improvement project.

Romania

With the end of the Yugoslavian war, the director of Romania's main port at Constanta—the second largest in Europe after Rotterdam—turned to the UN for help in resurrecting its once flourishing FTZ. However, because the zone was a joint venture run by the government and several private Austrian, German, and Australian firms, it was recommended that the zone's rehabilitation be placed in the hands of private interests. Accordingly, the zone's managers contacted me for help.

After a stop in Dijon, France, for an International Fiscal Association meeting in 1998, we visited Constanta, in southeastern Romania on the Black Sea, 130 miles east of Bucharest. Both the port and the zone suffered severely from the war sanctions applied against the former Yugoslavia, since many of the latter's transshipments from central to western Europe use the 42.2-mile Danube-Black Sea Canal, which shortens the route taken by Europe-bound cargo from the Far East by twenty-five hundred miles. In 1994, the sanctions against Yugoslavia caused a 25 percent drop in port traffic, resulting in $2.5 million in canceled contracts and lost transit fees. With the lifting of sanctions, the port has recovered rapidly, and new projects with an estimated value of more than $3 billion are being undertaken. Moreover, Romanian exporters have begun systematically exploiting world markets after a slow start following the overthrow of the Communists.

35. Dorothy conversing with the representatives of the French delegation after a discussion on French-American cohesiveness in tax policy at the Dijon Joint Conference of the French and American councils of the International Fiscal Association, before leaving for Romania in 1998.

There efforts have involved rehabilitation of noncompetitive facilities and attracting foreign capital from joint venturers, especially for the ports and FTZs.

After constructive discussions with Romania's transportation minister, Traian Basescu, and the trade minister, Constantin Foda, who praised Constanta as an oil terminal capable of handling 250 million metric tons of cargo a year, a visit to the port was arranged for us. We were picked up at the hotel early one morning by Ionica Bugur, the port's marketing director, and driven the 130 miles on the potholed highway to the Black Sea. There, with the port's managing director, we spent most of the day on the choppy Black Sea inspecting the facilities by motor launch—every terminal, landing, warehouse, shed, docking pier, crane, and administrative and commercial building.

The journey back to the capital that evening was as hazardous as any we ever made. Since the marketing director was not returning with us, the driver used the occasion to show how fast the port's Mercedes could go. Romanian taxi drivers like to stop in front of the palace that housed the government offices and proudly point out the landmark rooftop where Nicolae Ceauşescu and his wife were hung on display after being shot by the insurrectionists.

With the end of the Yugoslavian war, Romania's free economic zones at Constanta, Sulina, and Tulcea (there are six others of lesser importance) are being restored as key links in East-West trade. Generally, though, the Romanian economy has risen only slowly from its decades under communism. American investment in Romania has been slack.

In 1987 the president of the Romanian Chamber of Deputies, Adrian Nastase, came to Washington, D.C., and New York and promised that Romanians would "fully privatize about seven thousand enterprises." Only then did the outlook for American private capital improve. He declared that Romania had already placed three thousand state-owned ventures in private hands. Of the thirty-eight thousand foreign joint ventures in Romania, only twenty-eight hundred involved American firms. Somewhat defensively, Nastase stated that his government was "turning more to structural reform, a sorely needed device that could once and for all end the menacing centralized system of rules practiced under the former Communist regime."

Under democracy, Romania has been making monumental changes that are preparing the ground for a market economy similar to Germany's. There is no doubt that the entire economy needed restructuring. When we were there, wages were lower than anywhere else in the former Soviet bloc and one-twentieth to one-thirtieth of wages in Western Europe. As an example of the incredible difference in prices, at the Bucharest Opera House we purchased two fourth-row orchestra seats for only $2.60 each for a magnificent performance of *Lucia di Lammermoor*. The same tickets in Vienna would have cost $200 each. Ceauşescu had been a tyrant, and under his heel the Romanian people had been deprived for decades of the amenities of life. One well-educated taxi driver told us he "was one of the few lucky people who had indoor plumbing."

The new coalition government was headed by two able economists, President Emil Constantinescu and Prime Minister Victor Ciosbea. Even so, the West was disappointed at the pace of Romania's transition. In 1997 the IMF and the World Bank stepped into the picture with an economic reform package designed to address Romania's structural and systemic problems. The government eliminated price controls, freed the exchange rate, accelerated privatization, and began encouraging more foreign investment.

When he visited the country in 1997, President Bill Clinton acknowledged the nation's progress in an address to the Romanian people. He told them "the United States not only supports but encourages Romania in its efforts to develop into a market economy." Clinton made it clear that "he was there to reinforce

U.S. support for Romania's political stability and economic reform measures." His address was received warmly throughout the country. Wherever we went, we heard praise for "your great leader." Constanta's managing director, Bugur, praised Clinton several times during the day we spent with him.

Bulgaria

Bulgaria was widely considered a leader in Eastern Europe when it came to successful FTZs, although its facilities were antiquated. It had six long-established entrepôts, and three more had been approved by the Council of Ministers. When we arrived in Sofia in 1998, Zheliu Zheliv, the Bulgarian president, had other issues on his mind. Attracting foreign investment was his principal objective. Years before, in 1982, he had sent his prime minister, Filip Dimitrov, to Geneva to meet privately with more than sixty international business executives in an effort to lure foreign capital to jump-start his ailing economy. Subsequently, in the same year, Zheliv sent Dimitrov to Chicago. As a guest of the Chicago Council of Foreign Relations, Dimitrov stated that "Bulgaria hopes a very liberal foreign investment law and expertise in high technology will attract outside capital to speed its push toward privatization." He added that Bulgaria was positioned within the old Soviet Council for Mutual Economic Assistance (commonly known as COMECON) trading bloc as the main supplier of computer equipment in Eastern Europe and as a leader in computing skills.

Contradicting the Eastern-bloc stereotype, Bulgaria has one of the world's most modern telecommunications systems. It also has exceptionally well-trained computer programmers. For these reasons, a number of American and European companies turned to Bulgaria for help in solving the universal Y2K computer problem, especially if their mainframe programming had been written in the 1970s or earlier using COBOL, a programming language popular at the time but less so today.

At a conference in Sofia, the chairman of Bulgaria's Foreign Investment Agency, Ilyau Vassilev, stated that his government was linking up with several electronics firms in other countries to expedite private investment. He indicated that his agency was opening offices in Tokyo, Thessaloníka, Paris, London, and Washington, D.C. This maneuver was an outgrowth of the Bulgarian Investment Forum sponsored by UNIDO, which was held while we were in Sofia and was dedicated to seeking funds for financing projects undertaken by the West.

Before leaving Bulgaria we were invited to review the competitive status of the nation's first and most important international free zone. It was near Ruse, in northeastern Bulgaria on the heavily trafficked Danube River. There was another zone at Plovdiv, the country's second-largest city, southeast of Sofia. We were also told of plans to establish a third zone at Varna, a busy Black Sea port. In each case, I emphasized that despite the five-year tax holiday offered companies operating in the zones, Bulgaria would have to adopt a viable export credit insurance system if it expected U.S. companies to build subsidiary plants.

As was usual, I had to explain to the Transportation Ministry and the Foreign Investment Agency that most American multinationals were looking for some type of government insurance against commercial and political risks. This insurance was one of three cardinal requirements for attracting foreign investment, the other two being tax incentives and the availability of FTZs. Experience has shown that unless these inducements are offered, prominent American firms often bypass opportunities to invest in foreign nations, especially developing nations.

ONE OF THE MOST enlightening aspects of our assignment in Bulgaria was to observe the people's reaction to their restored religious freedom. With suppressed religion, a benchmark of decades of Communist rule, the Bulgarians were forced to resort to the underground to practice their religion. Now they could openly revert to their religious beliefs and were proud to describe to us their historic houses of worship, whether cathedrals, churches, monasteries, or synagogues. At the invitation of our official guide, we visited one of Bulgaria's famous monasteries with its fresco-laden church built in the hills a few miles from Sofia, the capital. Cordial monks welcomed American guests by leading Dorothy to the sacred throne of their leader upon which she could be photographed.

Estonia

Following the 2004 International Fiscal Association Congress at Vienna in 2004, we flew to Tallinn, the capital of Estonia, to have on-the-spot interviews with government officials. Our research was used in new chapters on Estonia in our books, as requested by our publishers and subscribers. One of the three Baltic states, Estonia enjoys a most progressive and open economy that appeals to foreign investors from around the world. A primary reason for the wide interest is that it has become an offshore financial center, the only one in Eastern Europe since Hungary tightened its laws. It is the focus of foreigners because of its zero corporate income tax on reinvested or retained profits, a duty-free exemption for

36. Dorothy Diamond waving to a group of monks who had placed her on a throne in the famed monastery outside Sofia, Bulgaria, after Walter and she held discussions with government officials in assisting Bulgaria in accelerating activities in the nation's special economic zones.

almost all nonagricultural imports, a well-educated workforce, and a hospitable attitude toward direct foreign investment. Moreover, Estonian policies include free-market economics, privatization, and reduction of state bureaucracy and monopolies.

A former Soviet territory, which regained its independence after the disintegration of the USSR in 1991, Estonia was welcomed into NATO in March 2004 and became a member of the European Union in May of the same year. An average gain in gross national product of 6 percent annually in recent years, one of the highest in Europe, and a stable government, along with a liberal commercial code, provide foreign investors with the prospect of substantial returns on their assets.

During our discussions with Erki Uustalui, adviser to the Finance Ministry, and his close associate, Mark Murgatroyd, the legal and tax manager of Deloitte and Touche Eesti AS, it developed that Estonia's three FTZs at Muuga, Sillamae, and Valga (the zone at Vorga was closed down in July 2001) were not a great force in contributing to Estonia's trade and growth. Customs bottlenecks and lack of government enthusiasm were cited as reasons for the failure to take advantage of Estonia's zones, although they were originally created to enhance regional development through the excellent port facilities on the Baltic Sea.

With the obvious potential that the three zones could make a more definitive contribution to the Estonian economy, our discussions led to the conclusion that a preliminary recommendation be submitted for presentation to the UN for assistance in expanding or modernizing the zones or both. This report is now being prepared by me with assistance from the Association for World Free Trade Zones.

Not only was our visit to Tallinn a success in supplying us with information to fill the gaps in our Estonian chapters, but we were also rewarded with the opportunity to explore the fascinating Old Town, which has survived for many centuries under several foreign regimes occupying the country. The Old Town is noted for its unique fortresslike structure divided into two parts, the lower section that housed traders and workers, connected by a steep, cobblestoned road to the upper level, where the cultural and aristocratic people lived and governed the nation and had access to one of the extraordinary Russian-built gold-lined cathedrals.

≫ 14 ≪

Canada's Dilemmas

*L*ITTLE DID I REALIZE that the jovial man I met at the Gray Rocks Inn at St. Jovite on Lake Ouimet ninety miles north of Montreal on my honeymoon in June 1947 would be responsible for two future assignments to help the Canadian government. When I entered the barroom of this popular hotel, all eyes were on the flamboyant character and his cheerful entourage of six beautiful blonde women. I was told he was a prominent labor union lawyer in Montreal. This was Jean Drapeau, who was taking a short holiday from his battles with Quebec legislators. Politicians, he told me, were a thorn in his side: "They're all alike, greedy and self-serving."

Twenty years later, as mayor of Montreal, he found my press card in his files and called me to help extract him from a predicament. The same politicians he complained about earlier were now a "bunch of wolves" and were trying to "ostracize" him. He had set his sights on making Montreal's Expo '67 a world's fair "unlike any other in history." It would be his legacy. However, the fair had not drawn the millions of tourists he and his planners had anticipated, and the project was going deeply into the red. The banks and bondholders that had financed the monumental undertaking were at his throat.

By the time the fair closed in 1967, the outlook was bleak. Prime Minister Lester Pearson and Drapeau's political adversaries were harshly critical of how the event had been managed. The federal government would not come to the mayor's rescue, and the province of Quebec had already suffered severe losses. But Drapeau would not give in. He decided to reopen the fair in 1969. In October 1968 he turned to the press for help in resurrecting his dream and finding a way to placate his creditors.

Reviving Expo '67

After a mammoth press conference and reception on the fairgrounds, Drapeau's fortunes began to improve. He won over Dorothy and me, and we did our best to help him by writing articles about the reopened fair for our publications. Expo '69 (as it was now called) became a financial success that mollified even some of his harshest critics. By reorganizing its finances, cutting expenses, and adding new events and exhibits, the reopened fair lured new crowds from throughout North America. In the end, it brought in sufficient revenues, enabling him to make a reasonable settlement with his creditors.

Having recaptured his popularity, Drapeau went back to running an efficient government, one that attracted new investors to Montreal. During the 1970s he visited New York several times; there, with the Canadian trade commissioner, he attended press receptions where he commended Montreal's programs for attracting American investment. Whenever he came to New York, he let me know beforehand so that we could renew our friendship. He always thanked us for our help in resurrecting Expo '67.

In his later years as mayor, Drapeau turned Montreal from a provincial city into a world-class metropolis by hosting the 1976 Summer Olympics and a number of cultural events. Also, he was instrumental in drawing many important conventions to Montreal. In one particular case, the International Fiscal Association came to his city for its annual congress. The mayor arranged with the police to block off several streets in the Old Town, where two thousand delegates partied and danced.

After thirty-two years as mayor—the longest tenure in Montreal history—Drapeau had transformed his city into one of the great North American banking and commercial centers. The impact of this success spilled over to other parts of Quebec and into Ontario.

In 1979, at Drapeau's suggestion, Canada's Tourism Department and Air Canada invited Dorothy and me to inspect a unique international joint venture: the Swiss Auberge l'Abri Training and Conference Center, in the Gatineau Hills fifty-five miles north of Ottawa. This venue is recognized as Canada's leading skiing center for business people. Of the twenty-two million dollar project, a two million dollar communications system provides business executives with closed-circuit television, instant playback of proceedings, audiovisual tapes, and translation facilities accessible from anywhere in the hotel. Delegates can even hear and view proceedings between ski runs or while in their rooms recuperating from tired legs and sensitive tendons.

The Tourism Department and Air Canada's public relations manager in New York, Steve Pisni, arranged for our driver to stop at Camp Fortune outside Ottawa so that we could try some of the ski slopes there. Camp Fortune, a former military base only twelve minutes from Parliament Hill, is a favorite spot for old-timers and can handle eighteen thousand skiers an hour. Skiers who landed at the Ottawa airport or who check in at the major hotels can be taken to the slopes by complimentary buses.

On the evening of the same day we were guests of the federal government at a reception celebrating the hundredth anniversary of the National Gallery. The gallery had been closed for extensive renovations, and its reopening gala was a major social event that year. We were standing near the elevator in the main sec-ond-floor gallery when a jaunty figure stepped out of the lift, smiling broadly. "Who is that person?" Dorothy asked me. "I don't know him, but I would vote for him no matter who he is." It was the prime minister, Pierre Trudeau, who was adored by millions of Canadian women.

Trudeau, a former law professor and champion of liberal causes, was prime minister almost continuously from 1968 to 1984. Of all those years, 1980 would be the one of his greatest accomplishment: he gave Canada its own constitution. Until then, the country had been governed in effect by the BNA Act, an act of the British Parliament at Westminster. It was Trudeau who brought that act home to Canada, renaming it the Constitution Act of 1982. When Queen Elizabeth II signed it into law that year, Canada at last became completely independent of Britain.

Long before the North American Free Trade Agreement was established to strengthen trade between Canada, Mexico, and the United States, Canadian in-dustries were lobbying for FTZs. By the mid-1980s, tax-free customs areas were mushrooming around the world, and more and more nations—both industrial-ized and developing—saw them as a necessity if they hoped to attract foreign cap-ital. In 1970 the United States had only 7 FTZs; today, it has 265 full-purpose zones and more than 540 subzones. In the 1970s there were 70 FTZs worldwide; today, the number exceeds 750.

Ports Canada FTZ Turndown

The Canadian government's Transportation Ministry, which operated Ports Canada, believed firmly that FTZs were a matter for the private sector. Finally, however, it bowed to a joint Montreal-Toronto group and authorized a trade consultant to undertake a feasibility study for the Ottawa-Hull region.

After many months of somewhat caustic discussions involving several visits to New York by Ports Canada representatives, I submitted a fifty-seven-page plan for federal legislation that would establish an FTZ authority. Ports Canada accepted my report, but it made little headway in the Canadian Parliament; too many politicians contended that it would give Ottawa excessive authority vis-à-vis private interests. Others argued that FTZs should be a provincial jurisdiction and that they would generate too much competition among the provinces. Meanwhile, two provinces decided to go it alone, without waiting for a federal law. Canada now has two well-run and profitable international trade zones: at Stephenville in Newfoundland and Sydney in Nova Scotia.

Stephenville, a town of ten thousand on Newfoundland's southwest coast, opened its zone for business in April 1983. Zone tenants manufacture goods for distribution in Canada, the United States, Europe, and other major markets. The Sydport Zone near Sydney, on Cape Breton Island, 260 miles northeast of Halifax, is an industrial park covering 250 acres. Once they were running, I inspected both zones and was favorably impressed.

After my earlier recommendations failed to make it through Canada's Parliament, Ports Canada again approached me for my opinion about establishing a zone in Vancouver, on Canada's western coast. Like my previous proposal, this one caused controversy. Local supporters of the plan contended that a customs-free area in the Port of Vancouver would create a "boom of manufacturing and distribution operations in the Canadian Province of British Columbia."

Moreover, trade analysts in the Canadian West predicted that an FTZ in Vancouver would give Canada a competitive edge over two American ports, Seattle and Long Beach, where successful FTZs were operating under franchises from the U.S. Foreign Trade Zones Board in Washington. Although three hundred million dollars was invested in Vancouver to expand and improve the city's port facilities, Ottawa never authorized an FTZ there.

Epilogue

A Glimpse of World Leaders

Qualities

$\mathcal{S}$PECIALIZATION HAS ALWAYS PLAYED an important part in my book-writing career: the combination of journalism and international economics is a rare one. Even today, few journalists are experts in international taxation and trade. In seeking people to help us prepare our monthly supplements for our eighty-one books, we have had to look long and hard to find authors who can meet our standards as well as those of our five law publishers. We have tried to train a number of attorneys, accountants, and top-level MBAs, including some from Harvard and Yale, but many experts in international trade lack journalism experience, while the reverse is true and many journalism graduates are not sufficiently familiar with overseas business activities. As a general rule, the candidates we have tried to teach to take over the Diamond books lack the patience, perseverance, and work schedule to keep our books current.

To these discouraging circumstances (for our books, anyway), we have found a possible solution: specialized education. With the full cooperation of Syracuse University, we have established the Walter H. and Dorothy B. Diamond Institute of Taxation and Trade as an adjunct of the Syracuse University School of Management. Under this program, journalism graduates of the Newhouse School of Communications, or of other colleges offering comparable journalism courses, can earn an M.A. or Ph.D. by attending the Diamond Institute's School of Management's international taxation and trade courses. The reverse is true as well: graduates of the School of Management or similar business education institutions can apply for a postgraduate degree in international writing at the Newhouse School of Communications.

Also, we have been active at St. Thomas University in Miami. St. Thomas, founded in 1946 by the Augustinians, was Latin America's premier university until Castro evicted it from its home in Havana. At that point, the Florida Catholic Diocese took it over, and it has maintained its earlier prestige. The St. Thomas University Law School Diamond International Tax Program on the Internet, directed by Professor William Byrnes, now attracts practicing attorneys and accountants from all over the world.

The program was nominated for the American Bar Association 2004–05 Law Student Division Annual Diversity Award. Similarly, Wellesley College will in the future be benefiting from Diamond international scholarships, which are intended to further expand its highly regarded international affairs program.

Despite the obstacles encountered in writing our books and conferring with the leaders of the world, we have received great satisfaction from assisting underdeveloped countries in improving their economies, contributing toward strengthening their balance of trade figures, and fostering international business relationships that help stabilize world peace. We are also grateful for the recognition by U.S. Treasury officials of our efforts to help offset the critical U.S. annual current accounts deficit by serving on the board of advisors of the American International Depository and Trust created to repatriate offshore funds to the U.S. by exempting certain state income taxes for alien nonresidents of America.

The Greatest Leaders

Having met more than one hundred leaders from one hundred countries or territories in more than 120 visits, what has impressed me the most is that every one of them has wanted to give their poor and underprivileged citizens a better life. In nearly every developing country, its leader was deeply disturbed by the large percentage of people existing below the poverty line, generally ranging from 30 percent to as high as 70 percent in some nations.

There is no doubt that they are sincere. I cannot help but remember Argentina's president Arturo Frondizi throwing up his arms in despair when he greeted me asking: "Mr. Diamond, how can I help my poor people?" Of course, there were a few conniving dictators who were concerned only about staying in power, but they were very much the exceptions.

Presidents, prime ministers, finance ministers, and other world leaders are human: they try to avoid critics and obstructionists, and they want to hear good news, never bad. I have always found that the best approach to getting them to open up is to start our meeting with a sincere compliment.

My modus operandi: Always approach a dignitary with praise, never a complaint; otherwise, that person will immediately reject any notions of cooperation. For instance, say, "Your people are most friendly," "Your staff is exceptionally efficient," "Your secretary has been very helpful," "The parks in your city are beautiful," "I have been impressed with your industrial development," or "You have an incredible view of the city and harbor." At one time or another, I have used all of these opening remarks when greeting dignitaries, with excellent results. Once these government officials gain confidence in their visitor and are convinced he or she is on their side, these heads of state are quick to reveal their problems and elaborate on their goals for overcoming them.

All politicians tend to take credit for successful efforts, even when their subordinates have thought up the projects and done all the hard work. But in most cases—especially with presidents and finance ministers—their helmsmanship gives them the right to take deep satisfaction in the achievements of their aides.

The great leaders have always insisted that their advisers tell them the truth. During World War II, Churchill, Roosevelt, Truman, and Eisenhower were all great leaders because they were always ready to confront adverse conditions. Kennedy, Nixon, the first George Bush, and Clinton were weaker leaders, since generally speaking their staffs wanted to protect them from irritating problems.

Lyndon Johnson was not a great president. He made most of his own decisions, which sometimes got him into trouble, such as the Vietnam quagmire, but supporters of the underprivileged will long remember him for his "Great Society" and for the tremendous advances in desegregation that he pushed through during his tenure.

Reagan made his own decisions—mostly with Nancy's approval—regardless of what his aides told him; he broke the mold and was close to greatness. Reagan earned this status by rebuilding an ailing economy, restoring America's image abroad, and playing an astute hand in bringing down the Berlin Wall and ending communism in Eastern Europe. His advisers "wanted to win the cold war; he wanted to end it."

Brazil's president Kubitschek, Ireland's prime minister Jack Lynch, Puerto Rico's governor Luiz Muñoz Marin, Israel's prime minister Levi Eshkol, and Tunisia's president Habib Bourguiba, all of whom I had the good fortune to interview, were great leaders because they listened to others and saw for themselves their country's weaknesses and the world's shortcomings. Fidel Castro of Cuba, Anwar el-Sadat of Egypt, and Daniel Arap Moi of Kenya had no ear for bad news; the results are reflected in their countries' deteriorating economies and falling living standards.

Winston Churchill was perhaps the greatest statesman of his time because he would never waver in the face of defeat and inspired his people to act with one objective. Franklin Roosevelt was a close second for his determination to stop Hitler from ruling the world despite the roadblocks his opponents in Congress put in his way. Harry Truman will always be remembered by Europeans—both the Allies and Axis countries—for saving Western Europe with the Marshall Plan. And Dwight Eisenhower will always be a hero for his strategy and foresight in conquering enemies in Africa and Europe as well as for his precise military style, which carried over to his days as president.

But the leader who impressed me the most was Prime Minister Jawaharlal Nehru of India, whose compassion and philosophy for righting the ills of the world are a lesson for all the world to heed.

Terrorism a Major Concern

Terrorism was a major concern long before September 11, 2001. In the 1950s and 1960s, insurgencies were emerging all over Latin America, the Middle East, and Africa.

In Argentina, government and business leaders, as well as average citizens, exuded anger while they told Dorothy and me horror stories about family members or friends whom the Peronists had abducted, executed, or caused to disappear without a trace. Chileans had to endure the tyranny of General Augusto Pinochet, the dictator from 1973 to 1990, who overthrew President Salvador Allende in a bloody coup. In Colombia, because of rampant street crime, we were warned to stay off the streets of the capital, Bogotá. In fact, terrorism in that country was rising to the extent that we were advised to cancel our scheduled meetings in Medellín.

In the Middle East and Africa, it was obvious to us that Islamic fundamentalism was already flourishing in the 1990s. For almost every leader, from the shah of Iran and Morocco's King Hassan to Egypt's Anwar el-Sadat and Kenya's Daniel Arap Moi, avoiding assassination was an important concern. Throughout both regions, national economies were being influenced by the ideology, language, and tactics of the jihadists. Yet the Western world stood by and let the Islamists' rebellion spread around the globe.

Of all the African leaders, only Habib Bourguiba of Tunisia showed no fear of being assassinated, because his political opponents were few and his supporters respected him as one of them. In the Western world, such leaders as Winston Churchill, Charles de Gaulle, and Ireland's Jack Lynch, despite occasional labor unrest, lived without fear of assassination because they had instilled confidence in their people and were widely regarded as heroes. Prime Minister Nehru of India, the wisest and most compassionate of all the world leaders I interviewed, resisted thinking about being assassinated, even though his country was known for harboring insurgents.

Among the foreign leaders I interviewed, the most admired American statesman was President Harry Truman, because of his initiative in implementing the Truman Doctrine. More than once I heard Truman referred to as "the father of reconstruction." He rebuilt the world economy through the Marshall Plan, and as a consequence the United States was placed on a pedestal as a friend and ally by these world leaders. This respect would last for a half century.

World Peace Through World Trade

Most of the world leaders I met told me that to recapture its once exalted status as the entire world's friend, the United States would have to end its farm subsidies, ban import quotas (especially on cotton and lumber), and reduce tariffs on raw materials and minerals. Some of these trade restrictions were revoked by the United States in early 2005.

The road to world peace is through world trade, these leaders reminded me.

Index

Page number in *italic* denotes an illustration.

Women's Congress, 37

Woolworth, William, Jr., 105

World Bank: as cosponsor of Austria's export credit insurance system, 203; criticism of offshore financial jurisdictions, 145; loans to South American countries, 134; Romanian economic reform and, 274. *See also* International Bank for Reconstruction

World Economic Forum, 227

world peace, 287

world trade. *See* international trade

World Trade Institute: aid to Jordan and, 226; Walter Diamond as adviser to, 117, 179; Egyptian FTZs and, 236–37; Lithuania's FTZ and, 269; recommendation to Channel Islands, 208; South Africa and, 231; special economic zone in China and, 180; trip to Morocco and, 243, 246–47; Turkish FTZs and, 192

World Trade Organization, 227

World War I, 6, 57, 58

World War II: Allied headquarters in France, 202; battle of Okinawa, 163; Bretton Woods Conference, 70–71, 72; defense of Malta, 196; Walter Diamond's naval duty during, 60–88, 61, 75; effect on Dorothy's journalism education, 30; end of, 87–88; in England, 68–69; factories, 32; foreign aid to allies in, 120, 121, 159; German recovery from, 189; great leaders of, 285; Hitler's plans for New York, 76; impact on women in workplace, 27, 31; memories of, 6; Naval duty during, 18; Norway's

contribution, 186; in Pacific, 75–88; question of blond journalism student, 30; Sadat's imprisonment during, 237; San Francisco Conference, 71–73; Sicilian campaign of, 200; U. S. bases in Panama, 101; U. S. ships sunk by U-boats, 75; Vaughn's contribution to, 196

Wrigley, Bill, Jr., 105

writers: in Diamond family, 4–5; secrets of success, 5–12, 30, 94–95, 283–84

WSYR (radio station), 18

Wu, M. T., 170

Xiamen Zone, 181

Y2K computer problems, 275

Yamaguchi, Hideo, 52–53, 54, 55–56

Yokohama Specie Bank, 45, 46, 47

Young America (youth magazine), 30–31

Yugoslavia, 37, 193, 198, 211, 214–16, 272

Yugoslav Institute of Economics, 215

Zabala, Jose, 127, 130

Zagranicznego, Handlic, 264

Zambia, 235

Zatt International, 228

Zheliv, Zheliu, 275

Zhukov, Georgy, 257

Zijlstrd, J., 194

Zimbabwe. *See* Rhodesia

Zolotas, Xenafon, 192–93